I·B·M

Selected Works by the Same Author

The Worldly Economists
The Last Bull Market
Inside Wall Street
The Fallen Colossus
The Entrepreneurs
The Money Manias
The Age of Giant Corporations
Panic on Wall Street

I·B·M

COLOSSUS
IN
TRANSITION

Robert Sobel

A Truman Talley Book

Times
BOOKS

The author, editor, and publisher would like to thank the following for their kind permission to reproduce the photographs in the picture section.

Associated Press, 37. The Smithsonian Institution, 2, 8, 13. United Press International, 7, 10, 11, 12, 14, 16, 19, 24, 28, 35. *The New York Times* 27, 29, 33, 34, 36.

The picture section of this book was researched and organized by Rod Rodriguez of New York City. Our special thanks for his exceptional work.

Published by *Truman Talley Books* · *Times Books*, a division of Quadrangle/The New York Times Book Co., Inc. Three Park Avenue, New York, N.Y. 10016

Published simultaneously in Canada by Fitzhenry & Whiteside, Ltd., Toronto.

Library of Congress Cataloging in Publication Data

Sobel, Robert, 1931 Feb. 19–
    I.B.M., colossus in transition.

    "A Truman Talley book."
    Bibliography: p. *350*
    Includes index.
    1. International Business Machines Corporation—
History. I. Title.
HD9696.C641488   1981   338.7′62138195   81–50092
ISBN 0–8129–1000–1   AACR2

Manufactured in the United States of America

10 9 8 7 6 5 4 3 2

For Jean Keaveny and George Delhomme

—the best is yet to come—

Contents

Contents

PART IV
The Way to the Future

PART I

In the Beginning

1

Men and Tabulating Machines

ORDINARILY we label eras with the names of those individuals who appear to dominate them, and so the business scene shortly after the turn of the century and prior to World War I habitually is associated with such figures as John D. Rockefeller, J. P. Morgan, and E. H. Harriman. This kind of shorthand is useful but can also deceive; these were not the typical businessmen of their times, for had they been so, they hardly would stand out as they do. Rather, the Morgans and Rockefellers of this world write the rules, set the stage and often determine who will play upon it, and mete out justice. They also provide models for lesser individuals and establish the bounds of acceptable conduct for them.

Yet big business usually admits a few eccentrics, especially during boom times, so long as they do not transgress the more basic precepts. During the Age of Morgan readers of the Sunday supplements delighted to the antics of John W. "Bet-a-Million" Gates, who actually wagered that sum on which raindrop would roll down a pane of window glass first. But Gates's work as a leader of the barbed-wire trust is forgotten; in this role he hewed to the Morgan standards. Charles Yerkes, the traction magnate, was always good for a quote or two. "Buy up old junk, fix it up a little, then unload it with a profit on the other guys," was one of his favorite maxims. Still, those who came in with Yerkes on one or another of his schemes knew that while he might cheat the public and corrupt public officials, he was essentially clean insofar as his transactions with peers were concerned. Those who know the name of Diamond Jim Brady tend to think of him as a glutton, *bon vivant*, and sometimes squire for Lillian Russell and other actresses. Brady also was a skilled businessman, particularly when negotiating for syndicates, the way in which he obtained the means to indulge his taste for high living.

In some respects Charles Ranlett Flint resembled these characters. Eclipsed by Rockefeller and Morgan at the time and hardly remembered today, he nonetheless was a man who possessed considerable panache and whose accomplishments in various businesses excited admiration.

Flint was born in 1850 in a small town in coastal Maine and so was in his prime at the turn of the century. A small, compact person with fine features and carefully barbered muttonchop whiskers, he prided himself on being a man of action in all things. Long before Teddy Roosevelt popularized "the strenuous life," Flint delighted in physical sport. He was an excellent swimmer and runner, the owner of the nation's fastest racing yachts, and one of the first to obtain an automobile license (and a founder of the Automobile Club of America, which he expected to popularize motoring as a sport). Flint flew airplanes at a time when merely going up in one took considerable nerve. Almost every summer would be spent in Europe on working vacations, with most of the time at hunting lodges. Regularly Flint would plunge into the north woods for weeks of shooting and fishing. He never smoked tobacco or drank liquor. Coffee and tea were reserved for special occasions—when he needed stimulation while working long hours on business deals. A friend once remarked that he would live till Judgment Day and then have to be shot. Quoting Rudyard Kipling, a journalist said of Flint that:

> 'E's all of sand an' ginger when alive,
> An' 'e's generally shammin' when 'e's dead.

Flint seemed always on the go, continually involved in a dozen or so enterprises in various parts of the world. He boasted that for many years he would spend one week out of every ten on a ship, either on his way to a foreign venture or returning from one. Because Flint gloried in excitement, yearning to be at the center of activity, and was intrigued by all things exotic, he rarely could stay put for more than a few weeks at a time. "It has been said, perhaps too frequently, that a rolling stone gathers no moss," he wrote. "But I have never heard anyone speak about the fun the rolling stone has a-rolling."

Flint got his start in international trade, as a commission agent, and did most of his work with Latin American nations. Although he dealt in guano, nitrates, and other raw materials, he was best known as a supplier of munitions to warring factions. He would ingratiate himself with governmental leaders, undertake to represent their interests in America, and supply them with whatever they needed and could pay for. At various times he served as consul for Nicaragua, Chile, and Costa Rica, and on more than one occasion he supplied guns and ships to both sides in a conflict. Toward the end of the century he developed contacts in the Orient as well. In 1895 Flint sold vessels to the Japanese for use in their war against China, and a decade later he purchased warships for the Russians to use in their conflict with the Japanese. Later Flint organized a company to sell Wright airplanes in Europe, and he instructed the Kaiser on how they might be useful in time of war.

While all this seems sinister today, it was quite acceptable at the time, and Flint was proud of his accomplishments in the international arena. Had anyone called him a merchant of death, Flint would have wondered what the fellow had in mind. Such was the nature of the Western world prior to the Great War.

Although Flint was one of the more important international businessmen of his time, his reputation was made in the United States, where he was known as one of the most adept creators of industrial combinations, a man whom a Chicago reporter called "the father of trusts," a title that remained with him for the rest of his life. Even so, he was best known for the number of combinations he brought about, not for their size. If occasionally some of them appeared overpriced, rewarding the promoters unduly for their efforts, Flint would respond that creators deserved proper recompense for their efforts, and he initiated several lawsuits against editors who suggested there was something unwholesome about them. "He was an industrial capitalist who became a promoter on the fringes of finance capitalism," concluded business historian N. S. B. Gras.

But he truly was both more and less than that. Flint was rarely engaged in industry; only once did he operate a company directly after setting it up. Rather, he would put together deals and then peddle them to others. But no businessman of his time was so eager to defend large-scale enterprise and major combinations as was Flint, and he excelled in the work. In speeches before business associations, academic groups, and political gatherings he clearly enunciated his views of the benefits derived not only by businessmen but by consumers and workers as well when business became big. Articles by and interviews with Flint on this subject appeared regularly in popular journals, and he even testified before congressional committees on the ways mergers improved living standards and the industrial and financial climate.

Most of Flint's arguments were rather standard for the time and are familiar even today. He spoke of the economies brought about by mass production and the need for heavy capital investments in a period of growing industrialization. Big businesses could raise large amounts of capital to meet these needs. Flint was convinced that in order to exploit foreign markets, American industries would have to become rationalized and restructured, if for no other reason than to compete better with their European counterparts. And he vigorously denied that businessmen corrupted the political process.

Beyond that, however, Flint set down a vision of American corporations that seemed a cross between ideas then being promulgated by Thorstein Veblen and later to come from the typewriter of John K. Galbraith, although Flint's version was unique. At a time when even monopolists spoke well of the benefits of competition, he thought otherwise. An unregulated marketplace, especially for goods that required large investments of capital to produce, could be highly wasteful. Competition forced manufacturers to lower the quality of their goods so as to compete on a price basis, to waste money on frivolous advertisements to ensnare customers, and to pay workers the lowest possible wages. Flint believed in free trade between nations but wanted this to be conducted between large-scale enterprises.

To those who argued that big business placed too much power in the hands of a few men, Flint replied that just the opposite was true. Ignoring the differences between power and wealth, he disingenuously observed that since ownership of many major entities was spread out among thousands of shareholders, the profits from them would likewise be dispersed. He wrote:

> Never before was there such a wide distribution of manufacturing interests. The great bulk of the stock is held, not by the very rich, but by moderately well-to-do people. The control under the new system is not vested as it was under the old, in the hands of a few abnormally rich men, but it rests with the majority of stockholders, whose numerical strength is growing every day.

Like other businessmen of his time, Flint held that it was the duty of managements to bend to the desires of the owners—the stockholders in this case.

But in his talks and articles can be found a hint of his belief that the two were growing apart, that in the future managements would be more or less autonomous, while owners would settle for dividends and price appreciation from their investments. This, too, was for the best. A supreme individualist himself, Flint encouraged others to work as members of teams. "Viewing the matter from every standpoint, the business man is benefited when he operates as a member of a combination instead of as an individual." As such he can take advantage of lower transportation and interest rates available to large-scale enterprises, can bargain more effectively with workers, can afford to finance inventories in slack times, and can even go on vacations without worrying about who is minding the store. Those who trade their assets for shares in a larger entity can dispose of them with relative ease. "In case of his death or disability, he leaves to his family a property that runs along uninterruptedly." In place of ownership of a small, often vulnerable, and minor company, the entrepreneur who joined with others to organize a trust would have shares in a large, strong, and immortal enterprise, one better suited to fill the economic and social needs of the new century.

Everything about him seemed to justify consolidations. Flint often observed: "A trades union is a combination of labor, a university a combination of intelligence, and a bank a combination of capital." The trusts, he went on to say, were "combinations of labor, intelligence, and capital"; his implication was that they would in time become all-embracing entities. A believer in bigness in all things, Flint was also convinced that the future belonged to corporate executives who existed to serve the interests of the company and were willing to submerge their own interests toward achieving that goal, in return for which they would receive economic benefits and security. Even as he rejected such a role for himself (Flint hardly was the boardroom type), he devoted a major portion of his energies to hastening this evolution.

Flint's initiation into the field of industrial consolidation resulted more from serendipity than from design. In 1879, while purchasing munitions for the Peruvian government, he met Marcellus Hartley, an international tycoon who, among his other holdings, owned a large block of shares in the United States Lighting Company. The firm's assets and prospects were not as grand as its name. Hartley had hoped it would come to dominate the field of electric illumination, and clearly this was not to be. Perhaps, however, it could work out some arrangement with the Edison and Westinghouse interests which would reward the stockholders. Hartley knew the situation required the talents of a wheeler-dealer, attributes he perceived in Flint. So he cultivated the man and within a few months, presumably for friendship's sake, arranged for Flint to purchase shares at a concession from the market price. Given Flint's background, one might assume he hoped for a quick killing, but this did not transpire. Gradually he found himself involved in the firm's direction, and in 1880 he assumed the titular leadership of U.S. Electric Lighting, with a mandate from the board to seek an accommodation with Edison.

Attempts at merger or consolidation failed for a variety of reasons, the most important of which being Edison's refusal to come to terms with a weak rival. But Flint could not accept this and came away from the experience with the belief that he might have carried it off had he been a "disinterested intermediary." He had made a poor start in this new career but felt he had learned a valuable lesson. Never again would he become involved with the management of a company. Rather, he would perform the duties of an industrial midwife. With this in mind, he turned to another area of merger activity.

"After my failure to bring about the electric light and power consolidation," Flint wrote in his memoirs, "I made up my mind that I would profit from my experience and endeavor to bring about a consolidation of some of my crude rubber customers, the manufacturers of rubber boots and shoes." At first he arranged for meetings between leaders of the industry, at which he pointed out the benefits to be derived from a union of interests. Then he awaited a call to action, which came in 1892, when several of them asked Flint to set down a plan for mergers. "I did not go to see the manufacturers. They saw me. They gave me their detailed statements which I treated as confidential. Then I drew up a plan for the consolidation." Out of this came the United States Rubber Company, a firm that dominated the industry from the start.

Flint took great care to assemble a board that consisted of prestigious and trusted individuals, including J. Edward Simmons, an influential member of the New York Stock Exchange. The shares, once floated, contained a good deal of "water," which in the parlance of the time meant they were overvalued in relation to underlying assets. On several occasions Flint claimed there was nothing wrong with this—that the prices of securities offered to the public reflected such items as goodwill, trademarks, patents, management, labor forces, and market position as well as land, buildings, and cash accounts. His critics replied that all this was little more than sleight of hand and that Flint and others like him were more interested in the creation of capital gains for themselves than shoes or boots for consumers. As it turned out, the securities of United States Rubber did decline, but this was due more to a general malaise on Wall Street and in the nation than anything else. In time the shares rose sharply, thus rewarding Flint and his colleagues for their efforts.

Flint's major consolidations came after the economic revival of 1897–98, at which time the securities markets also underwent a renaissance. Flint played a prominent role in putting together National Starch and the American Caramel Company. His peak year for consolidations was 1899, when he created American Woolen, Sloss-Sheffield, United States Bobbin & Shuttle, and a handful of lesser entities, including a steamship operation and three coal mining firms. His prime creation that year was American Chicle. The tangible assets of the six companies that went into making the "chewing gum trust" were worth $500,000, but Flint capitalized it at $9 million. He justified this figure by claiming that "the principal asset was trademarks," which he estimated to be worth at least $14 million. A firm's reputation, like that of an individual, was worth far more than a mere collection of bricks and mortar, he said. And while this clearly was self-serving, it nonetheless often was the case.

In 1900, in what seemed one of his lesser efforts, Flint played the midwife at the birth of the International Time Recording Company, a New Jersey concern the sole business of which was the production and marketing of time clocks of the kinds found in many industrial and mercantile establishments. After several combinations and acquisitions, it emerged finally as the International Time Recording Company of New York, headquartered at Endicott, New York. It was the clear leader in a very small field. Flint nursed the firm along, expanding its operations to include even agents in Europe, and he bought out all its competitors. International Time expanded its operations in the early twentieth century, producing devices for telephone companies that measured the time of long-distance calls and turning out a line of measuring equipment for railroads. By 1910 the company dominated its industry and reported sales of more than $1 million.

The Computing Scale Company of America was another of Flint's creations, one that did not turn out as well as International Time. He organized it from four operating companies in 1901. Its primary product was a scale that came equipped with a chart. When used properly, this enabled a clerk not only to weigh an item but also to calculate its cost. Scales such as this were marketed to retail companies throughout the nation, but they were successful primarily in the Midwest, perhaps because the main plant was in Ohio. In addition to the scales, the company produced a line of meat and cheese slicers and related equipment for retail stores. None of these businesses was very promising, however, and in 1910 Computing Scale's future was bleak.

It was for this reason, perhaps, that Flint considered a merger of International Time and Computing Scale. Apparently he had no thought of economies of scale, market domination, efficiencies, or the like. In the past he and other organizers had brought together companies in the same lines of endeavor and so could make a case for the benefits of rationalization. Clearly, however, there would be none of this when and if a manufacturer of time clocks united with a firm that produced scales and cheese slicers, especially when the main facilities of each were separated by more than 1,000 miles and there was no community of interests to which the two managements belonged. A dozen years later Flint would claim that there were benefits to what he called "allied consolidations." Anticipating an argument used by conglomerators of the 1960's, he wrote that the new entity would own "separate and distinct lines of business, so that in normal times the interest and sinking funds on its bonds could be earned by any one of these independent lines," while in "abnormal times" one or the other of the units might be able to earn sufficient funds for the payouts. He also claimed that both firms were in the business of measuring things—that, in fact, there was a unifying thread upon which to hook the deal. But this was not stated in 1910, when his work began. Rather, it was generally believed that Flint's actions were dictated more by a desire for capital gains than by the dream of erecting yet another viable trust.

The proposed merger came to involve a third company, which, unlike the others, was not a Flint creation. Nor had he any prior connection with the Tabulating Machine Company; in fact, to this day we have no clear idea of how Flint met Herman Hollerith, the founder and president of Tabulating Machine. It appears, however, that Hollerith was short of funds at the time—he had been unable to purchase shares to which he had been entitled two years earlier—and might have been attracted by Flint's promises of great profits. As for Flint, he might have seen in Tabulating Machine a firm with unique products for which demand could be enlarged and production expanded—one that in 1910 was unable to keep up with its backlog of orders. Perhaps he mulled over the idea that profits generated by International Time could be used by Tabulating Machine and that the former company's sales force might be employed to distribute machines produced by the latter. This, too, is unknown, but chances are the idea did not enter Flint's mind. Although a visionary, he hardly could have anticipated

Men and Tabulating Machines

the potential in a product which in 1910 had limited application and few customers. In any case, Hollerith's firm became the third unit of the triad. The name selected for it offers a clue to Flint's state of mind at the time. He would not call it American Measuring Machines, United States Calculating Devices, or any other grandiose title such as those he had used in the past. For a firm that clearly had no unifying theme there would be an awkward title. Flint called it Computing-Tabulating-Recording.

While Charles Flint was the organizing force behind CTR, Herman Hollerith was its technological engine. Born of German immigrant parents in Buffalo, New York, in 1860, he was a decade younger than Flint, but appeared older. Hollerith was a man of medium and stocky build, whose hairline started to recede while he was in his early twenties, by which time he had grown a bushy walrus mustache. He could be gregarious and even humorous with family and friends but tended toward stiff formality in public. Moreover, he was a man quick to anger, take offense, and alienate people. He always believed, often with justification, that others were conspiring to steal his ideas and deny him financial rewards that were his due. Few people who worked with Hollerith had anything positive to say about his personality, often while they conceded his undisputed brilliance, even genius. But his scope was narrow. In a lifetime of invention he really had only one great insight (and that was not original) and turned out one important device based upon it. Perhaps this was due to intellectual limitations, but it also might have derived from his personality. The same man who spent more than a decade perfecting some of his tabulators once became so angry when his automobile broke down that he got out and walked away, leaving the machine to anyone who would haul it away.

Sometime in the early 1870's the Holleriths moved to New York City, where Herman first attended a public school for a while and then had a private tutor, since his deficiencies in spelling were causing him both embarrassment and poor performance in other subjects. Even then it was evident that he had a gift for things mechanical, but little else. He entered

Columbia College when only fifteen years old and was gradu-
ated from there in 1879 with a degree of Engineer of Mines.
During summer vacations he had worked in iron mines in Mich-
igan, and perhaps he intended to return there when he received
his degree, even though he had found the experience somewhat
distasteful. As luck would have had it, Hollerith completed his
studies in a year ending in nine, a time when traditionally the
Census Bureau prepared to undertake its decennial work. One
of his professors, William Trowbridge, was also the chief special
agent of the bureau in charge of conducting a survey of power
and machinery used in manufacturing. He invited his student to
come on as an assistant at a salary of $600 a year. Faced with
the choice of returning to the mines or working in a Washington
office, Hollerith promptly accepted the offer.

Hollerith's work consisted of preparing a rather dull and
detailed report on steam and waterpower that few people con-
sulted and fewer actually read. Of more importance was his
meeting with John Shaw Billings, who was in charge of vital
statistics. An army surgeon with a special interest in the classification of medical knowledge, Billings was involved in developing a procedure to sort out the millions of bits of information
that soon would flood into his office. This had been a problem
during the counting of 1870, for which chief clerk Charles
Seaton had developed a crude tabulating device. But it was
inadequate for the situation of 1880. Given new demands for
information and a larger population, it now appeared that the
current census would not be completed for at least seven or
eight years and that the 1890 census would still be in the process of tabulation by the time the year 1900 rolled around.

The situation was intolerable; something had to be done by
way of invention to alleviate the pressures. Billings, who was in
the middle of the mess, outlined his problem to Hollerith one
evening over dinner. "There ought to be a machine for doing
the purely mechanical work of tabulating population and similar statistics," he said. "We talked it over," recalled Hollerith
thirty years later, "and I remember . . . he thought of using

cards with the description of the individual shown by notches punched in the edge of the card."

An engineer, Hollerith knew of the Jacquard loom, a century-old device "programmed" by means of such cards to turn out desired patterns on cloth. Music boxes operated on the same principle, as did the player piano. Hollerith spoke with Billings about the possibility of constructing such a device and asked the older man "to go in with him." Billings wasn't interested in the process of invention, however; all he wanted was a machine to do a particular job. But he didn't forget the conversation. A few years later, while he watched a small army of clerks in his offices transferring items from work sheets to schedules and tallying the figures, Billings turned to an associate and said, "There ought to be some mechanical way of doing this job, something on the principle of the Jacquard loom, whereby holes in a card regulate the pattern to be woven."

Hollerith did not remain long in Washington. General Francis Walker, whom he had met at the Census Bureau, became president of the Massachusetts Institute of Technology and in 1882 invited him to come there as instructor in mechanical engineering. Hollerith accepted, and while at MIT he began work on the kind of machine he had discussed with Billings. At first he thought to encode information on long strips of paper but abandoned this as too cumbersome. The following year, while he was on a trip in the West, the solution was literally given to him. His train ticket contained what was known as a punch photograph, designed to discourage short-distance travelers from cheating on rates offered to those taking long trips. When a ticket was purchased, the conductor would punch out a description of the holder—whether he had light or dark hair, blue or brown eyes, a large or small nose, etc. By looking along the edge of the ticket, then, other railroad personnel could check whether the traveler had actually been the original purchaser of the ticket. This provided Hollerith with an idea: Each person interviewed by the census taker could be given a similar punch photograph, one on which were holes which would be clipped, each standing for a different attribute. The cards might then be placed in a sorter constructed on the model of the Jacquard loom. In the case of the loom, the cards directed needles and thread into proper holes; the Hollerith device would sort cards into stacks by means of punched holes. Thus, when properly programmed, the machine could isolate all individuals between the ages of forty and forty-five—or even all Caucasian males working in Pennsylvania coal mines. Only the number of holes and methods of programming would limit the scope of such a machine.

Shortly thereafter Hollerith abandoned his academic career —he really lacked the talent for and interest in teaching—and devoted all his time to a new pursuit, that of inventor. In order to support himself, Hollerith took a variety of jobs, including one at the United States Patent Office, but most of his time was spent in the laboratory. He developed an advanced electromagnetically operated air brake and a machine for corrugating metal tubing, neither of which proved commercially viable. In any case, these were not of primary interest; Hollerith remained committed to the development of a tabulator.

Later Hollerith would recall a friend telling him that "half the art of invention consists of knowing what needs to be invented," and this certainly was the case with the tabulator. Machines that could perform this function would be required by the Census Bureau, of course, but there also was a ready market from other government agencies, the railroads, and retail establishments. Hollerith was one of several inventors seeking an efficient device. Charles Pidgin and William Hunt, among others, were at work in the same area and, like Hollerith, were gearing their efforts toward obtaining a contract for the 1890 census. And although Hollerith maintained good relations with Billings, Hunt not only was an executive at the bureau but for a while was also a member of the committee charged with evaluating machines to be used in the next counting.

Still, Hollerith had a start on the others and, in addition, had a far superior machine. He took out a patent for his first model in 1884, and two years later it had a successful trial in the

Men and Tabulating Machines

Baltimore census. On the basis of preliminary reports the health departments of New York and New Jersey placed orders for machines to tabulate mortality statistics. Hollerith was receiving inquiries not only from other cities and states but from overseas as well. Even before the 1890 census it seemed clear he would not be able to turn out all these machines by himself. Some organization would be needed; the inventor soon would have to become a businessman.

Hollerith was awarded three additional patents in 1889 and exhibited his devices to delighted crowds in Washington. He won applause and acclaim, became the subject of interviews and newspaper articles, and was awarded an honorary doctorate from his alma mater. The following year his "census machines" were matched against models submitted by Hunt and Pidgin in preliminary work on the census, and Hollerith's were the undisputed winners. The census contract was his. Subcontracting the production of the keyboard punches to Pratt & Whitney and the electrical apparatus to Western Electric, he was able to turn over machines to the bureau on a rental basis before the first raw data reached Washington.

The 1890 census was a huge success. Tasks which a decade earlier had taken years to complete were now done in a matter of weeks by a relative handful of machine operators. Superintendent of the Census Robert Porter was delighted. The 1880 census had taken nine years to complete, and with the use of Hollerith machines the next one was done in fewer than seven. "For the first time in the history of the world," Porter said, "the count of population of a great nation has been made by the aid of electricity."

Others showed less enthusiasm. Some noted the 1890 counting was more costly than that of 1880—$11.5 million versus $5.8 million. Much of this was attributed to the use of mechanization. Porter responded by noting that although the Hollerith rentals came to $750,000, they saved the bureau an estimated $5 million in labor costs, in addition to doing calculations which otherwise would not have been possible in so short a period. Not only did they enable a more rapid counting, but the 1890 census was far more comprehensive than any that preceded it. Commissioner of Labor Carroll Wright also justified this new system. Utilization of the Hollerith machines, he wrote, provided "a much more complete presentation of the statistics of population [than was] made at any preceding census. . . ."

Wright and Porter were major figures in what amounted to a worldwide census establishment; their support of Hollerith all but assured him a contract for the next counting and, in addition, provided him with new contacts. In late 1890 Austria ordered machines for that country's census. Canada took five of them the following year, while orders came in from Italy. Hollerith's machines encouraged the Russians to undertake their first counting. Production at Pratt & Whitney and Western Electric was intensified. Hollerith achieved fame as the world's first "statistical engineer." Other honors followed. Personally, professionally, and financially, he seemed successful.

What did this mean? On the simplest level it would appear that Hollerith had recognized a problem at the Census Bureau and had resolved it with the creation of a set of machines, which then were sold or leased to other countries. But there was far more to the process than this, and it could be seen in three areas.

In the first place, the criticisms regarding costs were well founded and a preview of what was to come. More often than the manufacturers liked to admit, their machines provided accuracy and speed but did not cut costs. Without the Hollerith devices or others like them, the business of the census might have dragged on for decades. Once the machines were in place, the countings not only could proceed but could be conducted with dispatch. Yet the machines altered the nature of the process. Human tabulators were replaced by mechanical and electrical ones, and the format of the cards on which information was punched helped dictate the kind and amount of questions asked. In the 1880's the need for tabulating devices for use in the census resulted in the creation of the Hollerith machines. Thus, the content, in this case the decennial counting, dictated the form—the Hollerith census counter. Thereafter the process would start to become reversed—which is to say, the existence of such machines and knowledge of their capabilities would lead to searches for new ways to use them.

This was the second area in which the technology and the needs of parts of society dictated Hollerith's actions. He appreciated the need for tabulators in other fields in which the rapid and accurate gathering of statistics was vital. Even while placing his census machines in various countries, he modified them for use by railroads. Actually little change in the machines—the "hardware"—was required. Rather, Hollerith had to redesign the cards to tabulate commercial statistics instead of counting human beings—that is, he had to alter the "software." By so doing, he was able to demonstrate how his machines could prepare freight and passenger figures for use by railroads. Hollerith placed devices with the New York Central and Long Island railroads, and other orders followed.

The machines gobbled up enormous numbers of cards, each of which could be used only once. By 1895 Hollerith was able to report that more than 100 million had been used for census purposes alone. This was the third important aspect of this new technology. Hollerith observed that the sale or rental of each new machine provided him with a steady stream of card orders. He dimly perceived that sales of cards might easily prove more profitable than that of machines. Before King Gillette and his safety razor and George Eastman and his camera, Hollerith came to appreciate the profits that came from controlling the market for a disposable item used in conjunction with a device that promised efficiencies for its user.

Initially Hollerith gave little thought to a structure for his enterprise since he was busily occupied with invention and placement. He did organize the Hollerith Electric Tabulating System, which was not really a company, but rather the name for his devices and the place near his Washington home where he assembled and repaired the machines and turned out the cards. He entered into an arrangement with the Library Bureau, which had offices in various American and European cities, by which he agreed to handle statistical projects under terms of contracts; in effect, he formed a service division, although the concept hadn't been rationalized at the time. Then, in 1896, he incorporated himself as the Tabulating Machine Company, a New York concern with its main offices in the Georgetown section of Washington. After receiving the contract for the 1900 census, Hollerith discontinued his relationship with Pratt & Whitney and Western Electric and manufactured his machines in his own shop.

Business was booming. Not only did Hollerith continue to place machines with governments and railroads, but now he also sold or leased them to wholesale and retail merchandisers, who used them to maintain inventories, and to insurance companies for a variety of tasks.

Next to nothing is known of the finances of the company in this period, but Tabulating Machine was reincorporated as a New Jersey concern in 1905, apparently to take advantage of that state's beneficial corporation statutes, and this can be taken as an indication that the concern was quite profitable. Hollerith owned most of the shares, but a few were sold or given to old friends and associates. In 1908 he gave these individuals rights to purchase preferred stock, saying that the money raised by the sale would be used to create new machines to place on rental. Hollerith preferred leasing arrangements, believing that in the long run they would provide more income than outright sales.

By 1908 Hollerith had rented some machines to electric utilities, which used them for billing. He had some thirty commercial customers, to whom he sold approximately a million cards a month. Profits were good and demand was strong; Hollerith took pride in the fact that Tabulating Machine had no sales force—his clients came to his door seeking machines. The backlog of orders was high; most customers had to wait several months before delivery.

With all this the company was in trouble. Finances were tight as the result of heavy manufacturing costs that were not recaptured by outright sales. Also, the success of the original machines had attracted others to the field. Hollerith had a head start, but his inventive juices appeared to be drying up. New companies with improved machines were nipping at his heels. Most important, there were signs he might not be awarded the contract for the 1910 census. James Powers, who had worked on the 1900 counting as a government employee and had become familiar with both the advantages and the drawbacks of the Hollerith machines, offered to produce an improved set of models. S. N. D. North, the new director of the bureau, suspected that Hollerith's charges were too high, and he welcomed the competition, especially since it came from one of his own men. Moreover, Powers said he would sell his machines, observing that this would result in further economies. Finally, Powers would charge less for the cards, which, as has been indicated, were extremely profitable.

After a trial run North decided to award the contract to Powers. Angered, humiliated, and threatened, Hollerith brought a suit against the bureau, claiming that Powers had infringed on his patents. But this was little more than a holding action. Hollerith's patents soon would expire, and it was not at all certain that his flagging energies would revive. In other words, Tabulating Machine in 1910 was a profitable operation that was short of both cash and innovation. It was a firm that appeared on the verge of starting a steady decline.

As has been indicated, it is not known where, how, or even when Hollerith first met Charles Flint, but it is apparent that despite their differences in background and temperament, each man had something the other wanted. Flint was seeking candidates for his next deal while Hollerith must have realized that Tabulating Machine might never again be as valuable a property as it was in 1910; in addition, he was short of funds. Perhaps Flint sought out Hollerith, or it might have been the other way around. Whatever the chronology, Tabulating Machine became the last part of the triad that formed Computing-Tabulating-Recording.

The new company, then, consisted of a prosperous manufacturer of timing devices, a chancy operation that produced scales and slicers, and an interesting but sclerotic firm that turned out a line of tabulators and related devices.* It would have facilities in Ohio, New York, and Washington, D.C., and offices in several other cities. In all, CTR would have 1,200 employees and a board dominated by executives from International Time. Hollerith would be chief engineer; he would not be given a management position.

CTR was put together by a man who had no desire to run the company, one famous for putting together deals in order to reap profits. Its leading innovator and resident scientist was a person whom some suspected of having reached a dead end in his creative career.

It was not a particularly auspicious beginning.

---

* A fourth firm, Bundy Manufacturing, was also included in the combination. Once the parent of a component of International Time Recording, Bundy still owned stock in that firm, and apparently this was the reason for its having been accepted.

2

Enter Thomas Watson Senior

CTR's most important leader, and its major asset, would be Thomas Watson. Today recognized as one of the dozen or so great businessmen of his time, he came to CTR after having been fired from his previous position. Before that he had been found guilty of violating federal law. The verdict was under appeal, but at the time he assumed his new post Watson faced the prospect of a year in jail.

His record was not as poor as this sounds, however, and in fact, Watson's reputation among his peers was quite good. He had been dismissed by John Patterson, the czar of National Cash Register, who had a reputation for ejecting protégés on whim, and many of them had gone on to better things. Hugh Chalmers and Edward Jordan, both of whom founded automobile companies that bore their names, had been fired by Patterson. Alvan Macauley, who headed the Packard Motor Car Company, was dismissed from "the Cash," as was Charles Kettering, soon to be one of the movers and shakers at General Motors; in fact, the automobile industry in the first third of the century was studded with executives who had that experience in common. Patterson fired men who went on to head a wide variety of firms, including Addressograph-Multigraph, Monarch Machine Tool, Standard Register, and National Automatic Tool, while a score of others became divisional presidents and executive vice-presidents.

Sometimes the dismissal was performed in private, but often Patterson would subject the men to public demonstrations of his anger. Several arrived at their offices to find their furniture in the hall and a new name and lock on the door. Businessmen didn't consider a Patterson ejection a disgrace; rather, those who worked at NCR knew they did so at their peril, and they saved money and cultivated contacts against the day they would require both in finding new employment.

Given all this, why did they go to NCR? Patterson paid good salaries, but more important, he was perhaps the most imaginative and creative businessman of his time. A few years under him was the equivalent of today's M.B.A. from Harvard or Stanford. Patterson's impact upon American business derived more from the stamp he put upon several dozen executives than from what he accomplished in the way of producing machines, important though that was. When Watson left the Cash, he had $50,000 in savings, a house in Dayton, which Patterson had given him in happier days, and assurances of posts at other companies. Like those who preceded him and others who would come afterward, Watson vowed that Patterson one day would regret having fired him—he would outdo and outperform his mentor. But he would never forget the lessons Patterson had given. These would be applied at CTR, a company Watson proceeded to mold in the NCR image, just as he appeared to be a calmer, more civilized version of Patterson. One hardly can understand and appreciate the former without reference to the latter.

Enter Thomas Watson Senior

Patterson generally was conceded to be a business genius, a man of great originality who had little patience with those he considered his inferiors. He could be generous with men of superior intellect who would follow his lead in all matters. But he would not tolerate people who stood in his path, especially if they were employed by NCR. His admirers thought him forceful; others said he was a bully.

Throughout his life Patterson demonstrated an aggressive, even pugnacious personality, and it showed in his bearing and on his face. He habitually struck a stance in posed pictures that, even when he was an old man, gave him the appearance of a retired bantamweight and that bespoke a lifetime spent in vigorous sport and earnest clean living. Patterson's face, too, was strong—firm chin, fiery eyes, and a well-shaped nose, under which was a defiant grenadier's mustache. He invariably was well barbered and attired; even while horseback riding, he would wear stiff collars and neckties, and he demanded as much from his underlings. Men who were flabby or careless of dress or who imbibed in public had no future at the Cash. Favorites were expected to work and play hard, present an attractive appearance, be efficient, have well-ordered private lives, and show at least some measure of enthusiasm for Patterson's dietary and medicinal idiosyncrasies.

Patterson was born in 1844 on a farm near Dayton, Ohio. He attended Miami University in nearby Oxford, served as a volunteer during the Civil War but saw no action, and then went to Dartmouth. This last experience gave him a lifelong intense dislike and mistrust of formal education. "What I learned mostly was what not to do," he later remarked. Far better than knowledge of Greek and ancient history, said Patterson, was the ability "to use small words and big ideas," a knack he developed after graduating from Dartmouth and purging his mind of most of what he had learned there.

For a while Patterson worked on his father's farm, and then he got a job as toll collector on the Miami and Erie Canal in Jackson County. This provided him with an office and a good deal of free time, both of which he used to run a coalyard. Soon

Patterson dominated this business in his small town, largely because he gave fair weights and prompt delivery and provided receipts for all transactions. He then took over several mines so as to obtain a sufficient quantity of high-grade coal. In addition, he purchased stock in and managed properties for the Southern Ohio Coal & Iron Company, the dominant force in Jackson County. As such, he had to manage the company's dry goods store, and he discovered that an operation that should have shown annual profits of $12,000 actually was losing $6,000. The reason soon became apparent: Dishonest clerks had their hands in the till.

About this time Patterson read that James and John Ritty had invented a machine that tabulated and registered sales. Ritty's Incorruptible Cashier, as it was called, sold for $50. Initially it had been produced by the Rittys' company, which they called National Cash Register. In 1882, however, the brothers sold an interest in it to others, who reorganized the firm into the National Manufacturing Company. In any event, the machines had virtually eliminated all theft at a saloon owned by James Ritty. Thinking it would do as well at his store, Patterson ordered two of them and at the same time hired new sales personnel.

Overnight the store's deficit turned into a profit. Thoroughly impressed, Patterson ordered machines for his retail coal offices. Swept by enthusiasm for the device, Patterson purchased shares in National Manufacturing, took a seat on the board of directors, and prepared to organize a sales effort geared at placing registers in shops throughout the nation.

The company's president, George Phillips, showed little interest in Patterson's plans. A prominent Dayton merchant, Phillips was involved in real estate speculations, the creation of a local telephone company, and other projects that appeared to him more promising than cash registers. Disgusted, Patterson sold some of his stock and resigned from the board. Yet he could not forget the machines. In the autumn of 1884, on impulse, he went to see Phillips with an offer: He would pay $6,500 for Phillips's stock, take control of the company, and become its new president. Phillips quickly accepted the terms. According to one story, Patterson soon regretted the deal and tried to back out of it, offering Phillips $2,000 to be set free. "You have purchased the stock," said the relieved merchant. "If you had paid for it and I had turned over the shares to you, I would not have them back as a gift."

Now Patterson had to make the best of what appeared on the surface a bad deal. He set about revamping the shabby and poorly organized production facility, which, according to company legend, consisted of a few semiskilled workers, a varied collection of simple tools, and a converted storefront factory. Patterson changed the company's name back to National Cash Register and as a sign of his confidence sold off some of his coal holdings and used the money to purchase additional shares from anyone wanting to dispose of them.

There are no records of sales, assets, and production in 1885, but at the time no more than a few dozen machines had been placed, so that the annual gross probably was around $1,000, and assets were thin. By 1913 NCR had sold more than 1.2 million cash registers, another 13,000 a month were being turned out at the modern eighteen-building Dayton facility, and annual sales were at the rate of $21 million. Patterson rewarded himself with a six-figure salary.

Patterson claimed that all this had been made possible by the production of excellent machines that were far superior to those turned out by competitors. This certainly was not the entire truth, for although the NRC machines became standards, others produced by rival companies were every bit as good as, and some were clearly superior to, their NCR counterparts. What Patterson had that the others either lacked or could not duplicate was a vigorous and original sales program combined with what today at least would be considered questionable business practices. These—plus the creation of what might be deemed "the NCR man"—was at the crux of Patterson's success.

He started not with the machine but with the people who were to sell it. The NCR sales agents had to be bright, aggressive, persistent, intelligent, and, most of all, hungry for success and fortune. They need not have had any previous sales experience, and in fact, Patterson preferred novices, for they would have less to unlearn. "It is the men who are willing to accept information and profit by it that will get ahead in this world," he said. "I think that better salesmen can be made of new, green men, who are willing and energetic, than can be made of men who have had some experience in this business." Patterson scoffed at the idea that salesmen were born, not made, for he intended to mold his in the correct fashion. He was purveying what a later generation would term image and doing so through his field representatives. Each of these was to appear as though from the same stamping machine. All were dressed in dark suits, white shirts and subdued ties, and highly polished black shoes. Like the components of their cash registers, they were to appear interchangeable parts of a still larger machine—the Cash itself.

Patterson refused to allow any of them to carry screwdrivers or other tools when calling on prospects. An NCR salesman was not a mechanic who would repair a balky machine as a favor to a client, but instead a trained professional in the science of helping merchants increase their profits. "You must sell yourself first," he liked to tell newcomers, and the best way to do this was to impress the potential client with one's professionalism and self-confidence. Often he would send promising young men on company-paid vacations to New York, and while there they were to purchase wardrobes at his expense. Other businessmen thought this a flagrant waste of money, but Patterson knew that the salesmen emerged from this experience with a heightened sense of their own worth and an incentive to improve their standards of living. This would be possible only if they sold record numbers of registers. It was, then, a worthwhile investment.

Each NCR salesman was given a guaranteed territory. Others from the company were not permitted to canvass there, and unsolicited orders from merchants in the territory were turned over to the salesman, who received a commission for them. Patterson's rivals felt this was senseless since it removed a spur to greater efforts and rewarded salesmen unnecessarily. He, of course, disagreed, observing that most manufacturers looked upon salesmen as necessary evils, whose commissions came out of their profits and were not really earned. In the early years at NCR the conventional belief was that profits should accrue to manufacturers, not to distributors. Patterson felt otherwise; the product is worthless unless it is sold, he often said, and so the salesman is a vital partner in the enterprise. Besides, he combined the guaranteed territory with a quota system. At the pinnacle at NCR was the Hundred Point Club, comprised of salesmen who had exceeded their quotas. They received bonuses, trips to conventions in big cities, and coverage in the company newspaper as well as personal congratulations from Patterson. The next year club members would find their quotas even higher, so their efforts would have to be redoubled.

Because the NCR salesmen were among the best rewarded in the country, they had a great incentive to work hard, for without results they might be demoted or fired. Two decades before Henry Ford discovered the virtue of high pay for good workers and instituted the $5 day in his plants, Patterson had salesmen on his force who made upwards of $30,000 a year. And the more they earned, the happier he would be. Other merchants tried to cut back on commission rates for excellent salesmen, arguing that the results came more from the nature of the territory than the efforts of the individual. Patterson, in contrast, would give bonuses to good producers. "If you can sell a million dollars in a week," he told one star salesman, "we'll hire a brass band to take your commission to you."

The sales effort was supported by an imaginative and costly set of advertising campaigns, and in fact, almost as much money was spent in promoting the machines as in producing them. Patterson introduced aggressive promotion shortly after taking command at NCR. Recruiting ten likely candidates for sales positions, he began by dazzling them with visions of the great wealth that could be theirs if only they absorbed what he had to say and then applied his precepts. According to him, the nation needed at least one register for every 400 inhabitants. The candidates knew the approximate populations of their territories, and while they did the mental arithmetic to figure out how much they might earn, Patterson went on, asking each to provide the names of 500 prospects in his territory. Now he had a list of 5,000 names. The next step was to write and have printed eighteen letters, each of which outlined a different reason why the purchase of a cash register made good business sense. The letters went out, one at a time for the next eighteen days, in the first example of saturation advertising.

The method worked. An inquiry would come in and be given to the salesman whose territory the merchant was in. Then came the initial visit, the follow-up, and, if all went well, the sale, generally on the installment plan.

The NCR salesmen would keep in touch with purchasers even after payments were completed, assessing their business needs and keeping the information on file. Calls for repairs or temporary replacements were promptly and efficiently answered, and extensions of payments could be arranged if they were required. Patterson appreciated the need for good customer relations and a superlative corporate image. He believed he was selling a service, not a product, and if it didn't result in higher profits for the purchaser, NCR would lose not only a sale but possibly a market as well. If, on the other hand, everything went well, the salesman might in a few years convince the businessman to replace his current machine with a new one that offered additional features. Word-of-mouth advertising was also important, especially in an industry that was highly competitive, and this, too, depended more perhaps on NCR's customer relations than on the superiority of its machines. With some justification it was claimed that Patterson lagged in research and development and even that he stole ideas and products from his competitors' registers. This could not be said for his sales and advertising techniques, which were highly effective and often imitated.

In 1894 Patterson established a formal training school; thenceforth all salesmen would undergo indoctrination there. And the course of instruction clearly was geared toward indoctrination, not education or even training. Patterson didn't appreciate originality in his salesmen; in contacts with clients they were not to deviate from the company line.

That line was set down by Joseph H. Crane, who, in addition to being NCR's crack salesman and director of the school, was Patterson's brother-in-law and one of the few men he deferred to in matters of sales technique. Several years earlier Patterson had asked him the secrets of his success, and Crane responded by delivering his sales pitch, honed to perfection by years on the road. Impressed, Patterson said, "That talk would induce me to buy a cash register," and asked Crane to repeat it for another executive. While this was being done, Patterson had a stenographer take it down verbatim. The talk was then printed as "The N.C.R. Primer: How I Sell a Cash Register," and distributed to all salesmen. Later the pamphlet became a basic text at the NCR school, where all potential agents were required to memorize it for later testing and evaluation. The speech was not to be analyzed, then, but was to be accepted as holy writ. "We had a primer of about 450 words, which it was necessary to be able to say word for word," recalled a graduate of Crane's course. "You were not considered bright enough to become an N.C.R. man if you could not recite it well. On the other hand, it was not well to be too bright. A happy medium was the proper thing. Then you might make good."

Patterson liked to post slogans in various places at company headquarters. One of these, outside his office door, read: "Be Brief. Omit all compliments about welfare work." The most prevalent one, however, consisted of a single word: "THINK." But this was not taken seriously at NCR, for Patterson was more interested in acceptance and obedience than intellectual endeavors of any kind.

Patterson was addicted to what he called chalk talks. Blackboards and pedestals for flip card presentations were placed in most rooms at corporate headquarters, and he took them along on his many trips throughout the nation. "The optic nerve is twenty-two times stronger than the auditory nerve," he liked to say, and all his talks were accompanied by scribblings on blackboards and reference to the flip cards.

Invariably the points made on the cards came in sets of five. Apparently he was intrigued by the number, though how this came about is impossible to say. Some believe the fixation originated from the time he would tick off ideas on the fingers of one hand. Others have noted that there are five senses. More important, perhaps, there were five kinds of money (gold, silver, copper, nickel, and paper), five kinds of fractional currency (pennies, nickels, dimes, quarters, and half dollars), and a like number of retail transactions performed on registers: cash sales, credit sales, purchases on account, bill collections, and money changing. Patterson stretched matters somewhat when he told a writer that agents at the school were instructed on the reasons merchants should have registers, and naturally, there were five of these—general instructions, objections and answers, selling points, closing arguments, and "miscellaneous." Whenever possible, he divided states and even cities into five territories. All registers were priced in multiples of five, and points in the NCR club were accrued in units of five. Finally, the flip card talks were structured so that all could be fitted on precisely five cards.

This was the company Thomas Watson joined in 1895, the erratic man who dominated it, and the training program he underwent.

Watson came as close as anyone to being the quintessential NCR man. Twenty-one years old at the time, he was earnest, intelligent, and highly ambitious and prepared to accept instruction. Watson was one of those highly disciplined individuals whose appearances change remarkably little over the decades. The outlines of the elderly tycoon of the 1950's were quite visible in photos of the young trainee of 1895. Both were tall, erect, lean, and strikingly handsome, with square-cut features and quick, piercing eyes. Throughout his NCR career and later Watson favored dark suits, stiff shirt collars, and subdued ties. As a youth he experimented with a mustache, but this frivolity was soon abandoned. He would appear at NCR clean-shaven.

Photographers rarely caught Watson in a moment of repose or with a smile on his face. Instead, most photos of the man, whether candid or posed, have him with a faint, almost forced grin, and his eyes were never playful. This was a person serious in all he did. And what he enjoyed most, and did best, was selling. Years later he told a reporter that he had a positive penchant for "collecting salesmen," that he liked to hire and train them whenever he could. In common with Patterson, Watson tended to believe that merchandising came first, that the function of the factory and laboratory was to discover and produce products for the sales agents to peddle.

Even Patterson, who continued to hold that salesmen were made, not born, might have made an exception for Watson. With all his varied interests later on, Watson was a natural salesman with a keener eye for development in this area than anything else. He had been born in Steuben County, a rural and wooded area to the southwest of the Finger Lakes in upper New York. Watson's father, also called Thomas, was in the lumber business and ran a small farm. The son tried his hand at farming and lumbering, rejected his father's suggestion he become a lawyer, and played with the idea of teaching school. He took a few courses at a local business school and in the spring of 1892 became a bookkeeper in a meat market in the rustic town of Painted Post, a job and place he thoroughly disliked.

Watson had an itch to seek new places; like thousands of young men of the time, he thought traveling salesmen were romantic figures. They would go about the countryside, staying at hotels and eating in restaurants, always meeting people, selling goods, and then moving on to another place. Watson would gladly have given up Painted Post for this kind of life. His chance arrived only a few weeks after he began work in the meat market. Watson ran into a salesman, George Cornwell, who had just taken a job peddling pianos, organs, and sewing machines and needed an assistant. He offered to take Watson on at a salary of $10 a week, which was almost double his earnings at the meat market. Watson quickly accepted, and in the summer of 1892, at the age of eighteen, he set off with Cornwell in an open wagon. It was not as romantic as he had hoped it would be. Since the territory covered was in the Painted Post area, there would be no long train rides to big cities, no conversations with fascinating people, and no dinners in fine restaurants. Instead, the two men slogged along country paths and tried to peddle musical instruments and sewing machines to stolid and indifferent farmers. The prospects weren't good. Nor were the rewards.

Still, Watson was being initiated into the fine arts of salesmanship, and when Cornwell left for a better-paying position, he took over, at a salary of $12. He was content enough with this to stay on for more than a year. Then, in conversation with another salesman, Watson learned that most people in his line of work were paid on a commission basis. That night he figured that by taking a straight salary, he had been badly cheated. Feeling quite foolish and angry at both himself and his employer, he quit his job and took the train to the big city—Buffalo—in search of another, one in which he would be paid commissions.

It was a reckless step. This was 1893, a period of economic hardship and mass unemployment, the worst time in a generation to be out of work. Watson went from one firm to another in the downtown area but had no luck in finding a job. After close to two months of this he was ready to write home for money to buy a ticket back to Painted Post. It was then that he was taken on as a commission agent at Wheeler & Wilcox, for which he was to peddle sewing machines. This didn't last long; but while it did, Watson met other traveling salesmen who operated out of the Buffalo area, and one of them, an older man called C. B. Barron, took him under his wing. Barron had a quick line of patter, a way with a story, and a talent for making friends, all of which impressed Watson. The man was a classic drummer, the kind of person who inspired stories about traveling salesmen that were stock-in-trade for humorists of that period. He seemed to float through life with ease and was a devout optimist, a trait which impressed his customers and resulted in sales. Watson had never met anyone quite like him before. Barron also dressed the part—silk hat, cutaway, spats, and all—and if some-

what garish, he also fairly reeked of what went for flashy afflu-
ence.

Watson was flattered when Barron suggested they join
forces in a new enterprise. He talked the Buffalo Building &
Loan Association into giving them commission work selling its
stock. Then the two men took to the road. Bold and gregarious,
Barron would say and promise almost anything to extract a sale,
and Watson took all this in. He tried to imitate Barron's approach, if not his actual words, and found it worked well. Watson started making sales of his own and in the process earned
more than he had ever thought possible. It was an exciting and
fruitful experience, one he would never forget. "They say
money isn't everything," he recalled a half century later. "It isn't
everything, but [it] is a great big something when you are
trying to get started in the world and haven't anything. I speak
feelingly."

Part of this new wealth went into the purchase of a wardrobe; Barron made certain the last vestige of hayseed was eliminated. "Clothes don't make the man," said Watson, "but they go
a long way toward making a businessman." And that was what
he meant to be now—not merely a salesman, but a true tycoon.

At this time chain stores were coming into vogue, and Watson tried to get in on the boom. The rest of his savings together
with some money borrowed from his father went into the establishment of a butcher shop in Buffalo, the first of what he hoped
would be a group. Now he had to learn all he could about the
business. Drawing upon his Painted Post experience, he hired
personnel and tried to supervise their work. This would be difficult because he and Barron were on the road much of the time.
To ensure their honesty, Watson purchased a secondhand cash
register.

It was an ambitious and sensible plan. Watson would plow
back into the shop earnings to which would be added commissions from stock sales. Soon there would be sufficient funds for a
second shop, and then the process would be repeated. Within a
few years, assuming all went well, he would be the meat king of
Buffalo.

In the Beginning

Watson's entrepreneurial career didn't last long. True to type, Barron slipped out of town shortly after the opening of the first store, taking with him all of his and Watson's funds. The young man never saw him again. Then Watson lost his job at the Building & Loan. The meat store failed. Watson was broke. But he did have that new wardrobe and the self-confidence and patina of success bestowed upon him by Barron. It was 1895. The depression was still on, and unemployment remained high. A new job would have to be found, and this time he would stick to what he knew best: sales.

Before this could be done, however, Watson would have to liquidate whatever remained at the store. Fixtures were sold, and those purchased on credit were returned to the sellers. The cash register was one of these. Watson carried it down to the local NCR office and, on a hunch, decided to apply for a sales job there. He was interviewed by John Range, the district manager, who had a reputation of being one of the finest developers of salesmen in the organization. Range was not impressed by the failed merchant and dismissed salesman and told Watson he was not the kind of person NCR was looking for. But Watson persisted, returning again and again, until he was taken on for a probationary period. Range handed him a copy of "The N.C.R. Primer," told him to absorb its message, and then put him on the road selling cash registers.

Watson's experience with Barron had exposed him to the world of salesmanship; the primer provided him with elements of theory propounded by NCR. Range showed him how to combine both the rigid principles of Patterson and the showmanship of Barron, and in the process he transformed Watson into a smooth, scientific salesman. In his new pupil he found a man of latent talent, great ambition, and stamina, who was prepared to accept instruction. When Watson came back after ten days on the road without having sold a single machine, Range went out with him and showed him how it was done. Watson said he didn't know what to do when a prospect told him he didn't want to buy a cash register, and Range demonstrated the proper response. He would smile, get the customer's confidence, tell a few jokes, and then say, "I know you don't. That's why I came to see you. I knew if you wanted one, you would have come down to the office and picked one out. What I've come for is to find out why you don't want one." It was Range, recalled Watson, "who taught me to use that important word 'why' in selling." This went beyond the NCR manual, a pamphlet Range apparently realized was based upon the experience of a single salesman in a particular area of the country; it may have worked for him but had to be adapted to the personalities of others. Range was prepared to bend the precepts of Patterson and Crane, and so long as he produced results, who cared?

It seemed very simple, even then. Patterson had said in many different ways that NCR was in the business of providing a service for its customers. The salesman would have to demonstrate convincingly that the merchant would make more than enough money from each register to cover its cost. He would have to prove to skeptical clerks that the presence of a register didn't mean their employer thought them dishonest (even when he did) and then win them to his side. It was wrong to denigrate rival machines, said Patterson and Crane, for this was unprofessional. Range agreed—because such tactics rarely worked. The salesman would have to believe completely in his product and remain loyal to his company at all times. Watson accepted this wholeheartedly, as he did most of what Range told him. At times, of course, there would be dry spells when that faith would be tested. On such occasions Range would offer advice and often harsh criticisms, take Watson on the road with him, and provide yet another lesson and demonstration.

It was like a variant of the Horatio Alger story: The young man from the farm goes to the big city and makes good, through pluck and luck, with the guidance of a wise, experienced older man. Or at least that was the way Watson liked to recall his Buffalo experiences. In his heart he truly believed the simple middle-class maxims of the period. Watson prized hard work and loyalty above all, and this comes through in the thousands of speeches and remarks he was to deliver in the next half century. In 1952 he told a writer that Range's advice was the best he ever had received and would still serve salesmen well. It all boiled down to a single principle: "Pack your todays with effort —extra effort! Your tomorrows will take care of themselves. They will also take good care of you and your money."

There was more to it than that, of course. Watson often utilized such homilies in his public statements and let them go at that. As was and is the case with almost all successful salesmen, he paid great attention to appearances, trying to present a proper face to all, potential clients in particular. Underneath this was the shrewd tactician, continuously assessing the impacts of statements and movements, trying to read subtle signs sent out by the client, always with the goal of nailing down the sale. Watson appreciated that his middle-class customers prized sincerity, dedication, earnestness, and other such public virtues and that most even believed in and applied them to one degree or another. So did he. They would be impressed by a well-informed and properly groomed representative, which Watson had become. He knew the value of being able to listen to a story and then to laugh with conviction at the proper moment, for the right amount of time. Guile was necessary to sell machines, and so was flattery; but the successful salesman could not be obvious in their use. He had to accept all this but at the same time not become cynical about it.

The high-flown ideas Patterson espoused in his speeches and articles were fine in their place; but they had to be applied pragmatically and on occasion discarded entirely, to be replaced by inspired innovation. All this business about not criticizing rival machines and concentrating on expounding upon the virtues of one's own sounded impressive on the podium but made little sense in the field at a time when more than a dozen representatives for other firms were prowling the Buffalo area. Watson conceded he stole clients from fellow salesmen, and given the techniques and accepted traditions of the period, he must have been as ruthless and devious in his approach as was necessary. Beneath the skin of the scientific salesman was the soul of the drummer. Range and Barron both understood this, and they imparted what they knew to Watson, who in any case would have learned it on the road, if not from his mentors. For that matter, Patterson himself, though never a direct cash register salesman, appreciated the need for hardheaded tactics in the field.

Within three years Watson became the star NCR salesman for upper New York. According to one account, in a single record-smashing week he earned $1,225 in commissions, an astonishing amount in view of the fact that he got 15 percent on sales and that most NCR registers went for between $100 and $200.

Clearly he was ready for bigger things and greater challenges, or at least this was the thinking at corporate headquarters. Business was booming throughout the nation; the depression had ended, and opportunities abounded. Besides, Buffalo had become saturated with cash registers as a result of his and Range's efforts. Watson's talents were being wasted there. Finally, Range had recommended Watson for a promotion, and this was supported by many other people in the organization who knew him, including Hugh Chalmers. For all these reasons, in 1899 Watson became branch manager in Rochester, at the time not a very promising territory.

NCR's record in central New York was particularly poor; in fact, it was one of the worst in the nation, a source of deep irritation to Patterson. It was believed that the agent had done a poor job and had to be replaced. If Watson could turn Rochester around, he would not only be marked as a "comer" in Dayton but do well financially because as an agent his commissions would come to 35 percent.

At first Watson did quite well, lifting sales by hard work and the application of maxims and techniques from the NCR guides. But then he encountered a strong sales push from the Hallwood Company, one of NCR's chief rivals, which had an excellent machine that sold for a lower price than most others. Now Watson turned to the hard sell. He or one of his salesmen would trail the Hallwood representatives as they made their rounds, noting the firms they visited. Shortly thereafter the merchant would find at his door an NCR salesman, who would not only tell of the virtues of his machines but speak ill of the Hallwoods. In 1897 Patterson had brought a patent infringement suit against Hallwood, and that company promptly counterfiled under the terms of the Sherman Antitrust Act, claiming that NCR engaged in unfair competition and conspired to restrain trade. The NCR salesman would aver that the suit was about to be settled in his company's favor and, furthermore, that owners of Hallwood registers would be named as accomplices. Hallwood was in shaky financial condition, or so they would say, and in fact was on the verge of dissolution. If this happened, there would be no one to service its machines, which, once broken, would be worthless. Thoroughly frightened, the merchant was now set up for the clincher: an offer to sell him an NCR register at a substantial discount.

It was not a pleasant business, but it was the way such activities were carried out in this period. Watson was no better or worse than the Hallwood people, who responded in kind whenever they could. But he won out in the end; within a few months the Hallwood threat had been blunted. Watson felt proud of his men and the job they did. Somewhat disingenuously he later said, "I gathered some fellows around me, and when I left that territory, it was one of the best organized and cleanest territories that had ever been turned over to another man."

It was not the cleanliness of the Rochester operation that interested NCR management, however, but rather the way Watson had stifled the competition. For years Patterson had been involved in litigation aimed at sweeping out all other register manufacturers, while he tried to do the same in the field through his salesmen, of whom Watson showed the most talent at the task. In 1903 Watson was summoned to Dayton to confer with Patterson and other executives. Hugh Chalmers, who had just been elevated to the post of general manager, had devised a scheme to rid the company of troublesome competition, and he needed a man of Watson's demonstrated skills to put it into operation.

Enter Thomas Watson Senior

It seemed that over the past few years several firms had entered the industry through the back door. They had purchased used registers, rehabilitated them, and then offered to sell the machines at a low cost. Thus, it was possible for a merchant to purchase an NCR register from one of these companies at a price lower than that quoted by the firm's own salesmen. These companies were doing a good business, a fact that irked Patterson, who now meant to bring it to an end. "The best way to kill a dog is to cut off its head," he later explained, and Watson was told that he was to do the chopping.

According to the plan, Watson was to use NCR funds to establish a company to deal in used registers. This firm, which was to be known as Watson's Cash Register & Second Hand Exchange, was established in Manhattan, with the objective of destroying the competition in that major market. Watson's did not have to show a profit; success or failure would be measured in how many companies in the secondhand business were forced to sell out or liquidate. In their company-sponsored biography of him, Thomas and Marva Belden wrote: "Watson established stores next to successful competitors, copied their successes, discarded their failures, hired their salesmen, undersold them, eventually put them out of business." The pattern was then repeated in Philadelphia. The city conquered, Watson moved on to Chicago, a central point from which he directed national operations in the secondhand business.

Watson reported directly to Chalmers and was instructed to keep secret all his dealings with Dayton, never to let on that he was an NCR "front." Years later it would be claimed that at the time the young man didn't truly appreciate the implications of what he was doing, that he didn't realize such behavior was in direct violation of the antitrust statutes. But Watson never explained why he agreed to keep a closed mouth throughout the operation if there was nothing to hide. In mitigation of his actions, the Beldens wrote that Watson's settlements with competitors were "generous" and "honorable" and that he "always regretted and rarely mentioned" his experiences of this period.

This is understandable considering what came out of the episode. The fact remains that Watson engaged in underhanded behavior at NCR.

He also had a hand in one of Patterson's favorite campaigns, one that involved "knockout machines," also known as "knockers." NCR designed and advertised machines that were close copies of, but were priced far below, those produced and sold by competitors. These registers were not meant to be produced, but rather were supposed to cause clients to have second thoughts about purchasing anything but an NCR machine. For a few months, then, while a customer awaited delivery of a nonexistent NCR model, a competitor had to forgo the sale and the profits therefrom. If obliged to do so, NCR might actually produce the machine and make delivery. These cheap models didn't hold up, however, and had to be replaced, by which time the competitor might be out of business. The objective here was not to sell NCRs at a profit, but to deny sales to other companies. This, too, was in direct violation of the Sherman Antitrust Act.

The deception came to an end in 1907, when NCR finally announced that henceforth Watson would be in charge of the firm's secondhand business. He would be stationed in Dayton, close to the top of the executive pyramid, where he would work under Patterson and with Chalmers.

Life at that level of management at NCR was never dull or secure. Chalmers was fired after a policy dispute with Patterson, who took this opportunity to clean house of almost everyone who had anything to do with the departing general manager. Watson was one of the few to be spared probably because he was too valuable a man to lose, but he was exiled to Manhattan for a period. Then he returned to Dayton with the title of sales manager, one of the handful of executives in the inner circle generally considered to be Patterson's heir apparent—at least for a season or so.

It was 1910. Only thirty-six years old, Watson had already achieved much and clearly was one of the industry's bright stars. Then everything started to fall apart.

Enter Thomas Watson Senior

That year the American Cash Register Company filed complaints against NCR, charging multiple violations of the Sherman Antitrust Act. The second largest firm in the industry, American had been fashioned out of the Hallwood and other companies that had managed to resist Watson's take-over bids; its leadership was comprised in part of former NCR men, some of whom Patterson had fired. It was out to smash NCR, which by then had almost completed its mopping-up operations and was gearing up for the final push against American. The company knew where to find evidence to incriminate Patterson and Watson. Henry James, who initiated the suit, had once been one of the most successful NCR salesmen, and Hugh Chalmers had an important financial stake in the firm. Vowing revenge for the shabby way he had been treated in Dayton, Chalmers knew all the details of the Watson operations and the knockout campaign, and he presented these to Attorney General George Wickersham. So convincing was his case that in 1912 the federal government joined in the prosecution, charging that Patterson, Watson, and virtually the entire NCR ruling group had conspired to violate several provisions of the antitrust statutes.

The trial was held in Cincinnati and began in November. This was the height of the antitrust movement, and national attention was focused on the courtroom. James Cox, a former newspaper publisher and a longtime enemy of Patterson, was governor-elect of Ohio, and he made no secret of his desire to see the NCR chief behind bars. The press in general appeared to feel that Patterson was guilty, as much for his arrogance and dictatorial methods as for anything else. But even without this negative atmosphere, the evidence presented was damning. Chalmers, who had helped originate the secondhand and knockout operations (and who doubtless would have been indicted had he remained at NCR), revealed the methods Patterson had employed to force competitors to the wall and the way he threatened litigation against those interlopers who refused to bend to his will. The government produced evidence that NCR salesmen had interfered with and sabotaged their rivals, along with a string of snappy statements Patterson was alleged to have made about the way he did business. "We do not buy out. We knock out," was typical of the genre.

As for Watson, he remained in the background throughout the trial as befitted anyone in Patterson's employ at a time when the leader occupied center stage. But the evidence showed he was involved in the knockout and secondhand business. Like the others, he denied wrongdoing and his defenders later would observe that such operations as those he headed, while technically in violation of the statutes, were commonly accepted business practices of the period.

The verdict and sentence were handed down on February 13, 1913. All the defendants were found guilty, and Patterson and Watson were sentenced to fines of $5,000 and a year in jail. The fines had been expected, but not the incarceration; both men had received the maximum sentences, unprecedented in actions such as this one. Even some of Patterson's enemies conceded the penalty did not fit the crime. All involved appealed the verdict, which was scheduled to be considered by the court of appeals.

This was a trying time for Watson. Not only had he become alienated from Patterson during the trial, but he was also engaged to marry Jeannette Kittredge, the daughter of a local businessman. Watson suggested they break their engagement, but she refused to hear of it. The wedding was planned, even though the bridegroom faced disgrace and a jail term.

Nature and the court of appeals saved Watson. Dayton was hit by one of the worst floods in American history in late March, destroying more than $100 million in property and leaving 90,000 people homeless. The autocratic Patterson was the best kind of person to take charge during such a disaster. He threw his full resources into the effort to provide relief and save lives. NCR assembly lines were converted from the production of registers to that of rowboats. Thousands of Daytonians were housed in company offices, and virtually the entire city ate at the NCR cafeteria, which kept running around the clock. Only a few weeks earlier he had been castigated as a heartless tycoon; now Patterson became a national hero. General Evangeline Cory Booth of the Salvation Army heralded him as an instrument of God, who doubtless would be rewarded. The press hailed Patterson as a philanthropist and told readers he was a generous man. Even Governor Cox had some kind words to say about him. Incoming President Woodrow Wilson offered his congratulations and urged a pardon for his humanitarian work, to which Patterson replied, "Our case is still in the courts. I do not ask for, nor would I accept, a pardon. All I want is simple justice."

What Patterson and the others received from the court was not simple, and there were those on both sides who argued it wasn't just either. In 1915 the court of appeals handed down a decision that the original indictment was defective in several areas and that the trial itself had been conducted unfairly. For these reasons the judges ordered the government to seek a retrial. Given the atmosphere of the time, this would never take place. Thus, the NCR leadership was no longer guilty in the eyes of the law, but neither had it been declared innocent of the charges.

Patterson celebrated nonetheless. There was a parade in Dayton, climaxed by his speech. "I am thankful and grateful for the decision of the Court of Appeals," he said. "It was, however, what we had a right to expect from three just and able men." Patterson thanked the crowd "On behalf of myself, and twenty-one colleagues who have been associated with me during the last two years of strenuous times."

The number was inaccurate. After the flood rescue and before the second trial Patterson had conducted another of his regular sweepouts of the executive suites, and Watson was one of those who had been ejected.

From the first Watson had proclaimed he had done nothing wrong. He wrote one friend that "while I am under jail sentence, I do not consider myself a criminal," and to another he wrote: "I do not feel humiliated. My conscience is clear. . . ." Patterson appeared to have taken Watson's protestation of innocence as meaning he was trying to dissociate himself from the other defendants. On one occasion there was talk of plea bargaining; Patterson was interested, but Watson rejected the notion out of hand. Patterson had agreed to a consent decree to avoid further litigation; Watson refused to sign, and this angered the older man. Then there was the matter of the rescue operation. Watson played a role in it, dispatching food and supplies to Dayton from New York. Afterward Patterson came to believe that for having done this, Watson was seeking an undue share of the glory. Finally, the two men had a falling-out over sales strategy. In April 1914, at the age of forty, Watson was dismissed.

Doubtless he would have had to go in any event. Patterson had never permitted any of his subordinates to rise beyond a certain point, and as has been indicated, it was a tradition at NCR for heirs apparent to be axed. Watson was no different from the others in this regard. And like them, he vowed revenge. When he walked out of the NCR complex, he turned to a friend. "I've helped build all but one of those buildings," he said. "Now I am going out to build a business bigger than John H. Patterson has." And of course, he would do just that. Watson would become a greater force in world business than Patterson had been in his time. He would prove capable of bold, even forceful actions, but rarely was Watson as innovative and imaginative as his mentor had been. Lessons learned in sales would later be applied in his future post. Methods Patterson had used to turn back rivals in cash registers would be employed by Watson's son and his successors to deal with challenges in computers—to the point of using knockout machines in one contest with Control Data. Ironically, the leasing companies that eventually would bedevil the son might have learned something from a study of the operations of Watson's Cash Register & Second Hand Exchange. Finally, the cash register business at the turn of the century had its version of plug-compatible equipment. The context was different, but the problems were remarkably similar. For that matter, so were the solutions—including the antitrust action.

Enter Thomas Watson Senior

Patterson placed his stamp not only on Watson but on the company to which he was heading. Principles inculcated in Dayton would be applied in Endicott. Like so many dozens of other Patterson ejectees, Thomas Watson would remain an NCR man for the rest of his business career.

3

CTR: The Apprenticeship

THE NASCENT Computing-Tabulating-Recording Corporation appeared to be more an instrument for producing speculative capital gains for Charles Flint and his associates than a viable, if not vigorous, business entity. Not only were its component firms mismatched, but the balance sheet presented the picture of a classic scam, while CTR's original managers seemed to know they were transients.

The firm claimed total assets of $17.5 million, of which $16.5 million was represented by the asserted worth of the paper of the acquired companies. For this the owners of shares in International Time, Computing Scale, Tabulating Machine, and Bundy had received $10.5 million worth in face value of CTR stock. Flint had "written up" the values of the old stocks by some $6 million, and this was the approximate amount of water in the capitalization.

CTR: The Apprenticeship

At the time of its birth CTR had cash items of only $35,000, in addition to treasury bonds of less than $200,000 that were used as collateral for short-term loans. The firm hardly could have functioned for long without an infusion of new capital. Selling additional stock was out of the question, so Flint had to seek a loan. This was obtained from the Guaranty Trust Company, which had financed several of Flint's earlier ventures and took this one on perhaps as a concession to a valued client. Guaranty purchased a $7 million gold issue that matured in thirty years, with a sinking fund to begin in 1913. This was about as secure a lien as could be obtained. As for the interest rate, it was close to being usurious. A few years earlier J. P. Morgan had said that 5 percent interest could draw money from the moon. The Guaranty issue carried a 6 percent coupon.

George W. Fairchild, CTR's first chairman of the board, had a rich and varied business background, having published a newspaper in Oneonta, New York, and served on the boards of several local companies. Formerly the president of International Time, he had been largely responsible for that firm's success. A wealthy, vigorous, and experienced man of fifty-seven in 1911, Fairchild was the logical selection for the top leadership post at CTR. Given his outlook and knowledge, he might have come to dominate that firm, too, had he been able to devote full time to the job. But Fairchild had other interests. He had been elected to the House of Representatives in 1906 and was still there five years later. President Taft had named him to a ministerial post in Mexico in 1910, and Fairchild was embroiled in the affairs of that country while chief executive at CTR.

Flint understood that Fairchild would be a part-time, temporary leader, a figurehead to please the bankers and impress the stockholders, a large number of whom were Oneonta citizens who had turned in their International Time shares for those of CTR only after he had advised them to do so. Fairchild would not become involved in the day-to-day operations of the company. He signed some official papers as "acting president" until Frank Kondolf, the former chief operating officer at International Time, took over that job. An amiable man who later served for a while as president of Remington Typewriter, Kondolf had a good reputation within the industry and, had he been able to demonstrate his talents, might have been able to develop them at CTR. But he didn't impress Flint, so Kondolf understood that his was only a stopgap appointment, too.

Meanwhile, the company trod water. Largely as the result of continued strong sales of time clocks, there were profits at CTR. But Fairchild and Kondolf showed little interest in developing new products, reinvigorating Computing Scale, or marketing the Hollerith tabulating machines to additional customers. No attempt was made to integrate operations, harmonize product lines, or eliminate overlaps. In this period CTR did little in the way of what today would be called research and development. Earnings were not plowed back into the company. Rather, they were used to lower the debt and, in 1913, pay stockholders a dividend. These were typical actions of a firm out to impress bankers and the investment community, not one attempting to grow within the industry. Flint seemed more interested in boosting the quotation for CTR stock than in creating a viable business entity. It was of a piece with his reputation as a jittery wheeler-dealer. Wall Streeters might have been excused for concluding that he was planning to sell out at a high price and then move on to other things.

Yet with all this Flint went through the motions at least of searching for a new chief executive officer. And in late 1913 Thomas Watson was seeking new employment. Each man must have known of the other's needs. Mutual friends suggested they meet. Apparently Watson made the first move, calling upon Flint in Manhattan to inquire about the situation at CTR.

This was not a case of a down-and-out indicted, convicted, and disgraced executive coming hat in hand to petition a business czar. Watson had considered many offers since leaving Dayton, some from men who themselves had been fired by Patterson and knew what that implied. Furthermore, even then it appeared that either the antitrust decision would be reversed or the criminal penalties reduced; there was little chance that

Watson would be sent to jail. Still, he was under a cloud, and were it not for this, he might have aimed higher.

Watson didn't have to tell Flint of his work at NCR, for his accomplishments there were fairly well known within the New York business community. As for the reasons he had turned down other offers, Watson indicated that most of them involved working with a strong chief executive, were outside his special field of experience, and paid straight salaries plus bonuses. He was in a strong enough position to turn down any job in which he would lack the authority to carry out his programs. Watson had rejected attractive offers to manage firms in the boat, automobile, retail, and other industries in which his knowledge of business machines would be wasted. Still a salesman at heart, he wanted a "gentleman's salary" plus a share of the profits he helped generate. Thus, even though it was only a fledgling company and hardly in strong shape, CTR seemed ideal for Watson. Flint assured him that Fairchild would stay out of the way, that Watson would have a free hand in management, and that the question of remuneration presented no serious obstacle; he liked the kind of man who insisted upon receiving "part of the ice" he had helped cut.

Flint had to overcome objections from the board. "Who is going to run the business while he serves his term in jail?" asked one director. Another, knowing well the answer to his question but wanting to see how it would be fielded, asked why he had left NCR. "Because Mr. Patterson asked for my resignation," was the response. Watson spoke of Patterson's well-known eccentricities but added that he considered him an imaginative and resourceful businessman. Fairchild doubted Watson was the right man for the job. Not only was Watson tainted, but he clearly opposed a generous dividend policy, preferring instead to plow all moneys back into the business. What would his Oneonta neighbors make of this? thought the chairman. But in the end he and the others bowed to Flint's judgment.

Still, Watson would not be named president immediately; that would have to wait until the criminal charges were resolved. Instead, he would receive the title of general manager, along with a salary of $25,000, an option on 1,220 shares of CTR common, and a slice of the profits. Watson began work in May 1914, still uncertain as to what kind of future he had at the company.

Although Watson appreciated the strengths of International Time and the problems at Computing Scale, and attempted to exploit the former and alleviate the latter, he was most interested in the prospects for Tabulating Machine. Perhaps this was because the devices turned out by this company were more akin to cash registers than any other products produced by CTR, or it might have been that he recognized that they had an enormous potential market. Although it was true that in 1914 International Time dominated CTR in terms of both sales and profits, there were indications of restless activity at Tabulating Machine Watson must have found appealing and familiar.

Shortly after the amalgamation several leading figures at Tabulating Machine met in Washington to discuss the company's future. By then it had become apparent that Powers not only had superior models but was succeeding in selling them to clients who formerly had used Holleriths. The company still had a backlog of unfilled orders, but this would not last much longer if the company's stagnation continued. E. A. Ford, one of Hollerith's assistants, recommended the establishment of a research laboratory, but Fairchild and others in New York would hear none of this. Their attention remained centered on International Time, and in any event they would not invest new funds in any operation that could not promise additional profits in a short period.

The firm did have sufficient capital for a new sales effort, one that would not prove costly since the salesmen were paid commissions and not straight salaries. Branch offices were established in several eastern and midwestern cities, where salesmen were urged to investigate the businesses of prospective clients to find out whether or not they could profitably utilize one or more Hollerith systems. A general sales office was opened in

CTR: The Apprenticeship

Manhattan, not far from CTR headquarters, from which a small staff attempted to coordinate matters and open new territories. Tabulating Machine also attempted to exploit the foreign market, an area that Powers had virtually ignored. Because of a lack of funds, the company had to license others to produce and sell machines and so received only a small royalty. Still, new clients were being serviced, and whatever revenues did accrue pleased Fairchild and the others.

Watson must have reflected that this was the way NCR men operated. Although it was a barebones structure, it demonstrated that at least he would have a human foundation upon which to build; he would be able to mold some of those already working at Tabulating Machine into his version of the CTR man. To indicate his support, Watson permitted Ford to create an experimental laboratory. It was little more than one room with a part-time assistant, but the action was a direct challenge to Hollerith's authority. Watson made no secret of his intention to use Tabulating Machine as a base of operations, and in the process he displaced the company's founder. Just as Fairchild served as president of International Time while chairman of CTR, so Watson assumed the presidency of Tabulating Machine as well as the general managership of the mother company.

While displacing Hollerith, he wooed Flint, a potential ally in any struggle against the International Time faction, which he had come to see as a collection of opportunists. On learning that several executives there were planning to manipulate the price of the stock, Watson went to see Flint and threatened to tell what he knew to reporters unless there was a halt to such activities. There is no way of discovering what went on between the two men, but in any event Flint came down on Watson's side. Perhaps he now realized that no matter what had happened at NCR, Watson was a man of integrity who meant to run a clean operation at CTR. Or it could have been that the new general manager had convinced him that there was more money to be made by creating a viable company than in manipulating its paper. In any case the wheeling and dealing came to an end.

From that point on Flint backed Watson in most of his clashes with the board. During the next year he obtained funding for Ford's laboratory. Watson received money to train additional salesmen. Flint talked the International Time people into setting aside parts of their factory in Endicott and later into erecting a separate facility for the production of tabulators. Most important, Flint was at Watson's side in his struggle to stop the payment of dividends until pressing development needs were filled. There would be no payouts in 1914 and 1915, despite much grumbling out of Oneonta. In the latter year, after the NCR antitrust suit was set aside, Watson was elevated to the presidency, and this, too, was accomplished with Flint's sponsorship.

Several years later the then-retired Flint would single Watson out as the most creative businessman he had ever worked with and one of the true giants of American corporate management. He also reflected that CTR was his finest accomplishment. Whatever else he had done in his first year at CTR, Watson had managed to charm the corporation's godfather.

None of this would have counted for much, or indeed have transpired, had it not been for Watson's ability to show results, and in this regard his reputation was linked directly to the performance of Tabulating Machine. As it happened, he was given credit for accomplishments that were none of his doing. Watson had arrived there at an opportune time. As has been indicated, there was a strong demand for Holleriths—in fact, almost any kind of tabulator, so great was the need for them. While it was true that the Powers machines retained their technological and price advantages and that Watson would have to change this if he were to succeed, the outlook appeared bright. Not only were placements high, but Holleriths were leased, not purchased outright, so each customer provided the firm with a stream of earnings over the years. Furthermore, almost three-quarters of Tabulating Machine's revenues derived from the sale of cards, and this, too, represented a source of ongoing earnings.

The new sales push, the demand for machines, ongoing revenues from leases and cards—all this predated Watson's arrival. His real challenge would come later, when he had to provide salesmen with new machines to compete against Powers. For the time being, however, he could demonstrate that any funds invested in Tabulating Machine would return fine profits.

That this was true could be seen in some of the company's statistics.* In 1912, its first full year, CTR reported net profits of $541,000, more than two-thirds of which came from International Time. Profits rose to $635,000 in 1913, with virtually all the additional income deriving from operations at Tabulating Machine. The nation was entering a recession, and many businessmen must have concluded they could do without time clocks. It was different in the case of tabulating machines and counting devices and, for that matter, a wide variety of office equipment, from typewriters to adding machines to hectographs. These enabled employers to cut labor costs and conduct their businesses in a more efficient fashion. The business machine industry came as close as any in the nation to being divorced from the vicissitudes of the economic cycle, as would be demonstrated during the 1913–1914 slump and others that followed. In periods of prosperity, businessmen needed the machines to facilitate expansion and produce goods and provide services for growing numbers of clients; in slow times they enabled them to economize, especially when devices could be leased. And no matter why they were installed, once in place business machines would not be removed except for replacement by superior models. Employers who had accepted the typewriter would not entertain thoughts of returning to the quill or steel pens, and when a businessman became accustomed to tabulators and adding machines, he would not revert to manual counting. Apparently the same could not be said for time

---

* It must be realized that the accounting procedures of this period were different from those of today. Companies did not maintain depreciation schedules, and corporate taxes were negligible. What today are called profits then were termed net profit available for dividends. By current standards these usually were overstated, and of course, there was no Securities and Exchange Commission, no generally accepted accounting procedures. Thus, it was not unusual for a firm to report what appeared to be a return on sales of from 30 to 50 percent and a like percentage on invested capital.

clocks, as could be seen in a decline in total sales for 1914, a year during which the recession lingered. On sales of less than $4.2 million, CTR reported earnings of $490,000, and most of the slump was attributed to a temporary sluggishness in the clock sector. Meanwhile, Tabulating Machine reported excellent earnings, almost twice those for International Time.

Watson was still a new man at the firm in 1915, untested and very much on probation. He deferred to Fairchild on matters of overall strategy but increasingly took command of CTR's staff, placing his own men in important positions whenever they fell vacant. Money was tight, but despite this, he expanded the research facilities in Endicott. When, as a result of economic stimulation caused by the European war, America came out of its recession, Watson organized an effort to develop new tabulators, recorders, and printers, knowing they would be needed by a reviving industrial sector. Computing Scale would produce profits to be used in other areas of the corporation but receive little in the way of resources for its own growth. International Time would be nursed back to health, but Watson would concentrate his resources in Tabulating Machine. Little of this was reported in the general press or even the business magazines of the period (and no wonder; why should reporters and analysts bother about a firm of this size and a businessman of Watson's stature in the age of Edison and Ford?). It can be unearthed by a critical reading of corporation reports, by an analysis of balance sheets, and from the recollections of those who were at the company in its early years.

Watson's objectives were clear and simple. He hoped to create a sales force in the NCR mold, produce advanced machines superior to those of any rival, and, by wedding the two, become the prime mover in office machinery. Along the way he would develop new devices and additional markets and eventually transform CTR into an industrial giant, larger even than NCR. Not only did this seem possible, but Watson thought the development inevitable if only the people he selected performed well at their tasks.

Not surprisingly, some of Watson's closest associates at

CTR: The Apprenticeship

CTR also had received their basic training under John Patterson. One of these was Joseph Rogers, who, with the support of Watson and Flint, was named general manager for International Time, which he ran while Fairchild was away in Washington or elsewhere. Watson had met Rogers when the two men sold cash registers in central New York. They were the same age, shared the same ambitions and interests, and enjoyed each other's company. When Watson was placed in charge of the secondhand business, he had selected Rogers as his top assistant. They had gone through the antitrust action together, and both had been indicted and convicted. When Watson left NCR, so had Rogers. That Rogers would be offered a post at CTR was inevitable.

Rogers understood that he was Watson's "man" at International Time and that among his other duties would be helping develop the next generation of tabulators, printers, and counters for Tabulating Machine. In this task he would be assisted by Robert Houston, also an NCR graduate who had worked with Watson on the secondhand project. Houston had to leave Dayton once Patterson had determined to rid himself of the "Watson clique," and he followed Rogers to CTR. Other NCR men arrived later. A greater number of them would wind up at the automobile firms, General Motors and Dodge Brothers in particular, but there was a strong NCR influence at CTR in the early years.

This could be seen in the approach to research and development. The actual tasks of designing the new machines were left to E. A. Ford and several young draftsmen Watson had hired, the most important of whom were Clair Lake and Frank Carroll. But the general direction was provided by Watson and Rogers. Just as they once had ripped apart the superior Hallwoods and then incorporated their best features in NCR copies, so they now obtained Powers machines, turned them over to Ford, and asked him to do the same. This was to be a stopgap measure, for once Watson was able to obtain sufficient research funds, he would aim for technological leadership. For the time being, however, he would have to settle for this.

What emerged was a new line of Holleriths, machines the CTR salesmen might justifiably claim were every bit as good as their Powers counterparts. By offering lower prices and easy terms and applying the maxims learned from Watson and Rogers they were able to undercut the competition.

Watson initiated his first sales campaign in the late summer of 1915, shortly after he had assumed leadership at Tabulating Machine and even before Ford had started work on the new line of machines. From the first it was evident that here, too, he meant to apply what he had learned at NCR.

Watson's approach to motivation and sales came close to being a carbon copy of what Patterson had perfected in Dayton over the previous two decades. Slogans abounded: "Time lost is time gone forever"; "Teaching is of no value unless somebody learns what is being taught"; "There is no such thing as standing still"; "We must never feel satisfied"; "We forgive thoughtful mistakes." This small selection—there were many more slogans on the walls at Tabulating Machine in the early days—transmitted the essence of Watson's philosophy. Like Patterson, he employed chalk talks and flip cards. There even was the use of the number 5 in one of Watson's favorite admonitions: "Read—Listen—Discuss—Observe—Think." The last of this string, which was an important motto at NCR, served the same purpose at Tabulating Machine. And like Patterson, Watson stressed that thinking in and of itself was of no use unless and until it resulted in action.

In his chalk talks Watson stressed the importance of sincerity, integrity, and loyalty. His salesmen had to be well groomed, in good physical shape, and always alert. They were not permitted to drink—alcohol would not be served at CTR functions, even prior to national Prohibition. Smoking, too, was discouraged, and although Watson would employ single men, he preferred those under him to be married, both to remove temptation (or so it was assumed) and to provide an impetus for harder work since married men knew they had to provide for families. Watson tended to talk in slogans when appearing before his salesmen. "You cannot be a success in any business without believing that it is the greatest business in the world," he said. "You have to put your heart in the business and the business in your heart." He told his men, "Business is fun," and they should approach sales in the same way they might an athletic event or sport, the difference being that if the sale is made, both sides come out ahead. One of Watson's favorite mottoes, "We sell and deliver service," indicated that Tabulating Machine was in the business of assisting its customers, not merely in the placement of devices in offices. This, too, was a direct outgrowth of the NCR experience.

"A company is known by the men it keeps" was emblazoned on the wall of the training center. "We have different ideas, and different work, but when you come right down to it, there is just one thing we have to deal with throughout the whole organization—that is the MAN." So went one of Watson's most successful speeches of this period, which came to be known as "The Man Proposition." On the blackboard he would write a list of words:

> The Manufacturers
> General Manager
> Sales Manager
> Sales Man
> Factory Manager
> Factory Man
> Office Manager
> Office Man

"We have to deal with just one thing throughout the whole organization," said Watson, and this was the ingredient common to all these occupations: "MAN."

Such a statement, combined with the admonition to "THINK," might seem to imply that he encouraged his salesmen to innovate and be creative. "When practicing the art of selling use all your talents," he told a New York audience in 1917. "Put everything you have into your efforts; above all, put your personality into them. Never copy anybody. *Be yourself*." It might appear that Watson favored individualism, but this hardly was the case. Rather, he looked for salesmen whose approaches to problems were almost identical to his own—or who, if they were not, were willing to bend to his will and accept supervision and instruction. Watson ever stressed the importance of teamwork. "A team that won't be beat, can't be beat"; "Everybody in this company is the supervisor of someone else"; "No man is big enough to instruct everybody how to do his work." Although Tabulating Machine didn't have its version of the NCR holy books at this time and salesmen didn't have to memorize canned presentations, Watson wanted each link in the chain to be aware of how much it relied upon others and how they in turn counted on it. The individual was important, to be sure, but only insofar as he served the greater good of the whole. "Every individual member is an important cog in the wheel which all help to turn."

Except Watson, who was above the system. That is to say, he was needed by others but did not have to draw upon them for guidance and ideas. Others would cooperate; he would oversee. He told a group of salesmen of how he had learned from others and of the importance of wise supervision, from salesmen, sales managers, and general managers. "Now I happen to be in a position where I try to supervise the men who supervise sales managers, who in turn, supervise salesmen."

Decades later Watson would be portrayed by admirers and critics as a benevolent despot, with the stress on the noun and in such a way as to imply that in some way he had created the modern organizational manager, the man at the top of the corporate pyramid. This was not so; dozens of railroad tycoons, leaders of steel companies, and Patterson himself had perfected the role before Watson made his contribution. He simply was more outspoken than most and more adept at public relations than any of his predecessors. A superlative salesman, he knew how to attract and utilize the right kind of publicity. To be sure, his primary aim was the creation of a fine sales and service organization, but it did no harm for CTR customers to know of his creed of integrity, service, and efficiency. Yet there was more than a touch of megalomania about it all. Pictures of Watson were ever-present; quotations from his speeches sprinkled the conversations of men who hoped to be singled out for promotions and prime territories. To open sales meetings, there even were hymns of praise to the chief, one of which contains a revealing last line:

> Mr. Watson is the man we're working for,
> He's the leader of the CTR,
> He's the fairest, squarest man we know;
> Sincere and true.
> He has shown us how to play the game
> And how to make the dough.

If this sounds crass, Watson meant it to be so. He demanded hard work, dedication, and loyalty, all of which would help the firm prosper, but more important, success would mean prosperity for the individual who made it possible. Here again was Watson's penchant for combining individualism with group action. "In putting forth your best efforts, do not feel that you are working hard just to build up the company and make money for the stockholder," he told a group of salesmen, adding that they really were working for themselves.

His men were paid on commission, just as Watson's total remuneration was based on net profits. Like Patterson, he preferred hungry, ambitious salesmen who had the good sense to realize that they could not make money unless the enterprise as a whole prospered. NCR had its Hundred Point Club; Watson instituted a Hundred Percent Club, comprised of men who had met their quotas. Especially prized and singled out for honors were those who had multiple memberships, for the composition of the club changed every year. These salesmen would be honored at conventions, their names and pictures featured in company periodicals, and some even had songs composed in their honor. As was the case at NCR, their quotas would be raised for the following year. "Never feel satisfied," was another Watson slogan; he liked his men to be hungry and lean, eager for the next challenge. Those who failed to make the club were admonished to do so, while persistent failure usually resulted in a transfer to a less demanding position not involved with sales.

To be shunted out of sales meant to give up commissions and perquisites. It also was a clear sign of disfavor, and some resigned rather than accept the disgrace it implied. Still, unlike many employers of the period, Watson rarely fired people outright; they might remain with the tacit understanding that their prospects weren't bright. This approach may have derived from Watson's distaste for the way Patterson had discarded individuals. Then, too, as a perennial optimist and booster he hated to concede failure of any kind, even when it involved the abandonment of an employee.

Whatever the reason, it proved a sensible policy. Watson wanted CTR to be considered a paternalistic employer. Those who were hired could count on many benefits. In the early years these included premium salaries, low-cost meals in company cafeterias, and paid vacations and insurance, and later the benefits were expanded into such areas as memberships in company-owned and –managed country clubs and educational assistance. Patterson had provided many extras for NCR employees, but Watson outdid him in this respect. While costly, they were sensible investments, enabling CTR to attract and keep good employees, most of whom seemed to appreciate the conditions under which they worked. Although this was not Watson's prime motive at the time, such people also had less incentive to join unions when they appeared in the industry later. Finally, the company's paternalistic attitude enabled it to keep tabs on employees.

With all this, Watson's salesmen remained a special breed, apart from others in the organization. Just as the company rarely fired people, so it practiced a policy of promotion from within; those who aspired to top rank at CTR knew they had to begin there while still quite young and work their way up. CTR's executive suites would be staffed largely by former salesmen or at least by people who had got their starts in sales. Those with such ambitions also understood that the path to the top went directly through the Hundred Percent Club. Every division at Tabulating Machine understood that it was there to serve the salesman, and later this would be true for CTR as a whole. Watson said as much at one of the first conventions held by the club, at which time he told his stars that they had to set the pace for all others at Tabulating Machine. "What synchronism means to a clock, a convention means to our organization. It enables those who are behind to catch up and get in step with the others."

The company prospered during the First World War. From the depressed base of $4.2 million in 1914 sales doubled to $8.3 million by 1917, and in the same period earnings rose from $490,000 to $1.6 million. All divisions performed well. Several of Computing Scales's devices were adapted for use in shipyards and factories, where they were used to measure exact quantities of nuts, bolts, and fasteners. Additional demands from war-related industries helped International Time boost its sales to record levels, and the Endicott facilities once again were expanded. In 1917 the division opened a new factory and sales office in Toronto to serve the rapidly developing Canadian market, and this more than made up for the small losses experienced in Europe.

The biggest advance came at Tabulating Machine. By the end of the war the division had some 1,400 tabulators and 1,100 sorters on lease at more than 650 installations. Virtually every large insurance company and railroad utilized Holleriths, as did government agencies, especially the Interstate Commerce Commission. Tabulating Machine shared the Toronto installation with International Time, and by the end of the war it was selling domestically produced tabulators to Canadian clients. The Washington plant worked double shifts, turning out more than 80 million cards a month. So rapidly was this part of the business growing that a makeshift operation was set up at a Computing Scale plant in Dayton. By 1918 it was producing another 30 million cards per month for the midwestern market, but even this was insufficient to keep up with the demand.

Watson might have been forgiven his optimism of this period, but in retrospect it clearly was overdone. This record hadn't been accomplished through excellent salesmanship, but rather resulted from the superior production record, at a time when Powers was in deep trouble. Not only couldn't that company meet the demand for its machines, but on several occasions during the war its tabulating card operations broke down completely, so that it was unable to capitalize fully upon the bonanza.

Watson surely must have understood that part of the new business was directly related to the war effort and that this segment would be diminished once the fighting ended. Then there would be major falloffs at International Time and Computing Scale, and the federal government would cancel many of its leases for Holleriths. If the economy sank back to its 1913 level, the firms that had overexpanded would be in trouble. But this did not seem to have caused him any distress, and certainly his euphoria was not dampened.

In 1916 Watson reinstituted the dividend, the payout being at the rate of $4 a year for each of the 104,827 shares outstanding at that time. The following year he initiated a new construction program and built up inventories in preparation for a major sales push. The salesmen at all three major divisions were brought together in 1918; now CTR would have a unified force, all under Watson's direct tutelage. The company's inventories were three times what they had been two years earlier, and the cash position was weaker in 1918 than it had been then. The company clearly was betting heavily on continued prosperity.

In 1919, at the first meeting of the combined sales force, Watson unveiled one of his major reasons for this confidence. It was a new printer-lister, a device that presented the information gathered in the Hollerith tabulators and sorters. Not only was it superior to anything else on the market, but its price was below that of the Powers counterpart. This was the first concrete evidence that Ford, Lake, and Carroll were well on the way to creating a new line of machines to replace the old Holleriths. Within four years Watson had assumed the technological lead within the industry and had provided his sales force with superior products at competitive prices. The outlook had never been brighter.

Demand for the new printer-listers was higher than anyone had anticipated. Tabulating Machine's order backlog grew, and additional production workers were hired for the Endicott installation. Although domestic sales for International Time and Computing Scale declined somewhat in 1919, the reopening of some foreign markets enabled these subsidiaries to turn in respectable performances. And despite a hectic economic readjustment after the Armistice, there was no serious recession in 1919, a year during which CTR's revenues expanded. Net sales and rentals came to $13 million, and earnings topped $2.1 million.

Encouraged by this performance, Watson made plans for new production facilities at Endicott and funded a research program for International Time that would take the subsidiary into the business of producing metering devices for subways and buses, an area of great promise in the postwar world. All this required additional capital, which was raised through the flotation of a new bond issue and short-term borrowings from Guaranty Trust. In anticipation of excellent business in all of the company's divisions, this money was used to expand inventories. S. M. Hastings, the president of Computing Scale, assured Watson that all was well there and asked for funds to consolidate operations in Chicago in preparation for a new sales push. Although he had spent little time at Computing Scale, Watson went along with the plan, and this, too, strained CTR's resources.

As a result, the firm's cash position remained precarious through most of this period. This was not of great concern early in 1920, for both revenues and profits advanced. But the economy weakened toward the close of the year, the start of a recession that would carry through most of 1921. For 1920 as a whole CTR reported revenues of $16 million, or $3 million more than in 1919. Earnings declined, however, the pretax figure being $1.9 million, barely sufficient to finance all the new programs.

Still, Watson appeared unconcerned about the future. Sales remained strong at Tabulating Machine and International Time. Hastings informed him that Computing Scale would show revenues in excess of $5 million for 1921 and return record profits to the mother company. European sales were expanding, and the Canadian business remained impressive. In January Watson spoke seriously of doubling sales for the year.

He could not have been farther off the mark. Revenues declined by close to a third, to $10.6 million. Pretax profits were down by more than 40 percent to barely over $1 million, which after taxes came to a mere $430,000. Computing Scale was a disaster. Sales were below $3.5 million, the division posted a loss, and one of its subsidiaries, Detroit Automatic Scale, had to be liquidated at a cost of $216,000. Fairchild and his allies on the board insisted on maintaining the dividend, which cost the company more than $500,000. Because of all this, CTR showed a net deficit of almost $200,000 for the year.

Now Watson was obliged to institute a cost-cutting program, not only slashing away at deadwood but also discontinuing some of his most prized programs. The research and development division was virtually eliminated, and wages for everyone at CTR, from the president down, were cut by 10 percent. Some of the salesmen were "furloughed," while others resigned to accept positions which at the time appeared more promising than ones in commission sales. In a moment of despair Watson even stopped production of the new printer-lister, though demand remained strong, as he concentrated on slashing inventories in order to keep the firm afloat and solvent.

That CTR was able to survive was due in part to Watson's success in retrenchment and keeping creditors at bay. In addition, there were timely loans from Guaranty Trust, which also assisted Watson in refinancing the debt. Perhaps even more important, however, was the continued good business out of Tabulating Machine, which came through the ordeal in fine shape. Earlier suspicions that companies would accelerate office mechanization in time of recession were proved out in 1920 and 1921. Watson soon came to regret having discontinued production of printer-listers and related machines, and he reactivated this operation late in the year. Even so, he could not supply enough of them to potential customers in 1922, and this was one reason for CTR's slow recovery from the slump.

Another was Computing Scale's stagnation. The division's industry position remained strong, and given better leadership, it might have been able to regain an important measure of profitability. As it was, Watson's policy there was to cut back on and in some cases discontinue production and try to work off the inventory.

As for International Time, it limped along. Development work on new products was discontinued, and the office staff was pruned. Clearly Watson had decided to concentrate his attention and available funds at Tabulating Machine, and he permitted the other divisions to founder.

For a while there appeared to be a revolt in the executive suite. Fairchild and others of the old International Time management resented and disagreed with Watson's priorities. There was talk of a sellout to a Wall Street financial clique and even a rumor that John Patterson might purchase controlling interest and merge CTR into NCR. Whether or not there was any substance to such talk is impossible to say, but in any case by then Watson's position at the firm was strong enough to enable him to block any such action that might have been contemplated.

In spite of record sales at Tabulating Machine, CTR's 1922 revenues were only slightly higher than those for the previous year and were $5 million below the 1920 figure. There was substantial recovery in pretax profits, however, and these rose to $1.6 million. After payment of dividends and other subtractions, CTR was able to add $614,000 to its surplus. The company had recovered from its ordeal and was in good shape to capitalize upon opportunities during the booming 1920's.

Still, Watson carried the scars for many years. Never again would he permit CTR's cash position to fall as low as it had in 1919 and 1920. He would maintain a policy of low dividends, high reserves, and careful cost controls. Not for another four decades would the firm make so large a wager on the success of a new line as it had in 1919 and 1920. Watson would expend large amounts of money on research and development, but his company usually lagged when it came to the introduction of new products. Others would blaze the trail, while Watson took careful note of what was happening. Then, if all went well, he would enter the market with his version and try to take sales away from the innovator.

Most of his work would continue to be done at Tabulating Machine, and this was another lesson he derived from the experience. He had never doubted that CTR's future rested with this division, and now he would make the firm's major business the production and the leasing of tabulators, printer-readers, punchers, and related products. Computing Scale would remain starved for funds, while International Time would play a less important role in corporate affairs in the 1920's.

During his early years at CTR Watson had been considered a front man for Charles Flint, his nominal patron. He had been obliged to defer to George Fairchild on many issues and, of course, had operated from under the long shadow of John Patterson, whose record was always held before him as something to emulate. This period now drew to a close. Patterson died in 1922, removing from the scene not only the industry's leading figure but the phantom against whom Watson had had to race. Flint had suffered severe financial reverses during the recession and even came close to bankruptcy, being saved by loans from Watson and others; he no longer could be considered a dominant force at the company. As for Fairchild, he left Congress in 1919, indicating he planned to devote more attention to business affairs, those of CTR in particular. By then, however, Watson's position at the firm was strong, and in any case Fairchild had little interest in or stomach for the kind of brawl it would have taken to dislodge the president. In any event Fairchild died in December 1924, removing from the scene the last person who had acted as Watson's superior during the period of his apprenticeship. Shortly thereafter the board abolished the post of chairman, and Watson assumed the role of chief executive officer as well as chief operating officer. He was fifty years old at the time. The company was his.

There was an even more striking and obvious change at this time. Watson had never liked the company's name. Computing-Tabulating-Recording smacked of something that was jerry-built, containing as it did portions of the three major ingredients that went into the mix. A new name would be needed, something that not only was integrated but offered an indication of where Watson hoped to lead the firm. He had found such a title in 1917, which he bestowed upon the successful Canadian subsidiary. Later it was applied to a branch that handled the Latin American operations. Several months prior to Fairchild's death Watson asked the board to consider a new designation, and once again he had his way.

In February 1924 Computing-Tabulating-Recording became International Business Machines.

4

Enter the Electronic Revolution

THE BUSINESS CLIMATE of the 1920's was ideally suited for the development of the office equipment industry. That the decade was one of economic vitality cannot be denied. The gross national product rose from $69 billion in 1921 to $103 billion in 1929, while per capita income went from $641 to $847. There was tremendous, almost exponential growth in such industries as radio, motion pictures, automobiles, and home appliances, and impressive strength in chemicals, construction, steel, and a wide variety of others. Electrification proceeded apace; the nation consumed 53 billion kilowatt-hours in 1921 and 117 billion eight years later. Americans moved to their cities; 15 million more of them lived in urban areas in 1930 than in 1920, a period during which the rural population increased by only 2 million. The rapidly growing businesses of urban America required efficient offices and so were ready customers for typewriters, letter openers, accounting machines, bookkeeping equipment, tabulators, and many other devices. Sales, profits, and prospects for companies that produced and sold such machines were excellent, and their stocks were among the darlings of Wall Street.

Then everything fell apart. The private sector required few new machines during the Great Depression, but for some of the companies the New Deal provided a bonanza. Franklin Roosevelt may not have succeeded in his objective of providing economic recovery, but he spawned scores of new agencies staffed by brigades of bureaucrats, all of whom became potential customers for various kinds of business machines.

It might appear in retrospect that the office equipment industry could hardly have helped prospering during the interwar period, that several of the small entities of 1921 should have become medium-sized by 1929 and then, after stumbling in the early 1930's, gone on to turn in ever-greater sales and profits.

Certainly this was IBM's experience. Revenues for 1922 came to $10.7 million and, after rising, steadily peaked at $20.3 million in 1931. They then declined to $17.6 million in 1933, after which the New Deal-based recovery began. Revenues topped $31.7 million in 1937, and in 1940 they stood at $46.3 million.

The profits picture was equally impressive. These came to $1.4 million in 1922 and $9.1 million in 1939. Retained earnings for the same period went from $5.9 million to $28.7 million. While other companies cut or eliminated dividends during the Depression, IBM continued to pay $6 a share, combined with small extras in the form of stock from 1934 to the end of the decade and a $1.50 per share "bonus" for 1936.

It was not preordained that IBM should turn in such a performance or that it would emerge as the industry's leading firm on the eve of World War II. This certainly couldn't have been anticipated in 1922 or even during the prosperous years toward the close of the 1920's. This was a period during which older firms like Burroughs and National Cash Register appeared to have firmer customer bases and two potential giants made their appearances.

The first of these new firms was Remington Rand, which was put together by business machine tycoon James Rand, Jr., and several prominent Wall Street bankers and promoters. It even had the aid of Irving Fisher, an economics professor at Yale and one of Wall Street's favorite seers as well as a major force in his profession. Like the old Computing-Tabulating-Recording, this was an amalgam of formerly independent firms—Remington Typewriter, Dalton Adding Machine, Rand Kardex (which manufactured filing systems), several small office furniture and stationery operations, and Herman Hollerith's old nemesis, now called Powers Accounting Machine Corporation. Initially Remington Rand appeared more a promotion to sell stock and obtain market profits than anything else—in this, too, the company resembled the pre-Watson CTR—yet the components did appear to mesh fairly well. None of them was a leader in its particular segment of the industry; but all were related in one way or another to office equipment, and the same salesman who attempted to place an accounting machine might easily be trained to handle furniture, typewriters, and the like. These were highly competitive products, and profit margins were low. Remington Rand was a large company; revenues for 1928 came to slightly less than $60 million, three times that for IBM. But net profits were only $6 million, against IBM's $5.3 million. Still, given the right kind of leadership, this, too, might change. In 1929 several Wall Street analysts thought the challenge was being prepared, that during the next few years Remington Rand would make a major effort to displace Burroughs in adding and accounting machines and IBM in a wide variety of fields. Those who recalled the contest between Hollerith and Powers suggested the company might even attempt to win the contract for the 1930 census.

Underwood Elliott Fisher, the second of the new combines, was organized in December 1927. At the time Underwood dominated the typewriter business with its Model 5, considered the class of the field. It possessed a sales force every bit as good as IBM's and had a reputation that Watson might have envied. It was generally assumed that Underwood would be the senior partner in the operation, that it had acquired Elliott Fisher in order to broaden its line and provide its sales force with additional products. Kenneth Schley of Underwood became chairman, and two of his sons sat on the new board, which was dominated by Underwood men. But the president and general manager was to be Philip Wagoner of Elliott Fisher, who in nine years had turned that company into a medium-sized diversified manufacturer of a respected line of accounting and bookkeeping machines, calculators, cash registers, and typewriters. Considered one of the brightest and most aggressive figures in the business machine industry, Wagoner set out to use Underwood as a vehicle through which to introduce Elliott Fisher machines into offices and so take sales from Remington Rand, Burroughs, and other competitors. His was not a large company; sales for 1928 came to $19 million, but because of the high profit margins at Underwood, net income came to $4.9 million. This was a compact, well-organized and -managed firm, capable of dominating many aspects of the industry. For the moment it did not challenge IBM in any of its product lines, but students of the industry thought Wagoner would make a move in that direction early in the 1930's.

Wagoner posed a threat to Burroughs Adding Machine, by then the dominant force in that segment of the industry. A Detroit-based concern, Burroughs had grown with the automobile business during the century's early years. A careful, prudent management had made intelligent acquisitions, which in time provided Burroughs with a wide variety of office products, from calculators to accounting machines. In 1921 it acquired the Moon-Hopkins Billing Machine Company, and by the end of the decade this division had a near monopoly for its products, which were used by a wide variety of wholesale and retail establishments. Meanwhile, Burroughs adding machines were used throughout the world, and the company had manufacturing facilities in Europe and Latin America. More than any other firm in the business machine field, IBM included, Burroughs was an international operation. That it did not completely dominate the field was due to its management's overly cautious attitude toward expansion and a decidedly poor sales force. Within the industry Burroughs was known as an entrenched, conservative, somewhat unimaginative company which nonetheless had an excellent line of products and a good research operation. It was also a highly profitable concern; sales for 1928 came to more than $32 million, half again that of IBM, while its net profits of $8.3 million were more than $3 million better than IBM's.

The National Cash Register of the post-Patterson era was a foundering company, this condition being the cost paid for the founder's penchant for dismissing promising executives. In 1922 NCR had the assets, reputation, sales force, and even the leadership that might have enabled it to dominate the industry. But the old man was succeeded by his son, Frederick, who throughout the 1920's evidenced a paralysis of will when it came to making decisions. General Manager John Barringer pleaded with Patterson for permission to develop and market adding and accounting machines, but the new president and members of his family were reluctant to diversify out of cash registers, as though fearing disapproval from the shade of the founder. In the end Barringer had his way. NCR produced the Class 2000 accounting machine, which was a complex cash register that printed inventory, sales, and profits data on inserted forms, posted bills, and performed a variety of other tasks. The 2000 line was the most advanced in the field and, because of heavy development costs, carried high prices. Given a better economic environment, a well-mounted sales effort, and more attractive leasing arrangements, the 2000's might have served as the foundation for a reshaped NCR, which could have emerged as the industry's undisputed leader, a position it held during John Patterson's peak years. But NCR, like Remington Rand and Burroughs, lacked leadership of this kind and so stumbled.

NCR's malaise was not apparent during the first half of the 1920's, years of economic recovery and expansion, when placements of new cash registers were not difficult to make. Carried forward by the momentum generated during the John Patterson era, NCR's sales rose from $29 million in 1921 to $45 million in 1925, while profits climbed from $2.8 million to a record high of $7.8 million. But in this period NCR did little research and development, as the young Patterson hesitated and seemed incapable of making firm commitments. As early as 1924 rival registers were making inroads among NCR customers, and Barringer had no new models with which to meet the challenge. Although work began on the 2000 series, and in 1929 Barringer received permission to develop an even more sophisticated line, to be known as the 3000's, both sales and earnings stagnated. In 1928 NCR reported revenues of $49 million, while earnings were only a shade above the 1925 level.

Comparative Statistics for Selected
Business Machine Companies in 1928

(millions of dollars)

Company	Revenues	Earnings
Burroughs Adding Machine	32.1	8.3
International Business Machines	19.7	5.3
National Cash Register	49.0	7.8
Remington Rand	59.6	6.0
Underwood Elliott Fisher	19.0	4.9

Source: *Moody's Industrial Manual,* 1930

NCR was less prepared for the panic and depression than was any other significant firm in the industry. Beset by doubts and increasingly confused by events, Frederick Patterson cast about for assistance. In 1931, close to bankruptcy, he turned over control of NCR to Edward Deeds, one of the many men who had come up the ranks at the company before World War I only to be dismissed by his father. Deeds led a heroic and ultimately successful rescue operation, but NCR had lost its chance to become an industrial giant.

The IBM strategy was quite different from that of the other business equipment firms. There would be acquisitions; but none of them was of major importance, and all served to enhance existing enterprises. Watson did not hesitate to discard parts of the company that did not fit into his plans or were only marginally profitable. He continued to stress research and development; even when some of his projects led to blind alleys, he would not permit IBM to succumb to what might be termed the NCR malaise.

The overall strategy was simple. In the 1920's IBM turned out and rented machines that would gather and then process and present large amounts of data. Its products were not suitable for all offices and businesses, but in 1929 Watson estimated that his machines had been placed in only one of every five that could use them profitably. He was not interested in mass-produced machines, such as typewriters and adders, but was willing to expand into these products if and when they could be made part of an existing system. In other words, Watson tended to ignore lawyers, accountants, and school systems. Rather, he concentrated on larger businesses and government agencies with specialized requirements.

The IBM salesman would contact a manager and offer to analyze his operations on a noncommitment basis. If he was invited through the door, he would attempt to show how the use of IBM machines would speed the gathering and processing of data, increase efficiencies, and cut costs. Watson's men would tailor-make a system for each business from existing components. If all went well, the main office would be called in to arrange leasing terms, and these, too, were fitted to each individual need. IBM-trained technicians would install the equipment, accompanied by a service representative who would be on call if anything went wrong, and would offer advice on how best to alter or add machines as the business changed.

Originally Herman Hollerith had elected to lease his tabulators because the government saw no need to own census-related machines, but Watson saw how this approach could be beneficial in other areas as well and give him an edge over Burroughs, NCR, and Remington Rand, all of which sold their accounting machines. Not only would the decision to lease be easier to make than one to buy—it involved less initial funding and lacked an air of finality—but in time IBM would create a steady flow of funds into its treasury, one that would continue even after the machines had been fully depreciated. This meant the company would have to husband its financial resources, maintain high cash reserves, and measure its performance not only by net sales and profits but by the status of the rental base.

The rental rate included a finance charge, although this was not stated in the contracts. IBM might have sold the paper to a factor or arranged short-term credits from banks, but by the mid-1920's the company was financing most of its machine placements. Although the statistics for this period are sketchy, it would appear that IBM was turning a fine profit from this end of the business. As has been indicated, there was some question whether Watson was selling a product or a service, and it appears that the latter was the case. An equally important question, one with no simple answer, was whether he was in the business of turning out a capital good or running a leasing operation, with business machines his prime product. Such questions would be posed by students of American business three decades later, but they might have been asked in the 1920's as well. Had they been, and had Watson gone on record with responses, one might have more clearly appreciated the relative strengths of IBM when matched against those of its major competitors.

Then there was the matter of supplying the machines with cards. The early typewriter manufacturers understood this; almost all of them sold ribbons as well, and some diversified into the production of carbon paper. Each installation implied the purchase each month of many thousands of cards, almost all of which would be purchased from IBM. (Other firms tried to enter this business, but IBM retained a technological and price advantage and, as shall be seen, insisted its leasers use its cards.) This aspect of the business was close to being depression-proof. By the mid-1930's IBM was selling more than 4 billion of them a year, at a price of $1.05 per thousand.

The matter of cards convinced Watson that he had to remain in the time clock business. International Time sold rather than leased its products, and Watson might have let them go at cost, so profitable was the card business. Each employee who punched a clock needed a new card each week. During bad times fewer of them would be sold, of course, but at the bottom of the Great Depression of the 1930's some 100 million of these were sold, at a price of $1.40 per thousand. Of the company's total revenues in 1938 of $34.7 million, card sales accounted for some $5 million, and profit margins were higher than for any other IBM product.

Watson was willing to devote a substantial portion of his assets to International Time, hoping to broaden its scope and increase its profitability. In 1931, venturing into a new field, he acquired exclusive rights to sell and lease the Filene-Finlay translator, a system for transmitting simultaneous translations in different languages that was quickly adopted by the League of Nations. Two years later IBM purchased a dating stamp, a cost recorder, and a time stamp from the Instograph Company. These and other products were transferred to International Time, which soon took on the title of International Time and Electric Time Systems and, by the end of the decade, had become the Time Recording Division. This became an umbrella operation under which were gathered a variety of conventional and experimental products—Time Recording was the place to venture into new areas. By then it was selling fire and burglar alarms, automatic traffic recorders, and even music and speech equipment as well as a wide range of timing devices and the translator.

Computing Scale was another matter. Watson had no interest at all in cheese and meat slicers, and commercial and retailing scales didn't fit into his future plans. All these products were sold rather than leased, and none had a lucrative aftermarket. Despite this, sales at one subsidiary, Dayton Scale, actually increased substantially in the early 1930's, in large part as the result of the introduction of innovations in its product line. Grasping at the chance to transform an unwanted asset into yet another income stream, Watson sold Dayton Scale to Hobart

Enter the Electronic Revolution

Manufacturing in 1933, receiving 100,000 shares of the latter company's class B common stock. Hobart was a well-managed, conservative capital goods manufacturer, and its dividend appeared as safe as was possible in those parlous times. In return for assets carried on the books at a value of $4.1 million, Watson now would receive dividends at the rate of from $125,000 to $150,000 per year and was freed from the need to devote any part of his capital or attention to this peripheral business. Thenceforth IBM would produce scales for use in retail establishments on order and to specifications and then only as a concession to old customers.

Several years later Watson gathered Computing Scale's industrial products into a new subsidiary, which later came to be known as International Industrial Scales and Counting Devices. He had earlier set about acquiring other industrial scale manufacturers, most of them small and on the verge of bankruptcy. Automatic Scale Company had been purchased in 1930, and two years later Watson had bought National Scale. His enthusiasm for this business soon waned, however, and it never figured importantly in the company's plans.

IBM's heart was the old Tabulating Machine operation, now renamed International Electric Tabulating and Accounting Machines. Most of its growth came internally, but along the way Watson had acquired several small firms with special products, interesting notions, or key personnel. In 1921 he purchased the Ticketograph Company, which had a machine that printed rate schedules for factories and retail establishments. The following year Watson acquired Peirce Accounting Machine, which had an alphabetical device that meshed well with the new parent company's numerical machine. Peirce also owned a variety of patents for bookkeeping machines, and one of its prime assets was John R. Peirce, one of the industry's leading innovators, who would be partially responsible for several important product introductions in the 1930's, among which were test-scoring devices, a subtraction accounting machine, and a multiplying punch. Peirce and others developed a line of equipment designed for use in banks, featuring a proof machine that could sort and add checks, which was among the first IBM products successfully to challenge Burroughs in this area.

IBM started to lease its new alphabetical tabulating machine in 1932, and this was an outgrowth of parallel research at Peirce and the old Tabulating Machine center. Known as the 405, it became the workhorse of the industry, the standard against which the competition would be measured. Within six years the 405's were being placed at a rate of 1,500 a year, and this easily was the most profitable of the company's products.

In the 1930's, as earlier, the company's basic rental unit consisted of three interrelated devices: the punch, the sorter, and the accounting machine. The operator would first punch the cards, entering information on them in the form of holes, each standing for a different characteristic. When the time came for retrieval, the cards would be placed in the sorter, and they would go through at the rate of from 225 to 400 per minute, with the desired cards falling into the proper classification bins. These would be taken out and placed in the accounting machine, which would make printouts of various kinds, print checks, or perform other functions as needed. Many customers also rented verifiers, a device which attached to the punch and made certain the cards were properly prepared. There were add-ons for the accounting machines that enabled them to perform a variety of tasks or expanded their capacities.

In the nature of things there were greater demands for IBM punchers than for sorters and accounting machines. Those who leased them—especially government agencies, insurance companies, and railroads—would build up large data bases but not have to use them or parts of them more than occasionally. Initially they would lease a single IBM unit, but in time they would take on more keypunchers, often employing dozens of them in various parts of the companies or agencies and sending the cards to the sorters when information was needed.

One might learn to operate a keypunch in a matter of hours, and the sorter was just as simple a device in this respect. Accounting machine operation was more complex. Young women, who in those years dominated office staffs, usually began at the keypunch after leaving high school and then, if they showed talent, might graduate to the accounting machines. IBM would offer to train these young women at no cost, hoping in this way to accustom them to its products rather than to those of the competition. Then they would go through their business lives as "IBM operators," a designation that appeared in some want-ad columns in the late 1930's. This was not a new idea—Underwood had sold typewriters this way in the 1920's—but Watson perfected it in the 1930's and later.

It was part of a harmonious whole. Potential customers would lease IBM equipment for a variety of reasons, one of which was that initial capital requirements were low and another that operators accustomed to using them were available. The placement of the initial unit would set into motion one income stream, and this would be augmented by rentals of additional keypunches, each of which devoured thousands of cards—a second income stream. This system provided IBM with a stability the other companies in the industry lacked.

From the first CTR had produced electrically powered tabulators, and all of IBM's machines were electrics. In contrast, Powers had started with mechanical devices and had switched to electrics in the early 1920's, as did Burroughs and others. Watson had been at NCR when Patterson brought out his first line of electric registers. They were faster, more efficient, and, after workers were trained, easier to operate than the mechanicals, but their premium prices kept them at a disadvantage with the older, simpler registers. Still, large retail establishments and small ones in search of prestige did purchase the electric cash registers, which were the most profitable of NCR's products at the time of Watson's departure.

As has been indicated, Underwood was the nation's leading typewriter manufacturer, and all its products were mechanical. Had it not been for this, Watson might have been tempted to purchase some of his keypunch consoles from that company or from some other typewriter manufacturer. As it was, they did not fit in well with his electric machines. This was one of the reasons he purchased Electromatic Typewriter, one of the few companies then working on this kind of machine.

Electric typewriters had been around since the turn of the century, when small firms like Blickensderfer, Electric Power, and Ellis had tried unsuccessfully to market their machines. Ellis had experimented with a combination electric typewriter-bookkeeping and billing machine, and some of its researches had been carried on by Electromatic. But the company's prospects appeared bleak in the early years of the Depression. The electrics produced neater and more consistent images than the manuals; but there was little sign that secretaries wanted them, and ultimately, as in the case with other office equipment, secretaries were the ones who influenced purchase agreements. In addition, the Electromatics sold for $250, almost twice the price of the top Underwoods, and price competition, always important in this field, had sharpened during the Depression. The company fared only little better as part of IBM. Toward the end of the decade only 6,000 electrics a year, about 5 percent of total industry sales, were being placed.

More important, at least initially, was the wedding of the Electromatic keyboard to the punches and accounting machines; Watson was re-creating the Ellis machines of a generation earlier. One of his more daring ideas, moreover, was his attempt to unite the electric typewriter with devices produced by another of his acquisitions, Radiotype, one of whose researchers, Walter Lemmon, was working on a means whereby messages might be transmitted by shortwaves rather than by wires, printed out by one typewriter, and received on another. In 1938 IBM spokesmen talked of a time when many large businesses would have several of them (Electromatic typewriters combined with consoles), by which instantaneous, inexpensive communications between offices would be made possible. IBM did not conceive of just where this might lead: communications between the machines themselves, the transmission of data from one bank to another. This would come three decades later and in a different technological atmosphere. For the time being, IBM appeared on the verge of developing electrical mail, setting up what might be considered the post office of the future.

The project did not get beyond the experimental stage. Because of technological difficulties and patent problems—but more perhaps because of the need to turn out accounting machines during World War II—this research was shelved, and in 1945 Radiotype was sold to Globe Wireless.

By then the IBM electric typewriters had a firm grip on that expanding segment of the market. Underwood, Royal, Remington, and others entered the field with their versions, but they had little success. In part this was due to IBM's head start and the overall superiority of its models. Furthermore, a generation of office workers had grown up on Electromatics, and they weren't going to switch at this time or even when some rivals, Remington in particular, came out with advanced models at competitive prices.

The nature of the sales effort was most important. The IBM men were placing electrics, most of which would replace manuals, and they knew that once secretaries or typists became accustomed to them, they would not return to the old ways. Salesmen for other firms had been brought up on manuals, had built up a following in this line, and continued to sell them even when carrying their new electrics. The Remington man who placed one of his company's electrics in an office usually did so by forgoing the sale of a Remington manual, and Remington salesmen often were reluctant to do so.

That Watson was able to expand and innovate in this fashion even while the nation suffered through the Depression was a tribute to IBM's strengths, a reflection on the nature of its customers and clients, and a demonstration of the virtues of rentals versus outright sales.

The rental base held firm during the harsh years at the beginning of the decade. Customers would keep their machines, even when they cut back on their use, shown by declining card sales from 1931 to 1933. Rental income from accounting machines and sorters remained steady, while that for keypunchers continued to advance, going from $743,000 in 1929 to $1.4 million in 1931 to $1.8 million two years later. Sales were down for time clocks and scales, but losses here were compensated for by the strong performance at Tabulating and Accounting Machines.

IBM's Revenues and Earnings, 1929–1939

(millions of dollars)

Year	Revenues			Earnings
	Sales	Rentals	Total	
1929	10.7	8.7	19.4	6.6
1930	9.9	10.4	20.3	7.3
1931	8.8	11.5	20.3	7.4
1932	7.1	11.3	18.4	6.7
1933	7.1	10.5	17.6	5.7
1934	8.7	12.2	20.9	6.6
1935	5.0	16.9	21.9	7.1
1936	8.2	18.1	26.3	7.6
1937	10.3	21.6	31.9	8.1
1938	9.1	25.6	34.7	8.7
1939	9.9	29.6	39.5	9.1

Sources: *Moody's Industrial Manual*, 1930–1940; *Stipulation Between U.S. and IBM*, No. E–66–215, October 28, 1935

IBM's revenue decline was halted in 1933, and in the following year the company took in a record $20.9 million. Business recovery accounted for most of this, but throughout the rest of the decade IBM's placements with government agencies took on increased importance.

The Relationship of Card Sales to Total Sales for IBM, 1929–1934

(millions of dollars)

Year	Card Sales	Total Sales
1929	3.6	10.7
1930	3.9	9.9
1931	3.4	8.8
1932	2.8	7.1
1933	2.8	7.1
1934	3.4	8.7

Sources: *Moody's Industrial Manual*, 1932, 1936; *Stipulation Between U.S. and IBM*, No. E–66–215, October 28, 1935

Enter the Electronic Revolution

It is common knowledge that the federal government's intervention in the economy during the New Deal exceeded that of any previous peacetime period. In 1932, the last full year of the Hoover administration, budget expenditures came to $4.7 billion, some $400 million less than they had been in 1921. By 1936 the Roosevelt administration was spending at the rate of $8.4 billion a year, and then, after a decline, spending rose to $8.8 billion in 1939. The federal government employed 605,000 people in 1932; by 1939 the number was 954,000, and it would pass the million mark the following year. The rise was most notable in Washington, D.C., the nation's bureaucratic as well as political capital. As New Deal agencies proliferated, the 73,000 workers of 1932 expanded to 129,000 seven years later. Some of these were engaged in maintenance, manual labor, and related occupations, but in the nature of things most worked in offices—and used office machines, a good many of which came from IBM.

Despite the decennial revenues from the census, IBM's government business had been very small prior to this period. In 1930 and 1931, as usual, the federal government leased large numbers of tabulators and related equipment; but even then such leasings accounted for less than 2 percent of the company's total revenues, and in 1932 government business was less than 1 percent of income.

Because of the economic decline, most of the machines used by the Census Bureau were placed into inventory, where they awaited new leasers. This had happened ten years earlier, after the 1920 census, at which time Watson faced a near disaster. Despite the experience of that period, he remained an optimist. Furthermore, the IBM of 1932 was in better financial shape than CTR had been in 1921. Rather than cut back on production, as did Burroughs, NCR, and other competitors, Watson kept his work force intact, building up his inventory in anticipation of renewed demand from business once recovery commenced. Because of this, he was in good condition to meet the government's requirements after Franklin Roosevelt took office.

The early New Deal was a massive attempt to reshape several important aspects of the American economy and society, and all this required elaborate statistics, accountings, and enumerations, the kinds that IBM machines had been performing for the private sector in the 1920's. The National Recovery Administration (NRA), that centerpiece of the New Deal in 1933 and 1934, required many machines, and lesser amounts went to the Agricultural Adjustment Administration, the Civilian Conservation Corps, and other agencies. IBM had an edge in the competition, in part because its machines were best suited for this kind of work but also because it had good relations with government bureaucrats that went back to the Hollerith period. Moreover, IBM was able to deliver machines from inventory, whereas other companies usually could not.

By 1935, however, Burroughs and National Cash Register had recovered, while Remington Rand had emerged as a serious contender. All jockeyed to win a major contract from the new Social Security Administration. Although Social Security would not employ as large a bureaucracy as the NRA and some other agencies, it would keep tabs on every American worker and so would not only require large numbers of machines but consume ever-increasing quantities of cards. In addition, the economies of scale were such that the company that obtained the Social Security contracts would be able to maintain a price advantage over competitors for many years to come.

IBM won the contract, which was as meaningful for Watson's company as the census agreement of 1889 had been for the old Hollerith organization. Within two years Social Security offices throughout the nation had more than 400 accounting machines alone and three times as many keypunches. This opened the way for other placements with government agencies, some of which even sold their Burroughs, NCR, and Remington Rand machines to take IBM leases. Because of federally generated revenues, IBM was unaffected by the recession that began in 1937 and that further crippled other firms in the industry.

By the end of the decade IBM was the largest and most

Enter the Electronic Revolution

powerful business machine firm in America. (Remington Rand had higher sales, but some of these derived from office furniture and related subsidiaries.) A decade earlier it had posted lower sales than Remington Rand, NCR, and Burroughs and had been only slightly ahead of Underwood Elliott Fisher. During the 1930's Remington Rand and NCR had actually lost ground, while Burroughs stood still. Underwood Elliott Fisher had higher sales as a result of government typewriter purchases, but all of its other product areas were under siege, while its inability to take more than a small part of the electric typewriter sales from IBM later would be seen as the beginning of Underwood's decline. But as striking as were IBM's advances in sales, its profitability was even more impressive. So great were the company's earnings in 1939 that they surpassed those of the other four firms combined, a showing duly noted on Wall Street, where IBM common had become one of the few blue chips to emerge out of the Depression.

Comparative Statistics for Selected
Business Machine Companies in 1939

(millions of dollars)

Company	Revenues	Earnings
Burroughs	32.5	2.9
International Business Machines	39.5	9.1
National Cash Register	37.1	3.1
Remington Rand	43.4	1.6
Underwood Elliott Fisher	24.1	1.9

Source: *Moody's Industrial Manual*, 1940

Thomas Watson, too, received good notices, not only in the financial district but in articles in business magazines and the daily press. *The New York Times* hailed him as "an industrial giant," *Time* magazine thought him one of the "most astute businessmen in the world," *Forbes* wrote of the "master salesman," and *Barron's* considered Watson "a man of unusual vision." *Fortune* wrote:

Let him discourse on the manifest destiny of I.B.M., and you are ready to join the company for life. Let him retail plain homilies on the value of Vision, and a complex and terrifying world becomes transparent and simple. Let him expound on the necessity for giving religion the preference over everything else, and you could not help falling to your knees.

It would be too much to say that Watson served as a symbol for businessmen in general during the 1930's, for this was a period when such individuals were being regularly castigated and generally blamed for many of the nation's economic problems. Rather, he was considered an unusually enlightened and intelligent industrial tycoon, one of a new breed who not only understood the nature and potential of modern technology and the importance of planning, organization, and efficiency but realized that cooperation with government was necessary and could prove beneficial.

In later years Watson would be accused of harboring fascistic tendencies; critics would note the antiunion policy at IBM and its paternalistic atmosphere. Watson received awards from both Fascist Italy and Nazi Germany in the 1930's, and he was fulsome in his praise of Benito Mussolini. But this was a period when many Americans believed the Italian dictator to be a benevolent despot "who made the trains run on time," and in some respects Watson was a vain man who enjoyed receiving awards and honors of almost any kind; he collected these in much the same way as he did salesmen. Later, when the true nature of the regimes became evident, Watson returned the medals, confessing to associates that he should never have accepted them.

Watson was no fascist or for that matter a believer in any kind of abstract political theory. In domestic politics he was a Democrat, more because his father had belonged to that party than for any ideological reason. He respected power and always supported whichever leader happened to be in office; he considered himself a patriotic American above all else. This was not a pose or a ploy utilized to obtain contracts and favors. At a time when IBM had no important government business and was not seeking it, Watson praised Calvin Coolidge and Herbert Hoover, holding them up as exemplars for his salesmen and others at the company. A booster and a joiner, he became the president of the U.S. Chamber of Commerce and defended Hoover against those who criticized his handling of the Depression. Then, when Hoover left the White House, Watson had many kind words for Franklin Roosevelt, and he defended the new President against businessmen who thought him a dangerous radical. Henry Ford and others thought the National Recovery Administration would be Roosevelt's vehicle for seizing control of the economy, the first step in the nationalization of business. Watson called it "one of the fairest and squarest propositions that has ever been presented," and he pledged Roosevelt his full support. "To me, the New Deal is going to mean better things for the majority of the people in this country." For Watson it was simply a matter of organization, not ideology. "I am thinking about the NRA and the New Deal as a research laboratory, with President Roosevelt, the greatest research engineer that the world has ever known."

Roosevelt appreciated this defense of his policies and often referred to Watson as an example of the progressive businessmen who appreciated his actions and understood they were being taken to save free enterprise from its own excesses. The two men corresponded regularly, and in time Watson became a conduit to the business community for Roosevelt, who wrote the IBM head: "You go back and tell them that I have to think about millions of people, that my concern is to take care of them, and if I am successful, I'll automatically take care of the rest of you." Watson did just that, in words that seemed to suggest that he considered Roosevelt a colleague, that the President was trying to do for the country what he was attempting to accomplish at IBM—make it stronger and more productive and efficient and harmonize differences while taking care of workers in a paternalistic fashion. Watson was truly puzzled why other businessmen failed to see this.

Later Watson was considered for the post of secretary of commerce and for the ambassadorship to Great Britain, but he wasn't interested in a political career or one in public service. Also, why should he leave the presidency of IBM to work for another man? This was Watson's view of the matter. He had served his time under John Patterson, and never again would he return to a subordinate position. From his words and actions, it would appear that Watson made no clear distinction between being employed by a corporation or doing similar work for government. Both were organizations and were similar in structure.

Watson's critics have suggested that he defended Roosevelt for business reasons, one of which was his hopes of obtaining contracts. There is no evidence of this, and in fact, Watson criticized the President's actions in attempting to reform the Supreme Court at a time when a major Society Security placement was being negotiated. Furthermore, while Roosevelt and Watson corresponded with each other and worked together in apparent friendship, the Justice Department was prosecuting IBM under the terms of the antitrust acts.

The basis for the action was rather tenuous, open, and aboveboard and had been known within the industry for many years. It had its roots in arrangements worked out by CTR and Powers Accounting in 1914, just prior to Watson's arrival at the company. Although Powers had developed machines good enough to take the census contract from Hollerith in 1910, his line was incomplete. In addition, there was a need for his cards to correspond with those punched by Hollerith for the previous census. Because of this, CTR and Powers entered into an agreement whereby Powers was licensed to use CTR's patents for mechanical machines and, in addition, produce cards for use in them. In 1922 this was renegotiated, and in 1931 a new arrangement was worked out between IBM and Remington Rand, Powers's successor firm. The two companies cross-licensed some of their accounting machine patents, while IBM agreed to settle its fee claims against Powers for $300,000 on signing and $25,000 a year for the next five years. This was taken as an indication that IBM had become the industry's leader and that Remington Rand and other business machine producers would have to follow its lead.

Enter the Electronic Revolution

The Justice Department filed its suit two weeks after Roosevelt assumed office, claiming that the companies had conspired to restrain commerce. Specifically, it attacked the practice of leasing rather than selling machines, obliging users to purchase cards from the company that produced the machine, and refusing to sell cards to anyone else. The government was in a unique position during the case, appearing as prosecutor, litigant, and customer. Even while attacking IBM for maintaining unfair practices, the federal government leased additional machines and purchased hundreds of millions of cards from the company.

Although Remington Rand had been cited as a coconspirator, it was effectively severed from the case when it agreed to accept the decision as it affected IBM. As it happened, it really wasn't much of a case, attracting little publicity at a time when the nation's attention was focused on the economic problems of depression and recovery. IBM was obliged to produce a vast amount of material relating to its business, and the normally secretive Watson must have been irked to see it all put on the public record. From it emerged a picture of a powerful firm, which had close to 80 percent of the business in keypunches, sorters, and accounting machines used for tabulating purposes. Remington Rand and Burroughs were distant and relatively unimportant competitors, and neither offered a full product line. The government argued that IBM prevented customers from purchasing products from other companies when, in fact, there were no viable competitors in the field. It also became clear that had he desired to do so, Watson might have obliged Remington Rand to abandon parts of its operations simply by refusing to enter into the cross-licensing arrangements. On the other hand, the Justice Department did demonstrate that IBM made large profits on its card sales and that the company would breach no competition in this area.

As the case developed, most of the attention became focused on the issue of card sales, and in 1936 the Supreme Court decided the issue in favor of the government. Henceforth IBM could not oblige its customers to purchase its cards. But since there were no rivals in this field, and none developed afterward —when IBM cut its prices sharply—there was little effect on the business.

IBM emerged from the interwar period a powerful, well-entrenched corporation, with an undisputed lead in what even then was recognized as a major growth industry: office machines. It had outdistanced all competitors and had not been damaged seriously by Justice Department actions. These would be the two fronts upon which IBM's wars would be fought in the future. On the one hand, the company had to meet challenges from rivals, both the old ones and new entities that would appear during the next four decades. But its victories could not be complete, nor would they be celebrated, for the government was always prepared to initiate new legal actions against the company whenever it appeared to have achieved too great a success. And the other companies knew this. If unable to defeat IBM in the marketplace, they might always turn to the courts for satisfaction.

Watson was a healthy and vigorous sixty-five years old in 1939, unwilling to consider retirement, and in any case there was no heir apparent in the wings. He might have reflected that during the past quarter of a century he had created a superb research and production organization and a world-famous sales force, both of which were models of their kind not only for business machine producers but for much of American and even world industry. "The IBM man" was a reality in 1939, and the symbolism of that quietly efficient individual would grow during the next decades. The company itself was in excellent financial shape, its patent positions secure, and its reputation unmatched. Antitrust problems seemed resolved; there was no new litigation on the horizon. But Watson was prepared for such an eventuality. In addition to fine salesmen and production experts, Watson introduced a new factor in the late 1930's. From that time onward IBM would employ some of the nation's top antitrust lawyers.

PART II

The Computer Wars

5

The First Computers

LIKE MANY OTHER self-made men, Thomas Watson combined an almost instinctive distrust of academia with an attitude toward prominent campus figures that bordered on reverence and awe. On the one hand, he saw little use in much of what passed for deep, abstract thought, especially the kind that was encouraged at leading colleges and universities, while on the other, he admired individuals who engaged in the practice, and did so with style and ease, in such ways as to communicate their ideas and visions to people of action like him. Perhaps this was due to a recognition on Watson's part that excellence came in many forms, or it might have been that beneath his façade of boosterism and love of efficiency and order there existed a core of romanticism.

The same person who insisted upon a near-puritanical approach to business became an ardent and intelligent art collector, a benefactor of museums and symphony orchestras, and a contributor of time and money to educational institutions. Watson served on the board of Columbia University and assisted New York University and other schools. Along with many leading businessmen he possessed a sense of service and evinced a yearning for honors and recognition, for honorary degrees, medals, and citations to his civic-mindedness.

Watson also was one of the first men in his industry to realize that the right kinds of connections at institutions of higher learning could be good business as well. Such places could provide IBM with a small but significant market for its products and also be a source of concepts which might be used in the development of new machines and techniques. Watson quickly realized that assisting professors on various campuses could return large rewards; such individuals would in effect become valuable members of the IBM research and development operation.

Ben Wood was one such individual. A Columbia psychology professor who, as a result of his friendship with Watson, became one of the company's consultants and a major figure in educational research, Wood brought other academics into the company's fold. According to Wood's memoir, he met Watson in 1927, while searching for a company that might be interested in producing a machine capable of scoring tests then being devised at the university. At the time these were graded manually, at large costs and in operations that consumed much time. Wood thought that those taking examinations might place their answers in portions of a specially prepared form, using a lead pencil the marks of which could be "read" by a machine through which the papers would be passed. In this fashion the tests could be graded in fractions of a second rather than in minutes and at a relatively low cost per unit.

Watson immediately realized that such a machine would not only open the educational market to his company but also perform for testing of all kinds what the early Holleriths had done for the census: replace squadrons of semiskilled office workers with machines that could be leased, all of them processing tens of thousands of forms produced by IBM. He provided Wood with as many tabulators, accounting machines, punches, and sorters as he required and in other ways subsidized his work at the university. Watson spent much time at the laboratory, listening to Wood's ideas and attempting to find ways they might be translated into products and services. Wood directed him to other academics in the field, some of whom were hired by IBM or put on consultantships for this and related products.

Out of this experience came the 805 test scorer, a machine that for years dominated the field. It represented only a small part of IBM's total business, however, and in the late 1930's brought in less revenue than electric typewriters. Far more important than the machine and the test forms it processed was the new experience with academia. Throughout the decade and afterward IBM subsidized research at Columbia and other universities, often in areas far removed from the company's main lines of business and in areas of pure as opposed to applied science. Just as Watson earlier had collected salesmen, now he gathered in technicians and scientists, providing them with machines, grants, and consultantships. Most of their projects resulted in no great benefits for the company, but they provided IBM with a fine reputation that would serve it well later on, when such matters were of major importance. The company-university nexus also stimulated IBM's own scientists and did as much for Watson himself.

By the mid-1930's the Columbia University Statistics Bureau had received millions of dollars' worth of equipment and grants from IBM, while at the school's Thomas J. Watson Astronomical Computing Bureau several scientists, led by Wallace Eckert, were adapting tabulators and accounting devices designed for use in offices and banks for utilization in the study of the stars and planets. Working with IBM's Clair Lake, Eckert transformed these machines into a new form, a calculator, which could perform a wide variety of complex mathematical tasks in a short period. Eckert's calculator would not have appeared exotic to individuals used to many of the larger machines turned out by IBM, Burroughs, and other companies in the field. It was an electromechanical device capable of resolving problems that were fed into it by means of the familiar IBM cards and little more.

Still, this represented a new departure for Watson. In the past he had produced machines to fill specific needs of businessmen, obtaining many of his ideas from his salesmen. Eckert —who was soon to leave Columbia to take a research post at IBM—was concerned with pure mathematics, and he constructed his calculator without a thought to its commercial potential, but rather to assist astronomers in their work. As for Watson, he seemed to believe there was no market for calculators—no office, not even major government agencies, had need for such rapid calculations or would be willing to pay the cost of such a device.

News of the Eckert calculator and the activities at the Watson Bureau spread through the academic world. This machine was by no means the only one being worked on in America and Europe, but none of the other research was so well funded or conducted under such impressive academic and business sponsorship. James Conant, Harvard's scientist-president, and Harlow Shapley, also of that institution and one of the world's leading astronomers, came to visit Eckert and learn more of his work—and of Watson's willingness to fund such projects. Howard Aiken also visited Columbia. A young Harvard doctoral student in physics and a junior member of the faculty, Aiken had no great interest in astronomy but wanted to understand Eckert's calculator. Aiken had kept himself abreast of research into mathematical machines and had ideas of his own on what was both possible and useful in the field. He was shown around by Eckert and Lake and soon realized that his own concepts were in advance of any then being discussed at Columbia.

Even then Aiken wanted to construct a machine that would perform according to preprogrammed instructions and automatically, without any further input by the operator. Such a machine would stand in a similar relationship to the calculator as the automatic transmission in an automobile does to the clutch-activated transmission. It would be too much to say that it was capable of thought, but rather that Aiken had in mind a device that could retain a set of mathematical rules and then apply them to new data introduced later. And this is one of the essential differences between a calculator and a new kind of machine, the computer. The former lacks a memory, and this is at the heart of the computer.

It was not a new idea. Germs could be found in the work of Hero of Alexandria, Blaise Pascal, Johannes Kepler, and Gottfried Leibniz, all of whom were important figures in the history of science. Charles Babbage, who spent close to a lifetime working on his "Analytical Engine" in the nineteenth century, is usually credited with setting down the basic components for computers, even though he never completed his model. It was upon the work of such scientists that Aiken intended to proceed (although he later claimed not to have known of Babbage's work until well started on his own). Aiken was interested in Eckert's technology, to be sure, but even more in his sponsorship.

Conant, Shapley, and Aiken corresponded with Eckert and Lake, and in time Watson and one of his most important researchers, James Bryce, were drawn into the discussions. The way seemed open for an IBM-sponsored activity, one in which Aiken would play a role at Harvard similar to that of Eckert at Columbia. But several difficulties had to be overcome first. Watson insisted the machine be constructed at IBM's Endicott facilities, where he and his scientists would keep tabs on the work, while Aiken wanted a laboratory in Cambridge, Massachusetts. Both men were temperamental, arrogant, and blunt, and each disliked these qualities in others. Aiken needed IBM's money but would accept nothing else; Watson was interested in Aiken's theories regarding calculators and computers but avoided contacts with a person he quickly learned to dislike. Still, mutual interests drew them together, with Aiken obliged to give in on major points in order to obtain funding. He would receive whatever machines and money were required to construct what came to be called the Automatic Sequence Controlled Calculator (more commonly known as the ASCC and later as the Mark I), but the device would be put together at Endicott. Bryce would be directly involved in the work, as would other IBM scientists led by Clair Lake, who was to serve as chief engineer.

Work on the project got under way with a $500,000 grant in 1940. When the United States entered World War II, Aiken was called into active service by the Navy. Recognizing the potential usefulness of the Mark I to the war effort—and with Watson's prodding—the government assigned Aiken to Endicott, and so the machine was ready for demonstration in January 1943. Then it was dismantled and shipped to Harvard for an official unveiling in May of the following year.

Watson traveled to Harvard for the occasion, one he expected would publicize his company and provide him with new honors and recognition. He learned this was not to be. Instead, during a press conference Aiken took almost all the credit for the accomplishment. "I'm just sick about the whole thing," said an angry and hurt Watson. "You can't put IBM on as a postscript," he screamed at Aiken. "I think about IBM just as you Harvard fellows do about your university." Turning to Conant, he claimed that the machine was an IBM product, not a Harvard creation, and implied that future assistance should not be expected. Aiken cared little for what Watson thought of him. At the dedication he alluded to the role played by Bryce and other IBM men in the creation of the ASCC but did not mention Watson, who left the ceremony in a cold fury. Shortly thereafter he leased the machine to the Navy and for several months refused to discuss it or Howard Aiken.

What Watson thought regarding the potential market for such machines is unknown, although at the time they certainly didn't figure importantly in his plans. But in spite of his bad experience at Harvard, Watson continued to show an interest in Aiken's work, and he also encouraged other researchers in the field. During the war the Moore School of Electrical Engineering at the University of Pennsylvania had become closely involved with the Ballistics Research Laboratory of the Army Ordnance Department. Several researchers there, led by Herman Zornig, asked IBM to build special multiplying machines to their specifications. The order was accepted, and the machines were put together and delivered. In the process of working on them, several IBM scientists became interested in research and experimentation being conducted by a physicist, John Mauchly, and an electrical engineer, J. Presper Eckert. Several years earlier Mauchly had come across ideas set down by an obscure Iowa State College professor, John Atanasoff, who conceived of an electronic computer with a capacity and speed far beyond those later realized by the Mark I. Like Babbage before him, Atanasoff lacked the funds and technology to attempt construction, but thanks to the Army, Mauchly had both. Taking Atanasoff's basic plan and adding their own ideas, Eckert and Mauchly were attempting to construct a computer, which they called the Electronic Numerical Integrator and Calculator, or ENIAC.

In February 1944, as Watson was preparing to go to Harvard in what he conceived would be a triumphal visit, Colonel Paul Gillon of the Office of the Chief of Army Ordnance arrived at his office to ask IBM's help for the project. Watson realized that although the ENIAC was a military device, it also was similar to the Mark I in capabilities, though, of course, much faster and larger. He introduced Gillon to Bryce and other scientists, who agreed to supply the Army with whatever was required, and in other ways he helped initiate a correspondence between his people and those at the Moore School. Gillon was grateful, writing that although from IBM's vantage point the program "may appear to be a comparatively small one, its intrinsic importance relative to our overall ballistic computing problem is very great."

Gillon was mistaken if he thought IBM was extending itself only in order to help speed the war effort. Shortly after returning from Harvard, Watson decided on a new corporate approach to computers. Bryce was told that future contacts with Aiken were to be minimized and that IBM would produce a new computer on its own, in cooperation with Wallace Eckert and others at Columbia, to be based in part on concepts being tested on the ENIAC. Work began soon after on what would be known as the Selective Sequence Electronic Calculator, or SSEC.

IBM was not the only company to become involved with computer research around this time, and experimentation was being conducted at campuses other than Columbia, Harvard, and Pennsylvania. At Princeton's Institute for Advanced Study polymath John von Neumann was developing a device to be used in conjunction with the atomic bomb project. Jay Forrester of the Massachusetts Institute of Technology was at work on several military computers. Before the war George Stibitz, head of the Bell Telephone Laboratories, headed a team seeking a means to facilitate complex work in telephone operations, and by 1943 Bell had more patents and expertise than any other firm in the field. Stibitz, too, had been contacted by Colonel Gillon, and Bell cooperated with IBM and the Moore School scientists. Jan Rajchman was developing a computer for the Radio Corporation of America, which would be used to help aim guns. Howard Aiken didn't have to worry about the loss of Watson's patronage. The armed forces provided him with more than enough funds to develop a Mark II, and, later on, a III and IV as well. Several projects were under way in Great Britain, at the National Physics Laboratory in Teddington, at Cambridge, and at the University of Manchester. Scientists such as John Womersley, Douglas Hartree, and L. J. Comrie had worked on computers before their American counterparts, and now they provided the Moore School people with ideas and concepts. Alan Turing, a leading British mathematician, was setting down theories that would form the basis for a generation of computer designs after the war, and he, too, corresponded with the Americans.

There was nothing unusual about this; academic scientists had a long tradition of sharing information orally and by means of conventions and scholarly papers, and the practice was intensified by the war effort. So were the relations between corporations. American firms were supposed to compete against one another, and when two in the same industry agreed to share information and patents—as had IBM and Remington Rand—they might expect antitrust suits. During the war, however, the government encouraged them to work together and, moreover, to include the university scientists in their projects.

Although this form of cooperation had been practiced for several decades, relatively few corporations considered academic science an important part of their business. There were notable exceptions—the drug, petroleum, chemical, and food businesses had grown to expect information, ideas, and assistance from the professors. But most of the time, in most industries, academic researchers engaged in work pertaining to commercial products would be invited to leave the campus and take a post at the corporation.

IBM was no different in this regard. After the war Watson would offer employment to dozens of researchers at the Moore School, Harvard, Princeton, and elsewhere, and many accepted. Those who preferred to remain independent while engaged in interesting work found that IBM could be generous in making grants and paying for part-time consultantships. Academics would be invited to company-sponsored seminars and conferences, at which top scientists would be wined, dined, and wooed. The company had led the way in this regard during the 1930's, and its relationship with many academic scientists was strengthened during the war. As a result, IBM was able to put together one of the nation's finest research operations, and the corporation was in close contact with many of the world's leading technicians and theoreticians in fields affecting its products.

IBM emerged from World War II a far more powerful entity than it had been when the conflict began. Revenues from sales and rentals quadrupled from 1939 to 1945, rising from $34.8 million to $141.7 million, even though installations in Germany, Italy, and France were seized when America entered the war in December 1941. Factory space was tripled, and employment rose by more than 50 percent.

Watson took great pride in the company's contribution to

national defense. Early in 1941 he organized the Munitions Manufacturing Corporation, which during the war turned out a variety of weapons, from machine guns to hand grenades, for the Army. Watson limited profits on military contracts to 1.5 percent, and that went into a fund for the widows and orphans of IBM men killed in action. The wives of IBMers who entered the armed services received a week of their husbands' prewar salaries for every month the men were in uniform. Watson froze his own remuneration at the 1939 level and contributed generously to many war-related activities.

For the most part, however, IBM continued to produce the same kinds of machines it had turned out prior to the war, while it entered new fields in which military expertise could be applied later to the design of business machines. Only 10 percent of the company's wartime sales were derived from munitions and ordnance, and perhaps another 10 percent from other contracts for products directly relating to the war effort. This was more a result of government requirements than anything else. Other firms were better equipped for such tasks. In any case, the federal government's requirements for accounting machines, tabulators, and related devices expanded during the war, and IBM was asked to produce these rather than military items. The machines were leased at the usual rates, and this policy applied to electric typewriter and card sales.

IBM Selected Statistics, 1939–1945

(in millions of dollars)

Year	Revenues			Earnings		
	Sales	Rentals	Total	Pretax	Posttax	Net Assets
1939	9.9	29.6	39.5	11.2	9.1	79.0
1940	12.2	34.1	46.3	12.9	9.4	83.1
1941	19.6	43.3	62.9	19.0	9.8	97.6
1942	33.3	57.4	90.7	26.9	8.7	120.6
1943	65.2	69.7	134.9	37.0	9.2	154.2
1944	67.9	75.4	143.3	37.7	9.7	136.5
1945	55.1	86.6	141.7	36.4	10.9	134.1

Source: *Moody's Manual of Investments*, 1943, 1948, and IBM Annual Reports, 1939–1946

The First Computers

Were it not for the wartime excess profits tax, IBM's net reported earnings would have tripled from 1939 to 1945. As it was, the figure rose by only 20 percent. More important, however, the firm's net assets went from $79 million to more than $134 million in this period. In 1939 IBM had cash and equivalent items of $6.5 million, and in 1945, $23.5 million.

Watson had the products, patents, researchers, markets, ideas, and funds to take advantage of any new opportunities that came his way. Had he desired to do so, IBM might have undertaken a major effort in the field of computers. Work was proceeding on the Selective Sequence Electronic Calculator, and, with the possible exception of Bell Laboratories, IBM had closer contacts with the ENIAC team at the Moore School than had any other company. Bell did not pose a serious business threat; under terms of an agreement with the government its parent firm, American Telephone & Telegraph, had agreed not to compete in noncommunications fields, and Bell's leaders already had signaled that its computer work was directed toward internal use. There was a minor effort under way at RCA, but at the time that company was far more interested in television than in devoting resources to computers.

Selected Statistics for Business Machine Companies, 1939–1945

(in millions of dollars)

Company	Sales		Earnings		Net Assets	
	1939	1945	1939	1945	1939	1945
Burroughs	32.5	37.6	3.0	2.3	36.6	46.0
IBM	39.5	141.7	9.1	10.9	79.0	134.1
NCR	37.1	68.4	1.8	2.2	56.9	57.4
Remington Rand	43.3	132.6	2.1	5.3	43.2	75.4
Underwood	24.2	29.0	1.9	2.2	17.9	29.6

Source: *Moody's Manual of Investments*, 1943, 1948

There was little reason to assume that other business machine companies were about to make an important commitment to computers. National Cash Register merely dabbled in the field, while Burroughs didn't even do that. In any case, both were by then far smaller and weaker than IBM and more concerned with problems relating to conversion to a peacetime economy than in pioneering.

But there were stirrings at Remington Rand, which by then had become the second largest factor in the industry. The company still produced tabulators, and Rand Kardex, where president James Rand, Jr., had got his start, was the innovative leader in its field. Furthermore, during the war Remington Rand had obtained an Army contract for development of a missile guidance system, and now it had its own small team of electronics engineers and researchers. With the coming of peace these men were transferred to Kardex, where in 1946 they created the first electromechanical visible records system. Encouraged by its reception, Rand put them to work on a new electronic tabulator. This was a minor and peripheral effort, however, for Remington Rand lacked the will and resources to do more than this.

This absence of a competitive challenge may account for some of Watson's uncharacteristically slow movement in regard to computer development. Then, too, IBM's customers did not appear interested in such machines, and although the Atomic Energy Commission and other federal agencies wanted them, the market clearly was small. Always a salesman, Watson disliked committing the company to items his representatives could not immediately market. Also, there existed a strong demand for the current product line. Watson was interested in electronic calculators, tabulators, and accounting machines and did not see any forceful reason to proceed much farther than he already had with computers. He would develop the SSEC but not produce copies for the market.

Finally, there was the matter of his age. Seventy-one years old in 1945, Watson was healthy and vigorous enough to manage the company, but he had lost much of his zest for change. "It isn't a hard thing to build up a business if you are willing to do a reasonable amount of work," he said around this time. "The job is to protect a business after you build it up." This was what he was doing in the postwar period. Increasingly the day-to-day operations were handled by two vice-presidents, Charles Kirk and John Phillips. Both were completely loyal to Watson, and neither would undertake a new project without his approval, even though Kirk, who was only forty-three years old, was eager to go ahead with computers. He and Phillips, a more placid individual, went along with Watson's defensive approach, knowing it would not last for long.

One reason was that Thomas Watson, Jr., now home from the wars, had joined the firm and, despite official protests to the contrary, clearly was being groomed to take his father's place. This suited Kirk, who was entrusted with the task of preparing him for leadership. "He had a large desk," recalled young Watson later on, "and I simply had a chair pulled up at the edge of what he did."

This apprenticeship lasted little more than a year, long enough for Kirk to familiarize Watson junior with the company's operations, take him into the field to meet key executives, show him how headquarters was set up, and introduce him to the work in progress, particularly that relating to computers. The transition of power was well under way when, in the summer of 1947, Kirk died.

This was a shocking and serious blow, for it removed from IBM the one man with the power, imagination, and status needed to push ahead with development work on computers and related new products. Watson junior was by then a vice-president and member of the board, and although he was learning rapidly, he wasn't prepared to take command. Improvising to buy time, the elder Watson summoned John Phillips and told him that henceforth he would have to assume most of Kirk's responsibilities. Phillips was a retiring man, content with his previous posts as IBM's secretary and treasurer, and had no higher ambitions. Recognizing that he lacked executive qualities, Phillips first tried to convince Watson that his son should be moved into the slot and then accepted the assignment after this suggestion was rejected. Phillips performed his tasks well, but because he lacked Kirk's drive, the company started to drift, as though it were awaiting Watson junior's coronation. A move in this direction took place in 1949, when Phillips was promoted to the presidency while Watson senior assumed the chairmanship, a post that had remained vacant since Fairchild's death. In the order of things Watson junior became the new executive vice-president, his last step before taking full command.

During this interregnum IBM concentrated a good deal of its research and development upon the production of a line of electronic calculators. Watson's salesmen would have little trouble placing these with customers whose needs had previously been met by the electromechanical models and who would welcome the faster machines. Out of this came the 600 line of electronic calculators, the first of which was placed in 1946, and a huge card-programmed calculator which was created by meshing several new electronic accounting machines with a novel storage unit. The success of these and other devices which were little more than electronic variants of familiar machines provided IBM with a patina of modernity, leading *Business Week* to claim that it "remains in the forefront of technology" and, according to the *Wall Street Journal*, was "far ahead of its competitors" in terms of applying knowledge gained in wartime to commercial products.

More important developments in this regard were taking place at the Moore School, where the team of electronics researchers that had created military devices was about to be disbanded. Insofar as the University of Pennsylvania was concerned, scientists associated with the Ballistics Research Laboratory and the creation of ENIAC had been there to help out during a period of national emergency. Now that peace had arrived, their services were no longer needed. The scientists left the Moore School, some to take academic posts elsewhere and others for employment in large corporations. Several started businesses of their own. Most continued to be interested in computer development and were able to work in other locales on ideas originated at the Moore School.

Perhaps no figure in his branch of science had a greater reputation at the time than John von Neumann, who not only had won fame for his work in developing the atomic bomb but also had become a major theoretician in the computer field. However, even von Neumann had difficulties finding sufficient financial support for what he portrayed as an exploration into computer design and development, with no clear applicability to current problems and the costs of which were yet undefined. Bell Laboratories and IBM had profound respect for the man; had he so desired, von Neumann might have had a major research post at either corporation, but not necessarily in the computer field. Also, Bell and IBM already had ongoing programs in computer research and were reluctant to fund another inquiry of undetermined costs over which they would have limited control.

Von Neumann managed to obtain some help from Princeton and more from the Army and Navy, both of which were interested in the role computers might play in some future war. The Rockefeller Foundation turned him down, however, as did other such organizations. But von Neumann was able to interest Elmer Engstrom, vice-president for research at the Radio Corporation of America, in his ideas. After convincing his board of the soundness of the program, Engstrom told von Neumann that the company would pick up most of the costs for the experiments, and with this RCA made an important foray into the field.

As has been seen, RCA had conducted research in computers during the war and in Jan Rajchman had one of the nation's leading researchers. David Sarnoff, the company's chairman, intended to concentrate most of RCA's attention on television, but he also believed computers might prove profitable. He did not expect RCA to become a business machine company, however; his entire career had been in the field of radio, and Sarnoff wasn't going to change direction so late in life. Rather, he appeared to look at computers as vast arrays of cathode-ray tubes of the very kind his company was so expert in developing and as a natural outlet for the electronics capabilities RCA had acquired during the war. There was reason to believe that computer research would dovetail nicely with the work Vladimir Zworykin and his staff was conducting at the

RCA laboratories. What if the market for the giant devices turned out to be quite small? The knowledge gained from an involvement with von Neumann surely would be worthwhile if only a small part found application in television. And if indeed there were many potential customers for the machines—scientific laboratories, government agencies, the military—RCA might be able to enter a new field at low cost.

IBM and other companies in the industry paid little attention to RCA's dealings with von Neumann. Perhaps they understood that Sarnoff had no real intention of making forays into their markets, and they might have reflected that this new combination of scientist and electronics company only demonstrated that the expensive computers had little place in their own industry. It did mark an important development in the history of computers, however. IBM's interest in the machines derived from an expectation that at one time or another they might complement or even replace calculators and accounting machines in the nation's offices. As for RCA, it was seeking a means of applying knowledge to an interesting new product without first giving much thought to marketing it. As always, IBM started with its customer base and worked out from there; RCA and other electronics companies began with science and technology and then, having developed their machines, sought potential buyers or leasers. IBM remained primarily interested in corporate placements and future business requirements. In the nature of things, RCA and other firms that later followed its lead thought in terms of government sales, to the military and the Atomic Energy Commission in particular.

Design plans for the new computer were already being worked on at the Moore School when RCA agreed to provide funding. Now von Neumann invited many of the team's members, including Eckert, Mauchly, and a particularly brilliant young designer by the name of Herman Goldstine, to join him at the Institute for Advanced Study at Princeton. Goldstine agreed to come and became an important member of the von Neumann-RCA team that eventually produced the Electronic Discrete Variable Automatic Computer, or, in the shorthand of the day, EDVAC, which was completed in 1950 for use by Army Ordnance.

Eckert, Mauchly, and other Moore School scientists who had turned down von Neumann's invitation did so because their interests and ambitions were different from his. In particular, they believed computers could have important roles in private businesses and in this regard differed sharply with Watson and most other business machine executives. Under ideal circumstances they might have remained at Pennsylvania for a few years to work on their ideas and then have sought sponsorship from one or another corporation or even formed a new one of their own to produce and sell machines. The situation was far from ideal, however. For one thing, ENIAC had been constructed under a government contract at the university, and although there was some question of who actually owned the patents and product, they clearly did not accrue to the scientists. For another, it was becoming increasingly evident that Pennsylvania would like them to leave. Neither Eckert nor Mauchly had been offered a professorship at the school or given any clear sign his research would be supported in any fashion.

Both men had friends and associates at IBM who knew of their work on EDVAC and plans for commercial development of computers. Bryce, in particular, was most interested in their ideas and remained in close contact with the Moore School team. Earlier he had been rebuffed when he attempted to send observers to some experiments there. Now he had an opportunity to have the two leading scientists in the field at his laboratory, to help on the SSEC and to lobby for future machines. At his urging Watson agreed to meet with Eckert and Mauchly, and both men were offered employment contracts—to work on IBM projects relating to calculators and electronics. Unwilling to accept such conditions, they left IBM to seek assistance elsewhere and soon discovered that none would be forthcoming.

Eckert and Mauchly continued to develop ENIAC while scouting support and contracts for any computers they might construct. Nothing came of meetings with officials from Burroughs, NCR, and General Electric, although by then all three had pilot projects in the field. But several government officials who knew of the Moore School operations and were preparing to return to private business were mildly interested in investing funds in a new company headed by the two men. The Census Bureau told them they would be permitted to bid on contracts for the 1950 counting, and the Weather Bureau indicated it might want one or more machines designed to specifications. Northrop Corporation, a medium-sized defense-oriented aircraft manufacturer, wanted to know more about computers, but as a potential customer, not a source of funding.

ENIAC was finally completed and turned over to Army Ordnance in late 1945 and installed in early 1946. Now the university gave Eckert and Mauchly the choice of devoting more of their energies to teaching and pure research or finding employment elsewhere—and clearly hoped they would leave. This didn't come as a surprise; for months the Pennsylvania administration had complained the two were spending most of their time on outside activities of a purely commercial nature. They resigned to organize the first firm devoted solely to computers, which they named Electronic Control Corporation, with offices in Philadelphia and its only contract an order for one computer for Northrop.

Electronic Control was hardly a great success, but it did manage to survive. In April 1946 the founders went to Washington to make a presentation to the Census Bureau, which resulted in the award of a study contract and then an initial purchase order. Work proceeded on the Binary Automatic Computer (BINAC), which, as might have been expected, resembled EDVAC but had several improvements, among which was a magnetic tape input that replaced the more cumbersome card punches.

Even then the new machines captured the public's imagination. Articles on "mechanical brains" started to appear in popular magazines as well as in scientific journals. Together with atomic energy, computers seemed a major new wartime technology that would alter life in the postwar period. It would appear that Electronic Control had reason to expect additional orders. None was forthcoming, however. To capitalize on their growing reputation and product, the founders changed the name to the Eckert-Mauchly Computer Company, but this didn't help. In the late summer of 1947, by which time work had begun on the Census Bureau machine, Eckert-Mauchly was in a tight financial situation. Without an infusion of new funds it could not proceed with the development of what would be called the Universal Automatic Computer, or UNIVAC.

Help arrived in the form of a $500,000 investment by American Totalizator Corporation, a firm engaged in the manufacture of parimutuel machines used at the nation's racetracks. The company was controlled by the Mun brothers but was really operated by Henry Straus, who suspected that computers might be useful in processing information for the parimutuels. American Totalizator was a small company, unable to devote much of its limited resources to Eckert-Mauchly. But Straus persisted, the Muns went along, and in time American Totalizator took control of Eckert-Mauchly.

Operations were cut to the bone as the scientists rushed to complete UNIVAC, which they were convinced would not only revolutionize the 1950 census in much the same way as the Holleriths had changed matters in 1890 but produce a rash of new orders. The orders did arrive; but the money ran out before the first machine was completed, and for a short period work on it stopped as Eckert and Mauchly returned to American Totalizator with a new plea for help.

This time it was not forthcoming. Straus had been killed in an airplane accident that October, and the Muns, now without their company's driving force, were eager to unload what they considered a hopeless drain on assets. The brothers scouted around for someone who might be willing to take the company off their hands and found a buyer in James Rand of Remington Rand.

Rand had just released his new line of electronic calculators and was encouraged by the way his customers ordered them. Eager to explore related products and ventures, he entered into negotiations with the Muns. Rand learned that the first UNIVAC was a year away from completion and that the company had orders for six more, at a price of better than $1.1 million each. Eckert and Mauchly assured him their unit costs would be less than that but at the same time conceded they would need at least $1 million for the rest of 1950. Undeterred by reports that the total market for such machines couldn't be more than a dozen or so, Rand purchased 95 percent of the common stock in March and funded the project. Eckert was named vice-president of the new computer operation and promised more or less a free hand.

The initial machine was a huge success. Despite its late delivery in March 1951, UNIVAC took over a major part of the processing work, augmenting many Census Bureau machines and replacing others—among which were some IBM products. To those with long memories, it must have appeared that history was repeating itself. Just as Powers had mounted a successful challenge to Hollerith prior to merging into Remington Rand, so Eckert-Mauchly was doing the same, and once again success went to a Remington Rand subsidiary. Now Rand purchased the remaining 5 percent of the stock and enlarged the funding for additional research and development.

The Korean War was on by then, and Rand expected orders from the Army and Navy as well as from the civilian markets. Encouraged, he purchased another small computer firm; in 1952 Remington Rand acquired Engineering Research Associates, a St. Paul operation that had developed an advanced computer for the Georgia Institute of Technology and had recently entered into a contract for the development of military versions for the Air Force.

Remington Rand was not as large or powerful a firm as IBM. It lacked depth of management, appeared unable to increase its profitability, and for many years had lagged in product introduction and research. Its salesmen were deemed second-rate by IBM's standards, and more than a few were Watson rejects. Rand himself often found it difficult to concentrate for long on a single idea and then carry it through to fruition; in addition to office machines, Remington Rand produced electric shavers and several other items having little to do with its main line of business. Rand was ever on the lookout for mergers and acquisitions and at times appeared more a promoter than a manager. Wall Street knew the firm had not grown as rapidly as IBM, and its stock was not well favored by investors. But now matters seemed to be changing. On the surface at least, it appeared that Remington Rand had stolen the march on IBM in the computer field.

This is not to suggest that Watson had little or no interest in the new machines, but rather that he seemed content to permit research and development to proceed and even to put together some models for demonstration purposes or to fill government orders. If copies of these would be leased to old clients, well and good. He held back on a full-scale effort, however. Why do otherwise? The market for his 600 line of electronic calculators was expanding rapidly; by late 1950 IBM was placing them at the rate of 40 a month, and the number reached 100 a year later. His customers wanted these kinds of machines, not the huge, expensive computers.

This soon would change, at which time IBM would have to strain itself in order to catch up with the leader. For the moment at least, Remington Rand had the edge in one of the most important and profitable technologies of the twentieth century and had a fine opportunity to vanquish IBM on the eve of Watson's retirement.

6

The Brothers Watson

THOMAS AND JEANNETTE WATSON had four children. Thomas junior, who was born in 1914, was two years older than Jane, who was followed a year later by Helen. Arthur, who for most of his life was known as Dick, was born when young Tom was five.

Helen married the socially prominent Walker Gentry Buckner in 1940. The Watsons approved of the match and soon after took their son-in-law into the family business as an IBM director. Jane married the equally distinguished John Irwin II in 1949; he would hold several posts at IBM, and the Watson connection proved useful in his law practice. Each man was successful in his own right, and each knew he would play no major role at the company. Together with their wives and others in the immediate and extended family, they understood that young Tom was destined to succeed the patriarch, while some other less important and subordinate post would be found for Dick.

Years later Tom Watson would claim that the idea of assuming command at IBM—or even of working there—didn't occur to him until late in World War II, when, a veteran officer at the age of thirty, he was motoring into Washington alongside a general, who casually asked about his plans. Watson said he hadn't given the matter much thought, to which the general replied, "Aren't you going back to take over IBM?"

Everyone in the company knew this was the plan. Thomas Watson remained vigorous and unlikely to relinquish command to anyone yet, but the apprenticeship for the heir apparent had already been worked out. Like Rockefeller, Ford, and other industrial tycoons, Watson took it for granted that he would hand over to his elder son the reins of power at a time of his choosing. This had not been decided upon during the war or afterward, but rather was simply assumed when young Tom was born. Even in the highly unlikely circumstance that he truly had an open mind on the matter, Watson junior always knew of his father's plans, not only for him but for Dick as well. Both were highly spirited and independent young men, but neither had the temerity to challenge Watson senior on this matter. Early in life they became, in effect, IBM trainees. "The company," Tom Watson later conceded, "is in the family unconscious."

As a child young Watson visited IBM factories, went on company tours, and even attended Hundred Percent Club conventions, as though to expose him to the best people in the firm. Always he was prodded—and often not gently—by Watson senior and reminded of his status and the hopes held for him. Years later Tom Watson indicated that as a youth he stood in awe of his father, a man to be respected and feared as well as admired. The elder Watson clearly loved his sons but was somewhat awkward when it came to dealing with children and adolescents. He placed before his boys standards meant for exceptional men, and when they failed to measure up to them,

Tom and Dick would be bluntly criticized and punished, as men might be.

Amateur psychologists might conclude that individuals subjected to such strains either become stronger than they otherwise might have been or crack under the strain. Tom Watson did neither, although the experiences must have had an important effect. So had being pointed out as his father's son, the inheritor of power and wealth, at such an early age. Since many of the people he knew came from within IBM, he must have seen his father as a paragon of virtues, and this, too, would have impressed him. How could any son measure up to such a man? How could he expect to improve upon his record?

With all this, Tom Watson moved easily through his early years. He developed into an excellent skier and yachtsman and, in fact, was good at and enjoyed most sports. By the time he entered Brown University as a freshman in 1933 Tom was six feet two inches tall, possessed the figure and grace of an athlete, and was more strikingly handsome than even his father had been at his age. During the next few years he was more a play-boy than a student. Young Watson was at ease in parkas and tuxedos and certainly knew how to enjoy life. That he was personable, intelligent, and talented was obvious, but he lacked drive and ambition, or at least so it appeared at the time.

Tom Watson's behavior must have troubled Watson senior. His grades in school were poor, and his attendance there was erratic. But with the criticisms went pride as well. Tom Watson was, after all, a rich man's son—there was no way of escaping this. And if such was the case, at least he was turning out to be a decent specimen of the breed. Like his father, Tom had little interest in books and abstract ideas, but he did possess an agile mind, which in time could be trained. Besides, the two men had altogether different upbringings and experiences and were products of dissimilar eras. Watson senior realized that he lacked the ability to relax; he must have known this even as a young salesman in Buffalo. He was not built for leisure and frivolities and had little talent for small talk. Late in life he came to regret this. It was different with his elder son, and

Watson senior must have enjoyed hearing of Tom's escapades, even while he criticized and deplored them.

The two grew closer during young Tom's college years. As Tom came to understand business and think seriously of his future, he came to appreciate the magnitude of his father's accomplishments. He now knew where he was headed. Shortly before graduation in 1937 he asked his father, "How do you go about getting a job at IBM?" and, of course, knew what the reaction and answer would be. This act cemented their relationship. Watson senior was overjoyed. "The thing that I am looking forward to now with so much pleasure is having you to counsel with and help me plan my future programs along various lines," he wrote in an emotional letter soon thereafter. "I suddenly realized that now I have somebody in my life upon whom I can look with confidence."

As befitted the heir apparent, IBM accepted Tom with open arms, and he breezed through the schools there; no one would dare criticize him. Then he was assigned a territory in Manhattan's financial district, an area that employed many IBM machines, which were not so much sold as placed. Watson had no difficulty making the Hundred Percent Club in his first year, but he had no illusions regarding this record, understanding that the road to success had been prepared in advance. The following year he filled his quota on the first working day in January. Watson senior could not have been prouder and claimed that his son was making it on his own. "That is the only right way," he said. "Otherwise, people might feel that he had some special help, which he did not have." Tom knew better. "It would have been very hard for the son of the president to do poorly," he conceded.

Tom spent far more time in nightclubs than in corporate offices. Mention of his activities was more likely to appear on the society page than in the business section. In short, he was a playboy, skiing in the winter and yachting during the summer, and in between he would take orders for business machines. He piloted airplanes whenever possible. Given his choice of professions, Watson probably would have chosen that of aviator. He joined the New York National Guard to get in more hours in the air on a variety of planes, and he often volunteered for extra duty involving the transport of aircraft from one base to another.

In the autumn of 1940, when he was twenty-six years old and one of the nation's most eligible bachelors, Watson was called into service, entering the Army Air Corps as a private. After undergoing training, he was commissioned a second lieutenant and given an assignment as a transport pilot. Once America entered the war, he ferried planes across the Atlantic and soon after was selected to fly generals and other important figures back and forth from New York and Washington to London, Moscow, and other European cities. On one occasion he helped escort Winston Churchill from London to Teheran, and he flew into Moscow when that city was under siege.

These responsibilities and experiences caused Watson to cast off his playboy past. In addition, he married Olive Field Cawley a week after the Pearl Harbor attack, and she proved a settling influence. Now Watson rarely entered nightclubs where once he had been a regular; he cut down on his heavy drinking to the point where he all but gave it up for long stretches. At the time of his discharge Watson was a lieutenant colonel with senior pilot's wings. He also had a clear idea of what he wanted to do with his life. "Frankly I can hardly wait to begin," he wrote to his father shortly before receiving his discharge. "When I think of the difference in my general outlook now as against the 1937–1940 period, I am convinced that I am now at least seventy-five percent better equipped mentally to follow in your footsteps as I intend to do." After a short vacation he returned to IBM in January 1946, prepared to train for the company's presidency.

Those who remembered the easygoing Tom Watson of 1940 were somewhat surprised at the many changes that had come over him. Although he was only thirty-two years old, lines were beginning to appear on his face, and his hair was prematurely turning gray. He was a father now—Thomas III was born in 1944, and five other children would follow at intervals of roughly two years. Watson was sober, serious, and hardworking. In the Army he had become accustomed to giving orders and having them obeyed, and this was the IBM way, too. What the NCR experience in upper New York had done for the father, the war had provided for the son—it prepared him for a top post in business.

Given the fact that both men were proud, temperamental, and self-assured, their relationship was harmonious. As has been noted, Watson senior oversaw his son's executive training and moved him rapidly up the ladder. After Charles Kirk's death Watson was given new responsibilities, one of which involved computer development.

Watson junior had a more than passing interest in electronics because he had come in contact with many of the devices during the war. On one of their tours Kirk showed him experimental work on the 600 electronic calculators, and the two men prodded Watson senior into accelerating the research and then producing the machines, which, of course, were great successes. Kirk had also been instrumental in the company's commitment to the Selective Sequence Electronic Calculator, and after Kirk's death Watson junior urged his father to consider putting it into production. After being rebuffed, he had a survey done to determine the market for such machines, which showed that approximately seventeen might be placed, almost all of them in aircraft companies and none in offices. Watson senior and those who thought as he did considered this proof that the machines would never be commercially viable, while Watson junior argued that there would be many customers once they understood the kinds of tasks computers could handle.

At the time this division seemed to be along generational lines, with the old-timers on one side and the young Turks, many of them returned veterans, on the other. This generally was the case, but there was more than this to the contest. Watson senior was customer-oriented, as has been seen. He had a fine instinct for responding to the needs of the people who purchased or leased his machines. In Watson's view IBM should remain centered on the salesman, whose task it was to convince customers that the machines would be worthwhile investments. IBM funded the largest research and development operation in the industry, but like the other companies, most of the work was directed along hard, pragmatic lines. This orientation had served the company well in the past, and toward the end of his life Watson saw no need to alter it.

Watson junior appreciated the need to produce profits and considered himself every bit as practical as his father. Despite his initial indoctrination, however, his major interest was in the laboratory and the boardroom. As much as Eckert, Mauchly, and James Rand, he was convinced that in time there would be a tremendous market for computers, that they would be used not only in laboratories, offices, banks, and observatories but in factories as well. He was impressed by the ideas of men like von Neumann and Norbert Wiener, whose 1948 book *Cybernetics: Or Control and Communication in the Animal and the Machine* looked forward to the time when electronic brains would take over complicated as well as mundane tasks. Watson junior was intrigued by the idea of automation, a means whereby an entire assembly line might be operated by computers, and an oil refinery managed by several giant brains.

Such a major transformation could hardly be carried out by catering to the immediate and expressed needs of commercial customers, as had been Watson senior's way. A businessman who had been reared on stories of how John Patterson had sold cash registers to retailers and who was purported to be uncomfortable with electronic calculators, he could not have been expected to appreciate the "technological imperative," which holds that discoveries in science often lead to new technologies, which in turn result in new products and techniques. The corollary is that technology produces businesses and markets, not the reverse. This appears to have been Watson junior's point of view in the late 1940's, and it was quite different from his father's approach. Still, Watson senior capitulated under the prodding of his son.

Corporate legend has it that IBM moved into the production of computers shortly after the outbreak of the Korean War

The Brothers Watson

and that the move was triggered by a telegram Watson senior sent to President Harry S Truman, asking how IBM might contribute to the war effort. Soon thereafter Tom Watson and several executives and scientists went on a tour of defense plants and returned to tell Watson senior that they required computers in their work. "If this is what is needed, let's build it," was Tom Watson's recommendation, which, of course, was taken. Yet some IBMers claim that the decision to go ahead was based on the placement of the first UNIVAC at the Census Bureau, that Watson senior was angered by this challenge on IBM's home ground and was determined to meet it head-on. Scientists working on computers in this period generally believed that it simply was a matter of time before there would develop a need for the machines—along with Watson junior, they accepted the technological imperative.

In his own way, so did Watson senior. Prior to the war a research team at the Poughkeepsie laboratory altered an electronic calculator by adding programming and a memory unit. Known as the Tape Processing Machine, it in effect was the prototype for the initial line of IBM computers that reached the market in the mid-1950's. The development of the TPM was an example of the research Charles Kirk had wanted, and Watson senior had accepted so long as it clearly was experimental and little else.

By 1949—prior to the outbreak of the Korean War—Watson senior had agreed to fund work on scientific computers, the kind that might be marketed to industry. Design work on what would become the 701 was speeded up after the war began, but even then everyone involved knew the first machines wouldn't be ready for two or three years and so would have only limited wartime applications.

The 701 was a scientific machine, designed for use in laboratories and perhaps in factories, not in offices. Approximately twenty-five times faster than the SSEC and only a quarter of its size, the 701 would be the most complex machine IBM had produced to that time, and still, it was not as advanced as UNIVAC I. Furthermore, the 701 had only limited capabilities,

123

while the more flexible UNIVAC might easily be adapted to solve business as well as scientific problems. Remington Rand was preparing new models, several of which would be designed specifically to meet the needs of the offices of the future. It appeared that Remington Rand was approximately two years ahead of IBM in most phases of computer development, and it certainly had a greater commitment to production.

Watson junior appreciated the seriousness of the situation. But for all its drawbacks, the 701 met with a good reception since the cold war tensions had created a need for such a machine. Using this as a lever, Watson junior convinced his father that an all-out effort would be needed if IBM were to catch up and that the prize was well worth the expenses that would be involved. Building upon knowledge and experience gained in the TPM and 701 projects, he hoped to produce computers for offices and related uses and soon surpass Remington Rand technologically. Then, given IBM's superior resources and sales force, he expected to drive Rand and other competitors from the field.

All this would take enormous amounts of capital. Retained earnings alone would not suffice; IBM would have to enter the capital markets to sell bonds, placing the company deeper in debt than at any time in its history. Meanwhile, additional resources would be needed to turn out IBM's current line of machines, most of which were meeting with good receptions. Finally, the company was making a great effort to expand its overseas business, and this, too, would require large expenditures that might take years to recoup. IBM was about to enter a transitional period in 1950, in terms of leadership, products, organization, and scope. On Wall Street it appeared that the firm was treading water, perhaps even faltering, and its stock, once a glamour item, traded in a narrow range even as others in its group advanced.

Nevertheless, Watson senior was certain of his son's abilities and backed him before the board—that is to say, he was given what amounted to a blank check. Aware that his own time as leader of the company was drawing to a close, he approved a crash program to produce commercial computers. Besides, he had no intention of seeing IBM lose ground in any area, even one with uncertain prospects. Then, as a further signal of change, Watson junior was named president in 1952.

The IBM computer campaign was conducted on several levels. In the laboratories technicians and scientists rushed to complete the design for what would become the 702, a commercial version of the 701, while others started work on more advanced concepts. Factory space was set aside, and additional technicians were hired and trained. A special management task force was established. Louis LaMotte, a thirty-year veteran with a superlative sales record, was given overall responsibility for the campaign; a vice-president at the time, he now became head of the new Electronic Data Machine Division. Thomas Vincent Learson, a hard-driving sales manager at the Electric Accounting Machines Division, was to direct the sales effort and serve as general troubleshooter. Albert Williams, a former salesman who at the time was IBM's controller and a vice-president, had the most delicate and crucial task. As one who was particularly close to Watson junior and had been instrumental in preparing the case for computers, Williams was now charged with setting up leasing arrangements and creating a price structure.

Selected Statistics for IBM, 1946–1956

(millions of dollars)

Year	Gross Revenues	Net Income	Long-term Debt
1946	119.4	18.8	30.0
1947	144.5	23.6	50.0
1948	162.0	28.1	85.0
1949	183.5	33.3	85.0
1950	214.9	33.3	85.0
1951	266.8	27.9	135.0
1952	333.7	29.9	175.0
1953	410.0	34.1	215.0
1954	461.4	46.5	250.0
1955	563.5	55.9	295.0
1956	734.3	68.8	330.0

Source: *Moody's Handbook*, 1957, p. 193

The Computer Wars

There was no clear way of knowing the size of the market, how calculator and accounting machine users would react to computers, what competition might be anticipated from Remington Rand and others, or even the relative efficiencies computers might provide for users. Would commercial customers keep the machines long enough to return a profit to IBM? There was a temptation to ask for high lease prices, in which case many potential customers might be frightened away. On the other hand, the machines might be a constant drain on resources if rates were pegged too low. Some at corporate headquarters believed that only computers on long-term high-priced leases could be profitable, and then only if large numbers of them were placed, to cover the heavy research and development costs. This seemed to imply that IBM would do well to concentrate on placements in government agencies, and it appeared that LaMotte had been selected for his job because he knew Washington better than any other top executive. But it was also believed that Watson junior and Williams were committed to leasing machines in the commercial markets, in which margins were sure to be low and the outlook for large profits correspondingly bleak. In other words, the new president had embarked on as risky an undertaking as any in his father's time.

Some of the funding for the 700 series project came from the successful 600 electronic calculator series. These machines had driven the competition from the field and promised to be one of the most profitable products in the company's history. Would the 700's compete with the 600's and so destroy a valuable product? Watson thought not, and in any case, he believed that some customers then using 600's would be eager to accept computers once they were available. If they were not forthcoming from IBM, the 600's would be replaced by UNIVACs or models out of some other company. To prepare the way for change and as a stopgap measure, IBM produced peripheral equipment for the 600's which provided them with computer-like capabilities, while at the same time liberalizing leasing arrangements. Now the sales force had a product many businessmen would prefer over the still-unfamiliar, exotic, and more expensive UNIVACs. Well over 300 of the 650's, the most popular variant, had been placed by the summer of 1956, and IBM had orders for an additional 920 of them.

In time many of these would be turned in for 700 series improved models, and IBM would have to place the machines elsewhere, often at reduced rates. Thus, the transition to computers often resulted in losses or forgone profits on electronic calculators. But in the process IBM kept customers away from Remington Rand, maintained old ties, and established a beachhead in the commercial market.

IBM started taking orders for the 702's in 1954, before the machine existed, and this, too, caused Remington Rand no little distress. The first of what eventually would be fourteen placements was made in the spring of 1955, when Monsanto Chemical took delivery of what newspapers and magazines called "a giant brain," which was supposed to replace dozens of accounting machines while at the same time analyzing complex formulae. Even before the machine was shipped, Watson announced that orders would be accepted for two new models. One of these, the 704, was designed to replace the specialized 701 scientific computer. The second, known as the 705, was a vast improvement over the freshly minted 702 and in most respects a match for the contemporary UNIVACs in terms of speed and capabilities. The 705 was the product of three separate streams of research. Based upon developments at the IBM laboratories, it also contained components perfected at universities and used patented ideas purchased from other firms.

This was IBM's strongest and most impressive foray into the industry, and Learson provided the 705 with a strong sales effort. This time the demand was far greater than even the most sanguine executive could have imagined. Potential leasers literally lined up for their machines, jockeying for position to get the earliest possible placement. For the sake of publicity and to satisfy an old customer, Learson made certain the first of the 705's went to the Social Security Administration, where it replaced dozens of old IBM machines in the recording and storage of information regarding accounts. Others were placed in the offices of large corporations, and here, too, they did the work formerly handled by large calculators. The 705 did not provide IBM with new customers and revenue streams as much as it enabled the company to hold what it already had.

By 1955 what later would be known as the computer revolution was well under way. Bureaucrats, plant managers, and businessmen were coming to appreciate how the machines could fit into their operations, and the flexible 705, attractively priced by Williams to undercut the competition, had arrived at just the right time. A year or so later, and IBM would have found the Remington Rand position close to impregnable. As it was, UNIVAC was as close to being a generic term for computers as Xerox would be for copying machines a generation later. Thus, the Watson-Williams-LaMotte-Learson combination may have prevented IBM from suffering the same kind of fate that befell National Cash Register in the early 1920's, when NCR failed to take advantage of its commanding position to seize leadership in new areas.

Instead, the lead in computers passed from Remington Rand to IBM. In August 1955 there were more UNIVACs in service or on order than 700's; a year later IBM had the edge in installations by a margin of 76 to 46. More important, Learson had booked 193 additional orders against Rand's 65.

New production facilities were being erected, and additional personnel put on the payroll. The company was booming, with sales of cards and leases of calculators and accounting machines posting new records in every year of the first postwar decade. Such were the economics of leasing that many of the machines would not throw off a profit until several years after they were placed. On top of this IBM was losing money on computers, and there was no way of knowing when this drain would end. The company's line of credit was being stretched, but it remained strong, in large part as a result of the reputation IBM had earned under Watson senior's leadership. Like his father, Tom Watson refused to sell additional equity, but he did borrow money to an extent unknown in earlier times.

Electronic Data Machine seemed continuously in need of

funds. LaMotte argued that Remington Rand continued to be a strong contender; UNIVAC had an excellent patent position, and its current research was impressive. Other companies were preparing to enter the field or had already done so; RCA, Burroughs, NCR, and Bendix were in the forefront. There were rumblings out of General Electric, a firm the sales of which were five times those of IBM and the research and marketing credentials of which were impeccable. Watson did all he could to consolidate his lead, pouring additional money into the laboratories and luring major scientists with promises of prestige, recognition, and independence as well as remuneration. And he was succeeding. Watson senior may have been troubled about this enormous outlay of funds, but he openly admired his son's vigor, imagination, and aggressive leadership. Clearly the transfer of power had gone well.

Furthermore, it had taken place at an opportune time. Watson senior had run a company based on calculators, tabulators, accounting machines, and the ubiquitous cards and had done so by keeping most of the power in his own hands. Under his son's leadership IBM was being transformed into a company that would lead the way in computers, most of which soon would use magnetic tape rather than cards. In addition, the electromechanical age was giving way to one based on electronics. The salesmen remained important to IBM's success, but increasingly the firm had to rely upon scientists and academicians as well. And with all this came growth. In four decades Watson senior had taken the small CTR to a firm that grossed more than $333 million in 1952. Watson junior doubled that figure in less than three years.

The structure that had served the company well in the 1920's and 1930's was strained and clearly would have to be altered. No single man or even committee could oversee so vast and complicated an operation, which comprised dozens of product lines sold throughout the world. Responsibilities would have to be delegated, and power dispersed. This would have occurred no matter who was president and chairman in the late 1940's and early 1950's. As it happened, the change was initiated on what amounted to an informal basis by the father and completed by his son, who provided IBM with a new structure.

The change began in 1947 when Fred Nichol, a self-effacing vice-president and general manager, stepped down as a result of ill health brought on by overwork. Watson, who was seventy-three at the time, was troubled by this loss of an old friend and started to speak of the need for everyone to "slow down" and avoid undo strain. Charles Kirk took Nichol's place, and as has been noted, this hard-driving man died soon after at the age of forty-three. A shocked and saddened Watson now instructed his staff to permit line executives more authority. Where he once insisted upon having a hand in minor as well as important decisions, Watson now left the former to his assistants and permitted and even encouraged initiatives from others, though he retained a veto on their actions. Then the old Electric Tabulating and Accounting Machine Division was split into several parts, and the new Electric Accounting Machine Division was given greater autonomy. This enabled Learson to develop his own programs and demonstrate his talents in ways that previously would have been difficult to do. LaMotte had even more freedom at the Electronic Data Machine Division, and this liberalization was felt throughout the company.

Building upon this, Watson junior urged managers to use their imaginations and exercise authority without constantly asking for approval from the home office. Years later he would refer to the Danish philosopher Søren Kierkegaard's fable of the wild ducks that flew south at the onset of winter. Some ducks remained in the north, surviving by eating food set out for them by kindly people. No longer having to care for themselves, they became fat, lazy, and stupid, and once the feeding stopped, they perished, whereas the wild ducks that disdained help and practiced self-reliance flourished. The moral was obvious: Wild ducks can be tamed, but once this was done, they never again could be wild, a moral which to Watson implied that they lost their imagination, initiative, and drive. "We are convinced that any business needs its wild ducks," he said, "and in IBM we try not to tame them." In an address before a Hundred Percent

Club, he almost asked for controversy. "I just wish somebody would stick his head in my office and say, 'Tom, you're wrong!' I really would like to hear that. I don't want yes-men around me."

Those who took him literally found that Watson could be as temperamental and harsh as, and at times even more arrogant and self-assured than, his father. Still, he did make the effort. And the atmosphere at IBM's New York headquarters and its main plants at Endicott did change. It could be seen in such simple things as soft collars on shirts instead of hard ones; one day Watson junior arrived in a striped shirt, and reverberations went through the building. Even more striking was his attitude toward liquor; IBMers might now relax over an occasional drink without worrying about dismissal if discovered. In these ways, and others, the company was changing. The monolith was evolving into a hydra, and the change was accomplished in an orderly, carefully planned fashion, with a minimum of disruption and with the assent of Watson senior.

The old man looked upon some of these alterations with no little misgiving. But he did not interfere as Watson junior moved his own men into key posts, decentralized administration, placed increased emphasis on research and development, and enlarged the debt. By 1955 IBM had become Tom Watson's company, with the father only a shadow in the background, knowing he was out of place in the new order of things. Somewhat wistfully, he wrote that insofar as the company was then constituted, he would much more enjoy serving as sales manager than as chairman.

There was one major benefit from the decentralization that pleased both men. In 1949 Watson senior presided over the division of his empire into two unequal parts. The parent company, IBM, would conduct business only in the United States, which remained the primary market for its machines and services. The rest of the globe would be handled by IBM World Trade Corporation, the leadership of which was entrusted to Dick Watson. In this way the father tried to assure his younger son a degree of independence so that he would not have to live altogether in his brother's shadow. Tom agreed. "The more I think of it the better I think the decision was," he said years later during an on-the-record interview. "This for a number of reasons but particularly because if Dick were me and I were Dick—I would want an opportunity for independent operation."

It was a chancy and contentious move, one bound to cause unpleasantness for those involved and raise issues of nepotism. Of course, it had been the same when Tom arrived at corporate headquarters and rose steadily up the ladder. But he was self-assured and able to joke about the situation, and in any case he underwent a thorough and often grueling apprenticeship. Also, there was the tradition of having the oldest son succeed the father, even in large companies. Finally, Tom was given the opportunity and time to prove himself prior to taking command. Dick had none of these advantages. He lacked his brother's easy grace and good looks, tended to brood, and, despite his many accomplishments, was never quite able to achieve the kind of distinction he must have craved. In his prime Tom Watson appeared to be the kind of person who with different parents might still have risen to the top of a large corporation or one who could have gone far in politics. Under similar circumstances, Dick would have become an academic or a writer. Throughout his IBM career he appeared to know this; even in his moments of great triumph—when World Trade's record greatly surpassed that of the parent company—he seemed to know that he was being measured against the standards set by his brother and father and that those around him believed he fell short.

Dick Watson was thirty years old in 1949, when he took command at the newly formed World Trade and, in addition, became a vice-president and director. Periodically he would receive new titles and responsibilities—president of World Trade in 1954 and, nine years later, chairman. In 1966 Dick became vice-chairman of the parent company as well. But that was as high as he would go. He was outranked in the beginning by his father and brother and then by Tom alone. By the late 1960's he knew that he would be passed over for the top job when Tom stepped down, that he would never achieve independent power. In an admittedly fast field, he was an also-ran.

As has been indicated, Dick was five years younger than Tom. A natural rivalry developed between the two, but they also were friends, perhaps because of differences in temperament, interests, and talents. Tom was better at most sports while Dick excelled in intellectual matters. While at Hotchkiss Dick demonstrated a talent for languages, prompting his father to steer him toward a career in the foreign field. Dick attended Yale, where he majored in international affairs, and like his brother, he put considerable time in Manhattan's nightclubs and earned a reputation for heavy drinking. Slightly shorter and leaner than Tom, Dick was like his pale shadow. He was moody, irritable, and less likely to grin and make small talk; he might fly into rages with little provocation. Dick was a serious young man who found it difficult to relax except with close friends. His personality would change little over the years, and the same would be true of his appearance.

Dick Watson wanted to enlist soon after the United States entered World War II, but his father prevailed upon him to complete his school year first. He then entered the Army and was assigned to the Ordnance Corps, a branch that was far less glamorous than Tom's Air Corps. Dick would attain the rank of major, a notch below Tom's lieutenant colonelcy. He was sent to the Pacific and ended up at a depot in Manila; Tom crisscrossed the Atlantic, accompanying some of the period's important and glamorous figures. Still, Dick appeared to enjoy and profit from his military experiences—and the independence they afforded him. When the war ended, he asked his father's permission to remain in the Philippines, as head of IBM's small operation in that country. Had this been done, Dick might have headed his own division, gaining administrative experience out from under the shadows of his father and brother. Watson senior rejected the notion, telling Dick he had to come home to complete his education and enter the IBM training program. This he did, returning to Yale to study Spanish, French, German, and Russian.

Upon receiving his degree in 1947, Dick was enrolled in the IBM program and soon thereafter emerged as a salesman. He had a good record in the field—but not up to the standard established by Tom prior to the war. Dick married Ann Hemingway, and they eventually had six children. Rather than go off on a honeymoon, the young couple accompanied the senior Watsons when they embarked on a combination business-pleasure trip to Europe, and on this occasion Dick acted as his father's interpreter. From then until he took up his post at World Trade, Dick alternated between sales and serving as one of his father's assistants. Dick understood that he soon would have his own operation, but directly and through implication he was made to understand that even then he would be responsible first to his father and afterward to Tom.

World Trade was no small company or responsibility, but in 1949, the last year prior to its organization, foreign business exclusive of Canadian leases and sales accounted for only $6.3 million out of IBM's net revenues from all sources of more than $119 million. Its component parts were older than IBM, deriving from the firms that had come together to form CTR. Hollerith's work on the European censuses resulted in the establishment of agencies abroad. In 1908 he entered into a licensing arrangement whereby the independent British Tabulating Company received the exclusive right to manufacture and sell his tabulators and related equipment throughout the British Empire except for Canada. International Time had sales representatives in several foreign countries in that period, while in 1902 Computing Scale opened a factory in Toronto, from which a variety of products were shipped to European agents. All this was continued and expanded upon by Watson, who was intrigued with the idea of managing a worldwide operation. One of his major delights was visiting IBM installations abroad, where he made speeches and received awards and commendations.

After World War I the company erected small plants in Germany, France, and Great Britain, primarily to avoid the payment of tariffs, and, in addition, established agencies throughout Europe, Latin America, and parts of Asia. By the late 1930's Watson had started speaking in global terms, and his euphoria knew no bounds. As a symbol of this he renamed many of his subsidiaries. In 1937 the Japanese operation, which produced cards for the Asian market, was known as Watson Business Machines, and the same was done for branches in Sweden, Switzerland, Colombia, Turkey, Uruguay, and other countries. This was quickly followed by yet another change: In 1938 IBM established Watson Java in the Netherlands East Indies, to be followed by Watson Mexico, Watson Italy, and the like. If Ford could have his name on automobiles, why shouldn't Watson do the same for his business machines?

Whether this resulted from a business decision or megalomania is impossible to say. There was no indication at any time that Watson meant to alter the name of the parent company, however, or that he was attempting to create what amounted to "a cult of personality" overseas. Indeed, in common with the more enlightened American companies, IBM overseas hired and trained native individuals and more than most was willing to assign them to key managerial posts. Baron Christian de Waldner took over the IBM operation in France in 1934, for example, and by the end of the decade had become an unofficial spokesman for Watson in that country. Valentim Boucas, who opened the Brazilian branch in 1917, did pioneering work throughout Latin America, was a fourteen-time member in the Hundred Percent Club, and often was mentioned by Watson as one of the corporation's most valuable executives and salesmen.

With all this, IBM's foreign business during the interwar period was never truly important. The peak sales year was 1935, during which net income from all overseas operations came to only $1.6 million, with tabulator cards the greatest revenue producer.

IBM's facilities on the European continent and in Japan were seized during the war, but the plants continued to turn out cards and parts, which were used by the Germans and Japanese. Yet net foreign sales and leases grew rapidly in this period, coming to a shade below $2 million by 1945. This was due in large part to military orders filled at the old International Time facility in London. Before the war the German branch had accounted for half of all revenues (exclusive of the Canadian business). Now it was in shambles. In contrast, the small British operation had grown to the point where the Hammersmith facility was the largest IBM plant outside North America. At the time of Watson's first postwar European trip in 1946, it seemed apparent that the British business would remain important in the postwar world, while that in the Commonwealth would grow rapidly in importance. Clearly it would be in IBM's interest to renegotiate the 1908 agreement.

In 1949 Watson approached the British Tabulating Company with an offer. He would grant it a free, nonexclusive license on all existing IBM products as well as on some in the process of development. In return he asked the right to sell his products through IBM's own sales organization throughout the Commonwealth. In effect, a customer would have the choice of leasing an IBM-designed machine from Watson or from BTC—at least until new products made their appearance. A new entity would be formed, to be known as IBM United Kingdom, Ltd., and for the first time in its history, IBM would permit foreigners to purchase shares in a subsidiary.

BTC agreed to this arrangement. The directors must have felt that their knowledge of the market, relations with customers, and years of experience would enable them to throw back any challenge from this quarter. Then, too, there was the matter of simple nationalism: Why would a South African or an Australian lease a tabulator from an American firm when he might get the same kind of machine from a company owned and managed by fellow members of the Commonwealth? Yet Watson did win the contest, and in only a few years. This was accomplished by a combination of aggressive selling, superb service, and imaginative rates. Then, too, IBM United Kingdom was not a foreign company in the usual sense of the term; like BTC, it was run by citizens of the United Kingdom, and its salesmen were natives of the country in which they worked. Furthermore, it even was partially owned by Britons—at least until 1959, when the minority interest was bought out.

The Brothers Watson

IBM United Kingdom became the centerpiece for World Trade. On the first day of 1950 the parent company transferred all its foreign assets to this new wholly owned entity. At the time World Trade had ten factories producing machines and more than twenty installations turning out cards. Operations were being conducted in fifty-eight countries, and no foreign customer was more than a day away from a service center or a salesman.

Leadership of World Trade was a major challenge and an unusual opportunity for any executive, and so it was for Dick Watson. He would have the full support of the parent company, in terms of both products and financing. Otherwise, he was supposed to operate on his own. Initially World Trade would rely upon IBM for products and services, for in 1950 it still did not have the facilities to handle all of its clients' needs. This soon would change; eventually World Trade would have its own research and development projects, and its scientists and technicians would turn out machines some considered superior to their American counterparts. World Trade came to dominate the computer markets overseas, in many cases to an even greater extent than the mother company did in the United States. Still, Dick Watson received only a small part of the credit for this accomplishment. He was destined to go through life as "the other Watson."

7

The Shaping of a Giant

IN EARLY 1952 *Fortune* magazine labeled IBM the leader and major factor in what it called "the business machine industry," this by virtue of its successes in marketing tabulators and related products and services. Four years later a *Time* writer discussed "the $2 billion business equipment industry," in which such major firms as "National Cash Register, Burroughs Corp. and Remington Rand are busy making everything from adding machines to the new electronic computers." IBM had a commanding lead here, he thought, with approximately 25 percent of the total market.

Yet the business machine industry wasn't clearly defined in this period, which for all practical purposes also was the first decade of the computer age. Such usually is the case when a new technology or major innovation appears in an established field; old lines are dissolved, and new perceptions come into being. Furthermore, what economists, management experts, and others think of as industries often are merely collections of products and services that bear some relationship to one another, together with the companies involved in the operations. Thus, jet airplanes and railroad locomotives, and the firms that produce them, are deemed parts of the transportation industry, even while the former overlaps into defense and aerospace and the latter may be seen as an integral part of the coal industry. Similarly, a petroleum discovery firm could be placed in the energy, chemical, or engineering industry and, in fact, probably would be in all three and others at the same time, the primary one dependent upon the point of view of its leaders and those who interpret their activities.

In the nature of things the conception of an industry—be it "transportation" or "railroads," "business machines" or "computers"—will be accepted by the informed public even while their precise natures are debated by lawyers, economists, and scholars. Are interstate truckers part of a transportation industry or a separate category in and of itself? Is there a computer industry? If so, is it unique or a subdivision of business machines?

On the surface these may appear academic questions with only marginal application and of little interest to practical men and women. In fact, they are vital ones, and their answers have serious implications in the application of human and financial resources and the development of technology and organization.

Around the turn of the century what later would be known as the business machines industry was perceived as a subgroup of the much larger and more general industrial machinery category, special in the sense that business machines were operated by white-collar workers in offices rather than by laborers in factories. Some writers made the distinction between office and industrial machinery. The former included typewriters, pens, filing cabinets, forms, and even paper clips. The lines were sharp and well defined and were respected by most businessmen, who tended to stick to established products and markets.

For example, National Cash Register was not a business machinery manufacturer. John Patterson meant to turn out nothing but registers and to dominate that field and no other; he had few ambitions elsewhere.

Yet there were firms the products of which seemed to serve both office and factory, and two of these went into the creation of CTR. The time clocks produced by International Time, for example, were utilized in both offices and factories. Hollerith's tabulators—which today would appear clear examples of business machines—were considered special cases when they first appeared, designed as they were for the Census Bureau rather than for private offices; Tabulating Machine was not to be grouped with such firms as Underwood and Burroughs, the clear leaders in the field.

This perception remained even after Hollerith placed tabulators at insurance companies and railroads, and the reputation was inherited by IBM. Watson was able to lease tabulators to many large companies, and by the early 1930's the firm was producing a fairly wide variety of other machines as well. Still, as late as 1932 *Barron's* would write that "the company is a producer of primarily industrial rather than office machines."

The situation changed drastically in the next two decades, as tabulators, accounting machines, and the like became ubiquitous and offices adjusted to utilize them. In part this was due to developments in the private sector, but the driving force came from government agencies during the New Deal and defense operations in World War II. By then scholars and others referred to the business machines industry not as part of the industrial machinery complex, but as a separate entity on its own, with unique products, services, and goals. In addition, the old definition had been altered, from one that revolved around work forces to that of intent. Now business machines were those employed by privately owned companies and government agencies to gather, process, and present information relating to individuals and groups. Typewriters and tabulators clearly were business machines, as were copiers, adding machines, and files.

In 1950 the computer occupied a position within the business machine spectrum somewhat analogous to that of the tabulator a half century earlier; it was perceived as a specialized device, useful only to a handful of customers (in 1954 General Electric took delivery of a UNIVAC and so became the first private firm to employ a computer). Clearly it was not in the same category as the typewriter and the accounting machine. Like the tabulator market, its principal market appeared to be government agencies, such as Social Security and the Atomic Energy Commission.

It was at this point the comparison broke down, for although tabulators from the first could be adapted to the needs of commercial customers, the giant brains seemed worthwhile only for resolving questions relating to warfare and weather forecasting or the running of factories; that is to say, they were perceived as scientific and industrial machines rather than as devices of special uses in business offices. Tom Watson conceded the point but also talked of computers that would process mail, maintain airline reservations, and even write business letters. He had difficulties selling the idea to businessmen, who were wary of computers and by no means convinced there were places for them in their operations. To suggest the placement of a computer was akin to recommending the use of jets for commuter runs—computers simply were too powerful and expensive for the kinds of tasks most offices had to perform. As late as 1956 Watson was hard at work in his educational campaign, with few results to show for his efforts. "I think the next big field to fall to automatic data processing is the checking account," he told a reporter. But four years later only one out of every four banks with deposits of more than $500 million employed a computer, and there were hardly any in smaller ones.

Clearly this was a trying period for Watson, for he had staked his reputation on this matter. IBM might survive the relative failure of its computer operations; Watson junior might not, for critics would observe that he had taken the healthy and enormously successful operation put together by his father and frittered away its resources. This was a time when business publications were praising Henry Ford II for taking over and refurbishing a Ford Motor Company that was on the brink of disaster. Some hinted that Tom Watson might be performing a reverse task at IBM.

For all his doubts, Watson senior continued to stay on the sidelines and backed his son's gamble. "It is harder to keep a business great than it is to build it," he said in an oblique reference to the current situation. Given the problems of ego involved, the transition went more smoothly than might have been anticipated.

The one major issue upon which the two men disagreed involved an antitrust action brought by the government in late 1952 which was based upon just this set of questions and perceptions. Once again IBM was charged with monopolizing the tabulator market as well as that for cards, and the Justice Department demanded the company sell as well as lease its machines. Watson senior was indignant, and he hinted that this represented an attempt on the part of "reformers" to cripple IBM and punish him for his political activities. For years he had been one of Dwight Eisenhower's staunchest supporters, helping him obtain the presidency of Columbia University and then urging him to seek the Democratic nomination in 1948. A nominal Democrat for most of his life, Watson contributed to Eisenhower's 1952 Republican campaign, and in his view this led to retribution by a vengeful Harry Truman. While there was a certain amount of logic and evidence on his side, talk of a possible prosecution had filtered through Wall Street long before the election, and the action caused no great stir within the industry.

Watson senior blasted the government, both in private discussions and in a series of advertisements in major newspapers. Not only were the charges unsupported by evidence, he claimed, but the Justice Department's perception of the industry was simplistic and misguided. Competition was intense in the area of office machines, in which there were several strong firms, each of which had carved out a special niche. Why single out IBM for its domination of tabulators and calculators, he asked, and not go after Underwood, which had a commanding lead in manual typewriters? More important, was it right to deny his company the fruits of its labors, to oblige it to concede parts of a carefully nurtured market to those firms which refused to take risks and refrained from pioneering?

This view was shared only in part by Watson junior, who had been elevated to the presidency shortly before the government filed its brief. His reaction was different, in large part because of his perception of where the industry stood and where it was headed. The father was concerned with defending old products and patents and with justifying IBM's past actions; Tom Watson believed that within a short period much of this would be irrelevant. The government's case was based on tabulator leases and the sale of cards. IBM's lawyers believed computers and future products in this area were not included in the charge. Thus, even if the government won all the points, IBM would be free to take command of this new part of the industry. Moreover, the next generation of computers would not require cards or at least would use fewer of them. Thus, card sales might be expected to decline, as computers replaced calculators in many offices. Finally, few customers would elect to purchase tabulators and calculators, especially when leasing terms were attractive and generations of office managers had become accustomed to the practice.

For all these reasons—and a desire to make a clean sweep of things—Watson junior favored accepting many of the government's strictures, and he urged his father to instruct IBM's legal team to ask for negotiations on a consent decree, under the terms of which IBM would not admit to wrongdoing but would agree to alter its methods of conducting parts of its operations. At first Watson senior resisted this line of reasoning, but eventually he gave in under pressure from his son and the lawyers as well as under the growing evidence that the proposed decree would do little harm to the company. Furthermore, both men appreciated the importance of having a clear set of ground rules under which to operate, and the consent decree would supply this. For several years at least, the company might be free from legal harassment so long as it followed the text.

Toward the end Watson senior came to appreciate the logic of his son's position. While in court in 1956 to sign the decree, Tom Watson received a terse, typical note from his father:

100%
Confidence
Appreciation
Admiration

Love
Dad

The decree required IBM to sell as well as to lease its machines, and as Tom Watson had predicted, this had little effect on operations (although it would become important in the late 1960's, when IBM had to meet a new challenge from firms that purchased its computers and then leased them out on terms competitive with those established by the company). In addition, within seven years IBM was to divest itself of the capacity to produce more than half the tabulator cards in the nation. At the time this seemed the most important part of the decree insofar as the company's profits were concerned; card sales had accounted for almost a quarter of IBM's net income in the two decades after 1930. But the percentage had been on the decline since the end of the war, and Watson junior was willing to sacrifice part of this lucrative but mature business in order to obtain a freer hand in computers.

IBM agreed to establish what became the Service Bureau Corporation, a wholly owned subsidiary that would offer owners or leasers of equipment a wide variety of services, in competition with similar firms and the parent company itself. The government hoped the existence of SBC would encourage competitors to enter the field, and to some degree this may have been the case. But IBM was not constrained from undercutting SBC, and it did. The leaser or owner of a computer or calculator might purchase services from either the parent firm or the subsidiary, as well as from outsiders, and as it turned out, IBM got most of the business, often at the expense of SBC. In time Service Bureau evolved into a minor league for IBM technicians and salesmen and, more important, a "Siberia" to which out-of-favor employees were dispatched. Yet such was the IBM mystique that SBC quickly became the largest entity in its specialized field. Still, in 1962, its last full year as an IBM subsidiary prior to being sold to Control Data (as a result of yet another antitrust action), SBC's revenues were only $60 million, and its net, $1.5 million, out of IBM's gross income of $1.9 billion and earnings of $207.4 million.

Prefigured in these portions of the consent decree were the developments of the leasing and service segments of the industry, which would become most important in the 1960's and early 1970's. This could not have been foreseen in the mid-1950's, however, and in any event IBM's interests were not harmed under the terms of the arrangement.

Of more immediate interest was a provision that required IBM to grant licenses to any applicant that wanted them and was willing to pay the fee for all present and future tabulating, accounting, and computing machines. On the surface it appeared that the company would be obliged to throw open its patent books, to share its industrial know-how with other firms. But it was not as far-reaching as that, for in practice licenses would be sold only on inventions and innovations already on the market; business machine manufacturers that obtained knowledge in this way could utilize it to produce devices that would compete with well-entrenched IBM originals which in the already fast-moving industry were on the way to obsolescence. By so acting, seekers of patents would signal that they were laggards and, by using them, might have to accept runner-up positions insofar as the specific technology was concerned.

Remington Rand was hardly in such a situation. In 1947 the company had filed for several basic patents which, if granted, would provide it with what amounted to a lock on several key areas. Were this to happen, IBM would have to seek Rand's patents, not vice versa. Yet Rand monitored the IBM case carefully and in 1955 filed its own antitrust brief, which asked for complete access to IBM's patents free of charge.

When Watson signed the consent decree, Rand became convinced that full victory was possible and pressed forcefully for concessions. At meetings between the two firms in early 1956 the IBM team jockeyed for advantages of its own, such as access to the ENIAC and several UNIVAC patents. If these were granted, IBM would be ahead of Rand in technology, and have little trouble consolidating its already-impressive lead in placements and orders. Watson's lawyers suggested the two firms cross-license patents for calculators and computers on a royalty-free basis and, to sweeten the deal, offered Rand a payment of $2 million to drop its suit. When this overture was rejected, IBM went on the offensive with both a frontal and a flank assault. IBM countersued, charging that Rand had infringed on several of its tabulator patents, and at the Patent Office it challenged Rand's rights to specific ENIAC and UNIVAC concepts.

Caught off guard, fearful of protracted litigation which it well might lose, and seeing benefits to be obtained from sharing domination of the field with IBM, Rand was amenable to compromise. In August 1956 both IBM and Rand dropped their suits and agreed to cross-license computer patents applied for prior to the forthcoming October as well as specified technical information. If Rand were to obtain the long-sought ENIAC and UNIVAC patents, IBM would pay it a royalty of 1 percent of the manufacturing costs of infringing devices produced in the eight years after October 1, 1956—and so would foreclose the possibility of a suit for payments on machines produced prior to that date. Finally, IBM agreed to pay Rand $10 million during that eight-year period, with the understanding that it would be used as a down payment against any royalties that might be disbursed.

As in all such things, both sides believed they benefited from the settlement, but in fact, IBM received more than it gave up. As it turned out, Rand received its patents, and were it not for the agreement, IBM might have been obliged to pay out additional tens of millions of dollars on pre-1956 computer sales as well as damages. And in the matter of current patents, UNIVAC's proved more valuable. IBM might have dominated the field without them, but the task was simplified and eased with the patents in hand.

IBM benefited from the outcomes of these two antitrust actions in both the short and the long runs. Watson received what amounted to a go-ahead from the Justice Department in return for relatively minor concessions and outmaneuvered Rand at a time when that company was in its best position to press its technological advantage. Even then, however, it was by no means certain or ordained that IBM would become the leader in computers, for the industry was still in the formative stage, with many established and new companies seeking a strategy for entry and tactics to accomplish their uncertain objectives.

Almost all these firms fell into one or more of three categories. First, and initially the most prominent, were large companies with expertise in electrical and electronic products, obtained in either or both the civilian and military markets. Among these were General Electric, Westinghouse, Sylvania, Philco, Radio Corporation of America, Minneapolis Honeywell, Bendix, and North American Aviation. American Telephone & Telegraph's Western Electric subsidiary would have been a formidable competitor had it been free to enter the contest, but this was not to be because of antitrust considerations. All these firms possessed the research staffs, technical expertise, and financial resources needed to take the plunge. Most looked upon computers as scientific tools or devices useful to the armed forces; all were seeking outlets for their technological knowledge and were accustomed to finding them there. None had significant direct exposure to the office equipment industry. In order to be successful there, they would need reorientations in different managements and corporate styles, but given the will, these would not have been insurmountable problems. Such was lacking, however; each of these firms preferred to remain on the periphery of the industry, while devoting the bulk of its resources and energies to other, more familiar products and markets. By the time most of them decided to take the plunge it was too late; of the old-line electric and electronic companies, only

Honeywell was able to pose a significant challenge to IBM, and that came after almost two decades of deficits, frustrations, and false starts.

The value of Watson junior's vision becomes more evident when one considers that in the mid-1950's many of these firms were months or years ahead of IBM in most technological areas. In conjunction with the Massachusetts Institute of Technology, Sylvania developed a long-life vacuum tube far better than those used in the first UNIVACs and the initial IBM computers; since tube failure was a major drawback in the early days, Sylvania could have exploited its patents to obtain a toehold in the industry. Instead, the company permitted the opportunity to pass. The transistor was developed at AT&T's Bell Laboratories in 1948; but that company was more interested in using them in telephone switching devices than in the production of computers, and three years later the basic patents were licensed to other companies for a small fee. While IBM was perfecting the 709 around the vacuum tube, Philco, RCA, and General Electric tested transistors in experimental computers. Philco developed a commercial model, the S-2000, which was on the market in late 1958 and was far in advance of anything produced by IBM or Rand. RCA and GE followed with their products, and these, too, could have competed with the slower, less efficient, and more costly IBM models, given the proper resources. But these were not forthcoming. On several occasions one or more of them developed and marketed devices superior to the IBMs, but each time Watson was able to recover and counterattack successfully, saved by his firm's reputation, financial resources, and sales force.

The second category of challengers was comprised of the old-line business machine producers, such as NCR, Burroughs, Underwood, and Remington Rand, all of which were interested in computers. In the 1950's NCR and Burroughs engaged in research and development but did not mount an all-out campaign in the field until the following decade, while Underwood's efforts were halfhearted and came to an end as the company began its swift decline. The situation was different at Remington Rand, which led IBM in such areas as the use of transistors, memory systems, and the development of a new "language" with which to program the machines. Furthermore, by mid-decade the company was transformed into a new entity, larger, though more diffuse, than IBM, and in some ways better equipped for leadership in the computer age.

In 1955 Remington Rand merged with the Sperry Corporation to form Sperry Rand. Harry Vickers of Sperry was named president and chief executive officer, while General Douglas MacArthur, recently selected for the chairmanship of Remington Rand, took over that post at the new corporation. James Rand became vice-chairman and senior vice-president and was to have what amounted to a free hand in the computer area.

At the time it appeared to be a good mesh of talents, markets, and potential. Sperry had been a major military supplier during World War II, turning out a wide variety of electric and electronic gear, and was famous for its gyroscopes that were used in bombsights and torpedoes and that had other applications. The company had an electronic tube division and installations performing important research in the semiconductor area. Sperry's large plant at Lake Success on Long Island—which had been an early home for the United Nations—was deemed one of the nation's finest electronics research laboratories, and the company's Ford Instruments division had developed several novel uses for military computers. Sperry had close relations with influential Navy ordnance officers interested in electronic warfare and was considered a pioneer in that field. Its Vickers division manufactured hydraulic equipment of various kinds, and under Harry Vickers's leadership it had experimented with computer-directed machine tools, considered the forerunner of the assembly line of the future.

At the time of the merger Sperry was in better financial shape than Remington Rand, although its profit margins were lower and its prospects clouded. Like most companies the major business of which was in the military-industrial sector, it was subject to the needs of its prime customer, the federal government, and so underwent sharp swings in activity. Sperry's revenues rose from $24.4 million in 1939 to $460 million four years later and then declined to $65.8 million in 1946, the first full peacetime year. Cold war tensions led to new orders; Sperry grossed $464 million in 1953. Then, with the end of the Korean War, sales and activity declined once again.

Sperry had several subsidiaries the business of which was oriented to the civilian market—Vickers for one and the New Holland farm equipment company for another—but it remained tightly tied to the military. Unable to diversify successfully in other areas, it was prepared to discuss the merger with Remington Rand. For his part James Rand understood that the "fit" between the two firms was close to being ideal. He had an established position in the office equipment field; Rand might usefully employ some of Sperry's technological expertise in the design of future products, from typewriters to computers. In return he could offer Sperry a stable market, higher profit margins, and an outlet for devices that were originally designed for military purposes but were adaptable to civilian uses. Rand headed a company which was hungry for capital and had an aged management team that was dispirited and in need of reinvigoration. On its part, Sperry was cash-rich and in Vickers possessed a vigorous and imaginative leader who was eager to challenge IBM across the board.

At the time of the merger computers were still a minor part of the industry; the total retail value of installed computers in the United States was less than a quarter of a billion dollars, and most of these were being used by government agencies of one kind or another. In analyzing the merger and attempting to predict its consequences, Wall Street focused on such products as accounting machines, tabulators, calculators, and typewriters and concluded that Sperry Rand would be a formidable competitor; its stock advanced while that of IBM stagnated. *Business Week* wondered whether IBM would be able to maintain its lead against an anticipated new generation of Remington Rand equipment due out in the late 1950's. "It's a whole new ball game," said one financial newsletter, "and the office equipment industry is about to witness a bloody contest between the old champ and this new challenger." It went on to say that IBM would have trouble if UNIVAC were reinvigorated, General Electric entered the field, and the government won its antitrust suit. "The outlook for the company is hardly bright." *Fortune* appeared to echo this sentiment, concluding that the marriage of Remington Rand's sales force and Sperry's technological base might be too much for IBM to bear.

Whatever Sperry Rand's hopes and ambitions were in other fields and products, it remained a distant second in computers, and this would not change. Rather than being a laggard in technology, UNIVAC had consistently developed and marketed superior machines and did not require technological infusions from Sperry. In fact, the firm's primary weakness was in precisely the area *Fortune* claimed was its strong point—namely, sales. Watson junior and Learson had carefully nurtured IBM's calculator customers and were in the process of successfully weaning them away from those machines and introducing them to computers. At the time of Sperry Rand's formation the UNIVAC division had a mediocre sales force, many of the members of which didn't understand computers and showed little imagination in placing them. Insofar as computers were concerned, the merger was not only flawed but even misbegotten. UNIVAC would have been better served had Rand lured several dozen IBM salesmen to the fold than by being augmented by Sperry's technological staffs. As it happened, the two research operations in this area did not get along well together, and there was hardly any cross semination of ideas until much later, by which time UNIVAC was clearly out of the race.

In 1953 UNIVAC was the only entry in the field; anyone who wanted a computer had to get it from that company. At the time of the merger UNIVAC accounted for 39 percent of all installations measured in terms of retail value, while IBM had most of the rest. A year and a half after the formation of Sperry Rand, IBM had better than three-quarters of the market, while UNIVAC's share had dropped to less than 19 percent, with the remaining 6 percent or so shared by Burroughs, RCA, and NCR. Not only had the company not been turned around, but it actually was losing ground. Of all the new systems sold or leased in 1956, IBM accounted for more than 85 percent of retail value, and UNIVAC, less than 10 percent.

Clearly the old-line electric and electronic companies had a long way to go before they carved out positions for themselves in the new computer industry, and for the time being at least, little could be expected from the established business machine companies. Had there been a merger between General Electric and Burroughs in this period—or between NCR and RCA—the newly formed giant might have been able to compete successfully with IBM. This did not occur, and by the time sensible combinations of this kind were formed it was too late to challenge the leader. If technology were all that mattered or even of primary importance, Sperry Rand, RCA, and some other firms might have shared leadership with a strong but diminished IBM. As it was, customer loyalty, salesmanship, and vision turned out to be of vital importance. The major companies would absorb smaller entities that possessed technological expertise or outstanding scientists, and although such moves often proved beneficial, what they really needed were sales organizations and managers of the kind developed at IBM. It was in these areas that Watson and Learson had the edge, one they retained in the computer age.

This was the key weakness of the new companies in the field, which constituted the third category of challengers. During the next decade dozens of them would attempt to carve out a niche in a specialized segment of the market—small computers, giant mainframes, leasing, services, peripheral equipment, and the like. In the early and mid-1950's, however, a time when the industry was still in the process of formation, many had loftier ambitions, and their scientist-founders dreamed of taking leadership across the board. Almost all of them were undercapitalized, lacked sales organizations, could not sustain technological leads, and were mismanaged. These companies did not last for long; they would either collapse or be acquired by a larger entity, just as Eckert-Mauchly and Engineering Research

Associates had been absorbed by Remington Rand in 1952. Burroughs led the way, acquiring Electrodata, a small company that had developed a computer known as the Datatron, in 1956. Minneapolis Honeywell entered into an arrangement with Raytheon which resulted in the production of the Datamatic 1000 in 1957, and several years later it bought out the Computer Control Corporation. Likewise, NCR entered the field by obtaining the Computer Research Corporation. At one time each of these acquired firms appeared to have a promising future as an independent entity, but all succumbed in the end; data processing, like automobiles, required huge capital resources, far beyond their capabilities. As it was, they were more fortunate than scores of other firms—with names like Alwac or Viatron—which simply vanished from the arena without leaving a trace.

Control Data Corporation was the one outstanding exception. Like the other new firms, it was plagued by financial and sales problems in its early years, but unlike them, it survived and in the process acquired a half dozen less fortunate firms within a decade of its founding—Cedar Engineering, Control Corporation, Holley Carburetor, and C-E-I-R among them. In addition, Control Data salvaged personnel and products from the failed efforts of other, larger firms; it purchased a computer division from Bendix when that company decided to leave the field and later obtained the Librascope Group from General Precision.

Control Data was born—or, to be more accurate, reborn—in 1957. Most of its personnel came from Sperry Rand's UNIVAC operation; but prior to that they had been the nucleus for Engineering Research Associates, and its founder, William Norris, was soon elevated to a corporate vice-presidency and the UNIVAC general managership. From the first he and other former ERA men clashed with Rand and the old hands at Remington. Much of the reason for this derived from a natural antipathy that existed between scientists and businessmen, between the midwesterners at ERA and the Manhattan-based executives who ran Remington. Then, too, Norris had a quick temper and an abrupt approach to problems that irritated Rand and others. He was barely able to disguise his contempt for the managers and financial specialists, whom he considered short-sighted, penurious, and incapable of appreciating both the technological and the commercial potential of computers. In short, he was a computer man while James Rand came out of the old business machine industry, and in the early 1950's these were not quite the same. That Norris and other ERA scientists would leave Rand was evident from the first; the only questions were when and toward what objective.

When Norris opened his facility in Minneapolis, he announced that Control Data intended to "design, develop, manufacture, and sell systems, equipment, and components used in electronic data processing and automatic control." This covered a wide area, but at the time his goals were more modest and realistic: He hoped to produce large, fast computers to be used by government agencies and laboratories in the solving of scientific problems. The competition in this area was fierce; both IBM and UNIVAC had made important placements there, and both firms, of course, were well known and much larger than CDC. Norris did have three important advantages, however. In the first place, Control Data would not enter the commercial market, at least not initially. Commercial users had no experience with computers and so required a good deal of orientation, instruction, and assistance. This meant that IBM, UNIVAC, and others in the field had to mount intensive sales efforts, maintain large service and instructional staffs, and be prepared to move into the office at the slightest sign of trouble. All this might be profitable, but such support required large outlays of capital. Watson and Rand understood this and were prepared to make the investments; after all, they came out of the business machines environment and were familiar with the process, which had originated with John Patterson at NCR. Norris was able to forgo much of this kind of support. He was one scientist talking with and selling to another—a technician at the

Weather Bureau; a person who, like him, had a technical background and was on duty at the National Security Agency; an electronic engineer in charge of purchasing at an industrial laboratory. Whereas IBM or UNIVAC salesmen usually were businessmen who had learned as much technology and scientific language as were required to make placements, their CDC counterparts often were the actual scientists who had had a hand in developing the machines they presented and were at home using the profession's jargon. Control Data originated as a hardware company, one prepared to deliver a mainframe, show the customer how it operated, and then withdraw from the scene. In contrast, IBM and UNIVAC offered a variety of software—programs and instructions—which sophisticated scientific users might not really want or need.

Given Norris's narrow focus in the late 1950's, this was an important advantage. Later on, when CDC entered the commercial markets, he would have to alter his approach, and significantly, Control Data had far less success there than on its home ground. Initially, however, the strategy proved sound.

The second advantage was related to the first. More than the diffuse IBM and UNIVAC operations, CDC understood and knew the market for large, fast scientific machines. There were only a score or two individuals in various agencies interested in making purchases, and Norris and other ERA scientists had worked with many of them, understood their needs, and were prepared to meet them. The initial placements were made with the National Security Agency and the Atomic Energy Commission, and others of a like nature followed. It was a small but profitable market, and CDC had reasonable hopes of dominating it.

Finally, there was the matter of the actual machines. In the 700 series IBM had a basic unit that could be altered to meet the requirements of both scientific and commercial clients, and to a lesser extent the same was true for UNIVAC systems. Such was not the case with CDC's first important product, a large and fast system known as the 1604, at the time generally conceded to be the most advanced and economical computer in America.* Scientists and technicians understood this and appreciated the 1604's advantages, but commercial customers, accustomed to obtaining services and assistance from the IBM organization and needing even more support in a time of transition, continued to order the less efficient and powerful 650's and 704's.

IBM was not unaware of developments at Control Data and, in fact, had been monitoring Norris's work and ideas while he was at UNIVAC. Tom Watson wasn't certain there was a market for large systems. Already several major corporations had reported having difficulties with their machines—General Electric, hardly a small or unsophisticated firm, reported chronic breakdowns with its UNIVAC and was on the verge of returning it to Rand. Still, IBM could not afford to ignore a potential market. In 1955, under the terms of a government grant, Watson ordered work to begin on what would be known as the STRETCH computer, the history of which illustrated IBM's power, its ability to take a blow, the kind of competition other firms in the industry had to face, and the reason Control Data was able to grow as it did.

Watson's original intention was to design and possibly to produce a machine that was at least 100 times faster and more powerful than what would become the 704. It was understood that if all went well, it could be placed at the Atomic Energy Commission, but no other customer appeared on the horizon. In 1955 Watson thought that eventually eight or so STRETCHs might be leased, and after signing the consent decree, he said that its price would be around $13.5 million.

STRETCH proved a disaster. Powered by vacuum tubes at

---

* The early computers were given names, usually acronyms—UNIVAC, ENIAC, and the like. Later, when families of computers were produced, they were numbered—the 600's, the 700's, the 360's, and so forth. Although there doubtless was a certain logic to this, similar to Henry Ford's when he gave his autos letter designations, an element of playfulness also existed. Thus, it was claimed that Norris obtained the 1604 designation by adding CDC's address, 501 Park Avenue, to one of the systems he had produced at UNIVAC, the 1103.

a time when transistors were coming into use, difficult to program, and almost impossible to service, it was obsolete before it came to market, and even then it never met more than 70 percent of its promised specifications. IBM's loss on the project came to around $20 million, a sum that might have defeated many other firms but merely put a temporary dent in Watson's treasury. At the same time, however, STRETCH was not a total loss, for in its construction several teams of engineers and scientists gained the experience that would enable them to produce future series of machines that incorporated advanced concepts. "Our greatest mistake in STRETCH," said Watson in admitting the fiasco, "is that we walked up to the plate and pointed at the left field stands. When we swung, it was not a homer but a hard line drive to the outfield." He had learned a lesson. "We're going to be a good deal more careful about what we promise in the future." Watson reduced STRETCH's price to $8 million, but even this didn't help; in mid-1966 only seven of them remained in operation, and most of these were at government installations, on lease at giveaway rates.

Having been burned by STRETCH, Watson decided there was no really important market for giant systems. IBM all but abandoned this segment of the market and concentrated on the intermediate machines that might be favored by businessmen. This left the upper end of the market to Control Data and enabled it to survive and grow. Whether or not IBM could have defeated CDC at that stage in the company's history cannot be known. But Watson didn't really try. Troubled by STRETCH and restrained by antitrust considerations, IBM refused to make an effort in direction for several years, by which time Control Data had become a strong and well-known company, one that performed far better than any non-IBM firm in the industry.

The Control Data experience, and that of the other computer manufacturers, illustrated what would become an axiom by the late 1960's, when there finally was a well-defined computer industry. Firms that attempted to meet IBM in a head-to-head confrontation would be smashed. The only way to make the grade in computers, or so it appeared in that period, was to take IBM's leftovers and try to live with the giant. The computer wars that began in the late 1950's would leave few survivors, and those that came out of the decade that followed with their skins intact still wondered whether the profits from computers would ever match up to the risks involved and the huge losses sustained in their battles with IBM.

8

Snow White and the Seven Dwarfs

IN MAY 1956, shortly after celebrating his eighty-second birthday, Watson senior turned over World Trade to his son Dick and at the same time relinquished executive power at IBM itself to Tom. He retained the title of chairman, however, and indicated a desire to remain active in corporate affairs. "I'm not retiring," he told his staff late in the month, but to all at headquarters it was evident that the final transfer of power had been made. To all intents and purposes, Tom and Dick were on their own.

A month later Watson senior suffered a heart attack and was taken to a hospital close by his Manhattan home. The family was summoned, and last farewells were made. He died on June 19.

The newspapers contained the usual obituaries. The New

York *Herald Tribune* called him "a man who could well stand as a symbol of the free enterprise system," and both *The New York Times* and *Newsweek* said Watson was a "pioneer" in his industry. Referring to his paternalistic treatment of employees, *Time* called him "one of the first of a new breed of U.S. businessmen who realized that their social responsibilities ran far beyond their own companies." Two days later, at the Brick Presbyterian Church, the Reverend Dr. Paul Austin Wolfe eulogized Watson, telling the congregation (and dozens of reporters sent to cover the event): "He had a peculiar singleness of mind, and he saw things simply. It was because of that simplicity of mind that he could make decisions." But Tom Watson offered the best assessment of his father's position at the time of his death. A few days after the funeral he returned to his offices and, looking around, told a reporter: "It's going to be lonely around here. Whenever I got a real hot one it was always a comfort to be able to go upstairs and discuss it with my father."

This was not to suggest that Watson senior had retained a veto over his son's decisions or that his recommendations had been taken as mandates. Rather, toward the end he had provided moral support, not actual leadership. "We can be grateful that he gave us the responsibility he did," said Tom Watson. "Had he been holding everything, and died, we'd be completely lost. But there's no chaos. We think we know our problems, and we're going to drive harder than ever to solve them."

A structure to accomplish this had been established during a series of meetings held in Williamsburg, Virginia, shortly before Watson senior died. The father had always been loath to delegate executive responsibility; Tom Watson knew that this was necessary given the size and complexity of the new industry, and here, too, his ideas prevailed. The key figures in the organizational revolution—besides Watson himself—were Learson, Albert Williams, Louis LaMotte, and John L. Burns, a management consultant for the executive research firm of Booz, Allen & Hamilton, who at the time appeared to fascinate Watson with his talk of vast changes to meet "the challenges of the 1960s." "We had a superb sales organization," said Watson later, giving full credit to his father for this accomplishment, "but lacked expert management organization in almost everything else." Burns was there to help provide that. Watson invited 110 IBM executives to the conference, telling them that from the meetings would come a new company, dedicated to meeting whatever challenges appeared in the computer age. "We went in a monolith, and we emerged three days later as a modern, reasonably decentralized organization, with divisions with profit responsibility and clear lines of authority."

Under the terms of the vast initial corporate reorganization, electronic data processing operations were divided among five major units. The first of these was the Field Engineering Division, which sold and leased equipment to commercial customers. This was the largest entity and, in the elder Watson's view, the most important. Composed primarily of salesmen and service personnel, Field Engineering was to make certain that IBM's calculator clients had no difficulties switching from their old machines to computers. Field Engineering's salesmen were the envy of the industry, prizes sought by UNIVAC, Burroughs, NCR, and especially GE, Honeywell, and RCA, hoping they would bring some of IBM's magic to their companies. "At conventions, competitors have put envelopes under the door of every IBM salesman," said Tom Watson five years later. "They've got a few of our people, but you can't hire a whole force away."

The Federal Systems Divisions, geared to designing and providing services for government agencies and scientific facilities, was to have a secondary role, but it, too, was staffed by salesmen and technicians. Just as Field Engineering's major competition would come from UNIVAC, Federal Systems had the task of keeping Control Data at bay.

The machines themselves would be provided by two divisions, Systems Manufacturing and Components, both of which played a subsidiary role in Watson's scheme of things. They would produce the 600 and 700 series machines for Field Engineering and work on STRETCH for Federal Systems.

At the heart of the operation—at least in Tom Watson's

view—was the Research Division, which was given the task of taking IBM from an also-ran position in this area to industry leadership. Watson was keenly aware that IBM not only was behind UNIVAC in several respects but also lacked the products and research skills shown by other large and small entities in the industry. Salesmanship and reputation might carry the company along for a while, but without a major research and development operation, IBM's lead in computer placements necessarily would melt. Thus, Watson provided the Research Division with what amounted to a blank check insofar as installations and personnel were concerned. Just as rival firms periodically would raid IBM for salesmen, so Watson lured scientists from his competitors in his attempt to create the most advanced scientific complex in the industry. This is not to say that he slighted the salesmen; indeed, they were better paid and more praised than ever before. What Watson junior hoped to do was create a product line that matched his sales force, and this was to be his major contribution to the company.

Electric Typewriter, IBM World Trade, Service Bureau Corporation, and the Supplies Division (which produced cards, magnetic tapes, and related products)—all had roles to play within the revamped corporation. But such was not the case for the Time Division, which continued to turn out clocks. For the sake of his father Tom Watson retained this operation, but within a few months of Watson senior's death it was put on the block, and two years later it was sold at a token price. Thus, of the four divisions that went into the creation of Computing-Tabulating-Recording only the descendant of the old Hollerith operation remained. Data processing was to be IBM's future focus—all else would be discarded or function within that context, at least so long at Watson junior was in command.

From the first the Research Department understood the nature and dimensions of the tasks ahead, as for that matter did every other computer manufacturer and those electric and electronic companies thinking of entering the field. It was a matter of generations, a term thrown about freely during the mid-1950's, and it was to the credit of both Watsons that this referred to computer designs, not to switchovers in the executive suites.

As indicated, the first generation of computers was based upon vacuum-tube technology. These were gigantic, heavy machines, the component units of which usually had to be housed in several rectangular containers that could fill a fair-sized room. Uncovering their banks revealed a maze of spaghettilike wires and row upon row of tubes, which consumed large amounts of electricity. The machines generated a great deal of heat, so the computer rooms had to be air-conditioned, and the machines themselves cooled by water, thus often requiring extensive plumbing alterations in existing facilities.

This situation suited IBM, for its service staff was far larger and more experienced than UNIVAC's or any other company in the field. Corporate vice-presidents considering a switch to computers would hear about all this and naturally have doubts about making the move. If all went well, they would be rewarded, but a major error could result in the fading of a promising career. These people naturally turned to IBM.

The company had the best reputation in the industry, one earned by salesmen and sustained by service personnel. An executive who had ordered an IBM computer that failed to live up to expectations might at least argue that he had gone with the leader in a time of change. Often the vice-president who took a UNIVAC or some other machine produced by a competitor would be criticized for not having turned to IBM; the reverse rarely was the case. Thus, IBM was able to take the lead in placements even while its machines were inferior to those put out by other companies. In the vacuum-tube age it was simple: The salesmen would promise, and the servicemen would deliver. Competitors understood this and realized they had to operate under trying circumstances. Several years later Louis Rader, head of the UNIVAC division of Sperry Rand, would utter what by then had become a classic tale of woe: "It doesn't do much good to build a better mousetrap if the other guy selling mousetraps had five times as many salesmen."

What UNIVAC and the others needed were machines so clearly superior to the IBM 600's and 700's that customers would have to discount matters of reputation and loyalty in favor of performance and price. A new technology was needed to give these companies another chance, and one existed in the mid-1950's.

By then most of the companies, IBM included, were at work on what would become the second generation of computers, machines based upon transistors, which, as has been indicated, were invented at the Bell Laboratories in 1948 and were licensed to other firms in the field soon after. In 1956 the government ordered Bell to provide its patents on a royalty-free basis to anyone who wished to use them. By then the once crude devices had been perfected and were ready for use in a wide variety of products. In the following year the tunnel diode was invented, and it, too, found its way into the laboratories of computer firms.

Transistors and diodes were in every way preferable to tubes: They were dependable and smaller, ran cooler, functioned more rapidly and efficiently, and, given mass production and technological development, were less expensive as well. Business magazines and technological journals wrote knowingly of the coming transistor boom and of how the devices would affect the design, production, prices, and sales of a wide variety of products, from radios and television sets to missiles. As for computers, the advent of the transistor would be even more revolutionary than had been the arrival of tubes that replaced electromechanical relays. Few recent technological changes had been so widely heralded or closely tracked.

Transistors clearly were on the way to replacing tubes. Production rose from 1.3 million units in 1954 to 47.1 million in 1958, when the first of the second generation of computers was released. In the same period cost per unit declined from $3.89 to $2.40. Meanwhile, vacuum-tube production virtually stagnated, with 385.1 million turned out in 1954 and just 397.4 million four years later. Tube prices actually rose slightly in this period, going from 72 to 86 cents per unit. This, too, was taken as an indication of what was to come.

As had been the case with the vacuum-tube models, UNIVAC was one of the earliest companies to produce and deliver a transistorized solid-state computer; the first of its Model 80's was placed in August 1958. Pitted against the IBM 650, one of that company's most popular models, it clearly was smaller, less expensive, more efficient, and more powerful. Then RCA—which at the time claimed it had only a peripheral interest in computers—came out with its BIZMAC, while Control Data, never encumbered with tube models, released the 1604.

As had been the practice under Watson senior, IBM talked little about its own work in the field. It was evident to those within the industry, however, that once again IBM had fallen behind in research and development. The situation wasn't as serious as it had been earlier in the decade, when there simply were no IBM computers to match UNIVAC I, but in 1958 the stakes were much higher.

Watson and others at corporate headquarters noted that the order rates for the 600 and 700 series were declining. The 650 RAMAC, which had become the most popular computer in the world, was particularly hard-hit. In 1956 there were 470 of these machines in operation, and in 1957, 803. But orders fell off for 1958, and the situation in 1959 was disastrous. Thereafter the number of 650 RAMACs in service declined steadily.

Increased competition from UNIVAC was only one reason for this. More important was the fact that the product cycle for the first generation of computers was drawing to a close. The early models, the first of their kind, had blazed the path, but by 1958 most companies that wanted or could be sold computers on the basis of current business and prices already had their machines. How might they be made to switch? By offering a machine with a greater capacity for a lower cost, such as the UNIVAC 80. The renter of a 650 RAMAC might accept this machine on such a basis, and businessmen who in the past had resisted computerization might be tempted to install one if the price were right. The challenge to IBM was to produce a second-generation computer to match the model 80 and to do so before UNIVAC had made inroads into the customer base.

Watson took a major step in this direction in 1956, when he hired Dr. Emanuel Piore, a well-known scientist and manager at the Navy Department. Piore not only appreciated the potential of transistors but had a record of success. He was given a mandate to lead IBM in the development of a second-generation series of machines. As director of research Piore would be permitted to make large expenditures for both facilities and personnel, which for a while made him one of the most influential figures in the organization.

On the surface the situation appeared similar to that of the late 1940's, when Watson junior placed much of the company's resources behind the initial foray into computers. But IBM was much more powerful an entity in 1956 than it had been a decade earlier. Gross revenues had risen from less than $120 million to $734 million, and in 1957 IBM would pass the billion-dollar mark. Net income and working capital in 1946 came to $18.8 million and $13.2 million respectively; in 1956 the figures were $68.8 million and $124.2 million. The company was in fine shape financially and had no trouble paying for the new computer project out of earnings and cash flow. IBM's sales and rentals continued to climb, as did dividends. The company's long-term debt increased substantially during the research and development phase but then stabilized. To a far greater degree than almost anyone had anticipated, IBM was coming close to divorcing itself from long-term outside sources of funding and would remain in this happy circumstance for more than two decades.

The second generation would be financed in large part from the rental base built up by the 600's and 700's. Of the total computer-derived revenues of $881 million for 1958, $842 million, or better than 95 percent, came out of the rental base. Thus, the soon-to-be-replaced first-generation machines helped pay for their successors, to an even greater extent than the way they themselves had been financed from revenues derived from the old calculators and accounting machines of the immediate post-World War II period.

Snow White and the Seven Dwarfs

Selected Statistics for IBM, 1956–1965*

(millions of dollars)

Year	Gross Revenues	Net Income	Long-Term Debt
1956	734.3	68.8	330.0
1957	1,000.4	89.3	375.0
1958	1,171.8	126.2	425.0
1959	1,309.8	145.6	425.0
1960	1,436.1	168.2	425.0
1961	1,694.3	207.2	425.0
1962	1,925.2	241.4	425.0
1963	2,059.6	290.5	425.0
1964	2,306.0	307.0	425.0
1965	2,487.3	333.0	425.0

* Excluding World Trade
Source: *Standard & Poor's Guide*, 1956; IBM 10K Forms, 1957–1966

In the late summer of 1958 IBM installed the first of the large 709 vacuum-tube machines, which also was the last of its series; even then customers understood that the second generation was on its way.

IBM started taking orders for the large 7070 and 7090 soon thereafter, obtaining most from clients anxious to upgrade their equipment and a number from those who under other circumstances might have opted for the UNIVAC II or the Control Data 1604. Then Watson unveiled the 1401, a low-priced, powerful, and flexible office machine, and the 1620, its scientific counterpart. The 7070's and 7090's would appeal to government purchasing agents, bankers, and insurance executives who required major systems; the 1401 and its successors would fill a wide range of needs for many more customers, and this series quickly became the most popular in the industry, filling for the second generation the leadership position held by the 650 for the first.

The 650's had indeed been major successes. At their peak in 1959, approximately 1,500 of them were in service, out of a total computer population of 3,100. More than 250 of the 1401's were installed in 1960, slightly fewer than 1,800 of them were in operation by the end of 1961, and in 1964, when the computer census showed 16,700 systems in use throughout the nation, some 6,300 were 1401's, while another 700 were the more specialized variant, the 1640.

The 7000 series was no less popular in its category. By 1963 some 300 of these major systems were in operation. Rentals from the 7000's installed that year alone came to $33.2 million, against the $27 million for the 1400's and more than half of IBM's total for 1963 of $60.3 million. In fact, rentals for the 1963-installed 7000's were better than half again as great as the total for all system rentals by the other American manufacturers.

The computer industry was still in the process of formation when the second-generation machines appeared. At the time insiders spoke of "Snow White and the Seven Dwarfs," referring, of course, to IBM and its major competitors. The matter of imagery aside, the term was not wholly accurate around 1958, for there was then some question of the precise makeup of the dwarf contingent. No one would deny a position to Sperry Rand or, for that matter, to NCR, Burroughs, and Honeywell. But General Electric and RCA had yet to make full commitments to computers, Control Data hadn't proved itself, the Philco Division of Ford Motors looked like a major force, Bendix had several well-received machines, and there were many other companies with interesting reputations, credentials, products, and assets nibbling at the edges. Success seemed possible for North American Aviation, Bunker Ramo, Addressograph-Multigraph, International Telephone & Telegraph, the Monroe Calculating Machine Division of Litton Industries, Raytheon, and even General Mills, which made a small commitment to the industry. Along the way most either dropped out or sold their operations to others. A decade or so later there indeed were Seven Dwarfs—in order of importance, Sperry Rand, Control Data, Honeywell, Burroughs, General Electric, RCA, and NCR, which among them claimed about a third of the market. Philco dropped out after Henry Ford decided the stakes were too high, the risks too great, and the chances for success all but nil, and Sylvania did the same. As has been mentioned, Bendix sold its operations to Control Data, and the other companies simply

Snow White and the Seven Dwarfs

faded as a result of lack of financing, technology, marketing, will, or a combination of these factors.

Selected Statistics for Major American Computer Manufacturers, 1965*
(in millions of dollars)

Company	Gross Revenues	Net Earnings	Profit Margin	Working Capital
IBM†	2487.3	333.0	26.4%	698.7
Sperry Rand	1279.8	31.9	5.0	357.7
Control Data	160.5	7.9	12.2	98.0
Honeywell	700.4	37.5	10.2	215.0
Burroughs	456.7	17.5	8.9	130.0
General Electric	6213.6	355.1	10.4	1129.8
RCA	2042.0	101.2	8.8	511.1
NCR	736.8	24.7	7.5	156.5

* These figures refer to the entire business for each company, not merely to computers and related products and services. In 1965 this category accounted for a small fraction of General Electric's total revenues and all of those for Control Data. The other companies fell in between these two.
† Excluding IBM World Trade.
Source: *Moody's Handbook of Common Stocks*, 1966 ed.

Behind the Seven Dwarfs were some interesting new companies or small entities that had just started to find their niches in the hardware side of the industry. Among the more important of these were Digital Equipment, Hewlett-Packard, Scientific Data, and Varian Associates. Most of them concentrated on small machines; at the time none had the resources to mount an assault on the dwarfs. The same was true for Digital Equipment, a company operating on the principle that any direct confrontation with the majors was suicidal.

Market Shares in the Computer Industry, 1965

	Company	Share
1.	IBM	65.3
2.	Sperry Rand	12.1
3.	Control Data	5.4
4.	Honeywell	3.8
5.	Burroughs	3.5
6.	General Electric	3.4
7.	RCA	2.9
8.	NCR	2.9
9.	Philco	0.7

Source: *Honeywell v. Sperry Rand*, p. 157

By the mid-1960's IBM and UNIVAC had solidified a relationship that was unusual but mutually profitable. They were competitors, the leader and runner-up in what had become the fastest-growing industry in the nation. Their salesmen would vie for orders, but through cross licensing in the aftermath of the antitrust settlement, they had entered into an almost symbiotic relationship. UNIVAC seemed curiously comfortable in its secondary role; it was resigned to its status. No major firm within the industry was less aggressive or more willing to settle for what it had—namely, a special relationship with the leader, one that placed it in an advantageous and privileged position vis-à-vis the other old-line office equipment companies that were nipping at its heels. This was a realistic stance; for all its pioneering and the advanced nature of its machines, UNIVAC had not yet managed to turn a profit on computers. Sperry Rand's earnings were poor, in large part because of the UNIVAC drain. Each year during the early 1960's Sperry promised its stockholders that "the corner was being turned," but the losses continued until 1965, when UNIVAC posted a minuscule profit. Earnings from the old Sperry operation kept the company afloat, and all in the organization knew it. While IBM constantly turned in profit margins of around 25 percent, Sperry Rand's were below 7 percent from 1957 on through the 1960's.

Burroughs and National Cash Register were in better shape as a result of their entrenched positions in banking and, in the case of NCR, the retailing industry as well. These two firms managed to hold onto old clients as a result of experience in the fields and by designing computers that filled specific needs. Burroughs had the most complete line of banking-related machines, while NCR announced plans for cash registers that not only rang up sales but also kept inventory and performed other computer-related tasks. But neither company had the resources or the will to compete head-on, across the board, with the leader. Decades of experience had shown the executives at Burroughs and NCR the futility of such attempts. Like Sperry

Snow White and the Seven Dwarfs

Rand, but from stronger bases, these companies refrained from bold—and dangerous—forays during the 1960's.

The situation was different at Honeywell, RCA, and General Electric, all of which were newcomers to the business machine area, and, of course, at Control Data, the youngest of the dwarfs, the smallest in terms of assets and revenues, and the only one completely committed to computers. Each developed its strategy independently of the others, but all four had the same basic objective: in the short run to replace UNIVAC in the runner-up position and from there to go on to mount a serious, direct challenge to IBM.

General Electric certainly had the resources to become a major force in the industry, but the company lacked leadership to accomplish the changeover during the 1950's, and when the proper people finally arrived, it was too late to overtake UNIVAC, much less IBM.

Philip Reed, who had been chairman of the company since 1939, recognized that computerization would be part of GE's future. Under his leadership several IBM and UNIVAC machines were installed in plants and offices, and after the initial shakedown the experience proved financially and technologically rewarding. By mid-1958 *Business Week* was claiming that General Electric had become "the most computerized company in the world," a bit of hyperbole in view of the many machines then in use in various American Telephone & Telegraph facilities. Nonetheless, GE had taken delivery on eleven large systems and thirty-two medium-sized machines and had ordered three additional majors and thirty-eight mediums.

Most of these computers were used to process payrolls, maintain inventories, and assist in corporate planning. In the process GE developed a fine appreciation of the roles computers might play in business affairs and found ways of utilizing them that had eluded even the manufacturers. GE staffers also came to see their limitations. Many firms then taking computers did so with incomplete knowledge of what they were accomplishing. It was the vogue to install one, or even two, and the bigger

171

they were—and the more blinking lights and spinning tape drives they featured—the better they seemed and the more prestige accrued to the firm. In the late 1950's corporate executives showing visitors around their offices rarely would fail to make a detour into the computer room, where their latest acquisition was on display. Oftentimes they weren't certain exactly what it was the machines did, or could do, for the firm. They didn't understand that they required staffing, in particular the retention of a computer expert capable of instructing the old-timers on the machine's capabilities. A corporate vice-president hoping to impress his superiors might order a large computer when a smaller one was all that was needed and then see it go unused for days at a time because of a lack of work. General Electric was among the first to discover this syndrome, and it was reported upon in company publications before the problem became the subject of discussions in general-interest magazines and newspapers and at management seminars.

A business of the size and complexity of General Electric needed large computers, and so perhaps did another 200 or 300 major corporations and many government agencies. Another 1,000 or so medium-sized machines could be sold or leased elsewhere, but that was the effective limit to the market, or at least so it appeared to Reed and others at GE headquarters. Already the field was quite crowded, and among the leaders were firms that had been engaged in detailed computer research during the war—and GE was not of that number. IBM appeared destined to hold its position, followed by UNIVAC and other business machine companies. As far as Reed could tell, computers were here to stay, but the same couldn't be said of many companies then in the field. Why should GE take the risks when the rewards seemed so distant and elusive, the competition so intense, and there were better profit opportunities elsewhere?

Furthermore, Reed was half-convinced the nation would suffer through another depression—he had come up through the ranks in the 1930's and had never forgotten that frightening experience. Unwilling to permit GE to become financially vulnerable, he hoarded assets and was reluctant to make new commitments, especially to such exotic and expensive contraptions as computers. Instead, he concentrated on cleaning up his company's balance sheet. Reed succeeded admirably in this. At the close of World War II General Electric had a bonded debt of more than $200 million. By 1954 almost all this had been paid off—the debt stood at a mere $1.7 million. In this same period gross revenues increased by more than 350 percent, but working capital declined from $419 million to $364 million.

This was the financial profile of a timid or prudent company, depending upon whether one rejected or approved of the Reed approach. Whatever the case, a major foray into computers could hardly be expected from such a firm. Thus, the one large company capable of mounting a major challenge against IBM—which possessed the technology, capital, and sales force, as well as the reputation, for the effort—held back during the crucial first generation.

Reed stepped down from the chairmanship in 1958, to be replaced by Ralph Cordiner, who had been president for the past eight years. Cordiner immediately announced what he called Operation Upturn, geared at improving GE's showing, and he spoke of a thoroughgoing overhaul of the corporation. One of the changes would involve computers. As chief operating officer Cordiner had developed an interest in the machines, a respect for their capabilities, and the notion that Reed didn't appreciate the scope of the market. The outgoing chairman believed that soon there would be a backlash against computerization on the part of companies which were discovering they were expensive toys, uneconomical, and not really necessary in many applications. In Cordiner's view, the placement of computers involved the re-creation of the office and factory, the reeducation of staffs, and the training of new personnel. IBM and UNIVAC already had entered this field, and GE had experience in similar areas, which could now be related to computers. Cordiner also believed that his company had a unique advantage in possessing people who would be able to understand problems from the user's point of view, not only that of the vendor.

Cordiner took the plunge shortly after he assumed office, ordering a major program to develop a family of second-generation computers. These would match the IBMs and UNIVACs insofar as technology and price were concerned and would offer two important extras which GE felt would make them far more desirable. The company developed what it called the Datanet communications processor, which enabled the 200-level machines to "talk" with one another—to share information, sending it from one data bank to another. Not only did this enable users to expand their capabilities (or, if necessary, reduce them) without turning in their medium-sized machines for larger ones, but in time a computer at one installation would be able to transmit information to another one at a distant location. The other companies would follow GE's lead, but it was soon recognized as the pioneer in the area.

Of even greater importance at the time was GE's research into time-sharing, which enabled several users to draw upon the resources of the same machine. This was in response to Reed's criticism of large computers—that because much of the time they were not in use, they were uneconomical. Once time-sharing was perfected and implemented, idleness became a relatively minor problem; if the computer were "free," the owner or leaser might rent its spare time to others, and in this way a machine might be kept busy around the clock, seven days a week, if arrangements could be made.

The 200 series was followed by the 400's, which were more economical to lease than their IBM counterparts. Then came the 600 family, with time-sharing capabilities. GE also produced a small machine, the 115, and so was able to challenge IBM across the board. By 1965 it was in fifth place among manufacturers, ahead of National Cash and RCA and only slightly behind Burroughs. Scientific versions of the 600's were particularly popular, especially among researchers, who consistently selected them over the IBMs. Commercial markets were opening up, too, so that at mid-decade it appeared that GE was in computers to stay.

The venture was costly, however, draining tens of millions

of dollars from the firm. This had been expected; GE knew of UNIVAC's ordeal and was prepared for the red ink, which in any case did not cause a great strain on finances. Still, there was some question of how long such losses would be tolerated, especially as the firm's profit margins declined and there were demands from other sectors for additional financing. Always it appeared that the project was about to turn the corner, and then costs would mount once more. Losses on computers amounted to around $100 million in 1966, a year when GE's net income came to more than $355 million. Per share earnings that year were $3.74; without computers, it would have been around $5.00. The 1967 losses were more than $60 million, and there still was no end in sight. Stockholder grumbling had begun, and there was dissension from within the company as well. "How long can General Electric stand the strain and keep up the pace?" asked *Forbes*, which provided its own answer: "As long as it chooses to do so."

Like General Electric, Honeywell entered the competition late. Although the company had experimented with computers in the early 1950's, it made no clear commitment to the commercial and scientific markets until the acquisition of Datamatic in 1955. The Honeywell approach was somewhat different from that of General Electric and the other latecomers. For one thing the firm had more limited resources. Its gross revenues in the year of the Datamatic merger came to $244 million, its income was $19 million, and working capital that year was only $86 million, approximately a quarter that of GE. For all this, Honeywell was well situated technologically and had excellent leadership, and its view of the market was realistic. The company was by far the largest manufacturer of automatic controls, and its products ran from simple thermostats for houses to highly complex models that could direct industrial production and that bore a great resemblance to computers. During World War II Honeywell had worked on several projects dealing with missile and aircraft guidance, and it had a stake in the Vanguard program, one of the Department of Defense's most advanced projects, which involved the use of large and small computers. Thus, the firm had a work force knowledgeable in the area, especially after the Datamatic merger, and a management interested in expanding its base to include computers.

Honeywell planned to meet IBM across the board and, like GE, would produce and market computer series that would outdo IBM models in terms of performance and price. Expectations for success were based upon what amounted to a three-pronged strategy. In the first place, the head of what would become Honeywell Information Systems, Walter Finke, had an extensive knowledge of the first-generation machines and was well grounded in second-generation technology. He understood both the strengths and weaknesses of the 1400 and 7000 series models and felt it would not be difficult to produce similar models that could be sold or leased at far lower prices. Thus, Honeywell would "track" IBM in the matter of hardware, while keeping ahead of the leader insofar as pricing was concerned.

Next, Honeywell looked upon the government as its silent ally in the fight. It was common knowledge in the early 1960's that a group of New Frontiersmen in the Justice Department was eager to present an antitrust indictment against IBM. The newsmagazines dismissed such talk as wild rumor; after all, Tom Watson had strongly supported John Kennedy during the presidential campaign, and the men were on good terms with each other. In any case, the last consent decree was only a few years old, and that was supposed to safeguard IBM against new actions for the immediate future. The response was that IBM had been prosecuted during the Roosevelt and Eisenhower administrations, even though Watson senior was closer to those Presidents than his son was to Kennedy. Furthermore, there was no clearly discernible computer industry in the mid-1950's, and now that one had emerged, the government would have to intervene to assure competition. Then, too, although businessmen as a group had come to accept Kennedy toward the end of 1961, conditions changed the following year, when the President mounted an attack against the steel industry, which helped trigger the worst Wall Street panic since the end of the war. By the early summer of 1963 important segments of the business community considered Kennedy their enemy, a man capable of mounting a well-publicized crusade against them to divert attention from problems in foreign affairs and a possible economic downturn.

Top executives at Honeywell clearly read the meaning of all this and concluded it worked in their favor. They prepared to meet IBM across the board, matching most of Watson's top machines with their own. "We can't see putting so much effort into just the parts of the market that are left over," said one executive somewhat disingenuously. "Besides, if they develop into significant business, IBM will come in strong eventually, so it's no more than a temporary strategy."

There was more to it than that, however. Although IBM surely would compete in almost all parts of the market, it would do so with an eye to the Justice Department and possible antitrust prosecution. Just as the departure of American Motors or Chrysler might have resulted in an attempt to break up General Motors, so the demise of Honeywell could trigger a new antitrust action against IBM. General Motors had a stake in maintaining the health of its competitors, so the thinking went, and in a like fashion, IBM would have to concede part of the computer market to its rivals. Honeywell knew it could not hope to lead the industry, but under the proper circumstances the firm might displace UNIVAC. "We figured IBM was too smart not to let us take 10 percent or so of the market," said Chuan Chu, head of Honeywell Information Systems's technical department (who had been wooed there from UNIVAC). So the company proceeded with a great degree of confidence.

Unlike General Electric, Honeywell would not attempt to pioneer in such areas as computer communications and time-sharing. For one thing, the company lacked the resource base to support such an approach, and for another, Honeywell had little thought of surpassing IBM in terms of technology, sales, and leases. Rather, Finke understood that his success would be measured in terms of profits and that these would have to come quickly, for Honeywell couldn't stand a continued drain upon assets. After indifferent results with the Datamatics and the large 800 series, introduced in late 1960, he cut sharply into research, development, and organization to produce a new series, the 200's, which embodied a novel approach, one that would be followed by others in the 1960's and form the basis for a significant part of the industry during the following decade.

The first of the H-200s were introduced in late 1963 and were ready for installation the following March. They were targeted at customers who already had the IBM 1400's, had placed orders for one or more, or were considering them. The 1400's were the very heart of the IBM line, and in 1963 the 1401 alone accounted for some 20 percent of total industry placements. Of the company's service and revenue income of $1.4 billion, the 1400's provided about $390 million. According to some industry estimates, IBM had booked orders for an additional 10,000 machines, which represented another $400 million or so in rentals. If Honeywell could capture only 10 percent of this market, it would be catapulted ahead of such giants as GE and RCA. This was Finke's immediate ambition, and in early 1964 it seemed capable of realization.

The initial 200 was leased for $3,100 a month in its basic configuration, which was approximately 5 percent below the price for the popular 1401. The Honeywell was more flexible, could be obtained almost immediately at a time when there was a waiting list for the IBM machine, and was almost twice as fast as the 1401. In the past IBM had been able to come out ahead in similar match-ups with the UNIVACs, but this time it was different. The 200's were similar to their 1400 series counterparts; a programmer for one might easily switch to the other. More important even than this, Honeywell offered an inexpensive accessory called the Liberator, which enabled the 200's to utilize programs designed for the 1400's, and the tape sizes for the memories were identical and thus compatible. This meant that Honeywell had accepted IBM's versions of software and in other ways made certain its machines conformed to the other company's norms. At the same time it was signaling IBM's customers that it was possible to obtain more of a machine for a lower price without having to undergo the problems and costs of conversion.

It was not a new idea. The UNIVAC 80, introduced in 1959 at the dawn of the second generation, could handle IBM software, as could other models from different manufacturers. But Honeywell carried the concept farther than anyone else and hit IBM harder and in a more vulnerable part of the market than UNIVAC ever had. To a later generation this would be known as plug compatibility, meaning that the user might unplug his IBM machine one day, hook up the competitor's model, install the tapes and related paraphernalia, and process information the following morning without much of a delay. This was a major breakthrough and had important implications. For one thing, it meant the rest of the industry had just about decided to follow IBM's lead in this area; it also indicated that IBM in the future would have to meet the new challenge of plug compatibility by producing better and more inexpensive models.

Plug compatibility was the third, and in the long run the most important, prong in the Honeywell strategy. The 200's were huge successes. By the end of 1964 Honeywell had installed sufficient numbers of them to provide the firm with a rental base of some $56 million, and IBM sales personnel were reporting increased customer resistance to the 1400's. Watson learned that more than a few old IBM clients were turning in their machines and accepting deliveries on Honeywells. "It really hurts," said one sales representative. "You don't have to get many 1401s returning from the field, which means negative commissions for salesmen, for it to start hurting."

At conventions and in corporate meetings the decline in orders for the 1400's was attributed to the nature of the product cycle: The series had peaked and now was on the inevitable downward slope. Customers were resisting the 1400's, said one industry publication, because they believed the advanced third generation was on the way, and its machines would be far more economical to lease. But Honeywell actually fell behind in deliveries as a result of an upsurge of orders, many of which might have been won by IBM were it not for the Liberator. In 1965

Honeywell reported it was showing a profit in its computer division, an accomplishment that had eluded GE and the other majors.

Two years later Sperry Rand sued Honeywell for infringements of the ENIAC patents. Little more than a nuisance action, this also was a shot across Honeywell's bow and a sign that the firm was being taken most seriously by the runner-up in the field. Undaunted, Honeywell responded with a countersuit that threatened to shake the foundation of the industry: It charged that the Sperry-IBM cross-licensing agreement of 1956 represented a restraint of trade, an attempt by the two leaders to monopolize the computer industry and stifle competition. Now not only did IBM have to face a potentially dangerous competitor in the marketplace, but it also learned that Honeywell was prepared to use the powers of the courts to maintain its new position.

In 1954 RCA claimed it was the third largest factor in the computer industry, ahead of Control Data but behind Sperry Rand. In fact, the company was in seventh position, the next to the last of the Seven Dwarfs, ahead of NCR and behind General Electric, with less than 3 percent of the market. Still, Control Data had only 5.4 percent that year, so the confusion perhaps was understandable. Yet RCA had reason to believe it soon would leapfrog ahead of Sperry and perhaps even diminish IBM's role within the industry.

Watson understood the reasoning behind these ambitions but also believed them unrealistic. Nonetheless, no aspect of the competition engaged his emotions as much as that with RCA. IBM salesmen who lost out in competitions with GE, Control Data, or Honeywell could expect cool receptions from their superiors; those who came in second to RCA might undergo interrogations and tongue-lashings.

This was not because RCA had better machines or a superior sales force. Rather, Watson's interest in the company derived from his belief that RCA's management was devious and underhanded and unwilling to compete with him by the rules of the game as understood by IBM and most other companies in the field.

John L. Burns, who, as has been shown, was at the Williamsburg conference, was the central figure in all this, although in Watson's view David Sarnoff, RCA's aged chairman, also was at fault. In March 1957 Sarnoff appointed Burns president and chief operating officer at RCA, with several special assignments. One of these was to make a careful assessment of RCA's future role in the computer industry.

Only a few months earlier, Watson had contacted Sarnoff and asked whether RCA had any plans to enter the market for commercial computers. The implication was evident: If this were the case, then Burns would have to choose between the two companies, for to remain as an advisor with both would involve a clear conflict of interest. As he had on several occasions, Sarnoff assured Watson that besides BIZMAC and several other military projects, RCA had no intention of proceeding much further with computers. It was with this understanding that Burns continued to advise IBM and in the process became privy to the company's technology, works in progress, and future plans. More than most firms, IBM had a record of keeping such information confidential. Thus, Watson was enraged when Burns took his post at RCA.

In the late 1950's there was a joke circulating among managers to the effect that one had to be careful in taking on Booz, Allen consultants, for they had a record of going over to competitors and using one's secrets against one. Most people naturally assumed the story originated at IBM.

For all his knowledge and experience, Burns was unable to come up with a strategy that was original or more than occasionally effective. RCA would attempt to confront IBM in all product and service areas but, unlike GE, would do little pioneering. Rather, its machines would possess the same kinds of capabilities as their IBM counterparts but would carry lower price tags. Burns correctly understood that IBM's strength rested on its reputation and the sales force. So he hired as many key IBM salesmen as he could get (and of course, he knew who they were from his previous experiences) and set out to make as many placements as possible.

Placements were at the crux of his strategy. Burns would slash prices, make concessions—in fact, deliver a machine under terms which all but eliminated any reasonable hope of profit—in an attempt to make the RCA computers as ubiquitous in the nation's offices as the company's television receivers were in its homes. RCA's massive frontal assault was the talk of the industry in the late 1950's and early 1960's. It was one of the most daring gambles in American business history.

RCA expected to fund the campaign from revenues derived from its more mature operations, such as the National Broadcasting System and the sales of television sets. Just as radio had provided the resource base for television in the 1940's and 1950's, so television would bankroll this foray into computers. Close to retirement, Sarnoff already was considered one of the pioneers in his own industry and a great business tycoon. The gaining of a solid position in computers would be a grand climax to his career.

RCA released its giant 501 computer in early 1959, and the first placements were made that summer. This machine, which was designed to compete against the 7000 series, met with a favorable reception, in large part as the result of price concessions and aggressive salesmanship. The medium-sized 301, which was ready for market in early 1961, was matched against the 1401. Although somewhat more expensive initially, it was more economical to use, and quickly it, too, was subject to discounts.

The 501 was a major disappointment; not only was it unable to cut into IBM and UNIVAC sales, but it also did poorly in relation to the Control Data machines. The company fared better with the 301's. After a slow start, orders picked up, especially once discounting increased. But all this resulted in major financial losses, as had been and was the case at GE. During the early 1960's, as RCA reaped enormous profits from television, the company expended hundreds of millions of dollars on its computer operations. Clearly RCA would not so much as break even on these machines for several more years, if ever, but as was the case with General Electric, RCA remained in the field, still confident that success was attainable and that when it came, there would be a bonanza, in terms of both prestige and profits.

Rarely have so many astute big businessmen staked so much on what amounted to a fantasy. In retrospect one can see that they were dazzled by technologies they didn't fully comprehend and were chasing after phantoms—IBM's profit margin, sales and earning growths, and reputation with investors and on Wall Street. With few exceptions they didn't really understand what they were letting themselves in for, what the full implications of a foray into computers were, or how they could become almost inextricably involved in ventures that carried an inordinate amount of risk. Yet some of this was known at the time; they might have gathered as much from industry magazines and even general business publications. Each firm banked on an exaggerated notion of its own special strength—RCA thought aggressive marketing could turn the tide; GE counted on its reputation, resources, and new technologies; Honeywell picked its target carefully, adjusted to the IBM ways, and looked to the Justice Department for help; Sperry Rand expected to maintain its special relationship with the leader; Control Data would focus on the big machines, an area IBM tended to ignore; Burroughs and NCR would remain with their conventional markets for the time being.

And what of IBM itself? Watson understood that he couldn't afford to rest on his company's reputation and product mix. Nor would he ever forget that IBM still lagged in many areas of technology. The machines turned out by his competitors often were as good as, if not better than, his own, and until this situation was turned around, IBM would be at risk.

Dr. Piore and his growing staff had been given a mandate to change all this, and in the early 1960's it appeared that they would succeed, at least technologically. The sales force had been told to inform those clients unhappy with the cost performance of the 1400's in relation to competitive machines that a new generation was on the way. So it was.

In 1964 Tom Watson was still the heir, the son of one of the greatest businessmen the nation had ever known. Whether he was more than just a capable administrator remained to be seen. A decade earlier he had argued that IBM had to develop machines to go with its superior sales force, and whether or not he had done so to that point was questionable. Now he was prepared to shake up the industry, his own company included, by introducing a new group of computers. Honeywell, GE, and RCA had taken their risks. It now was IBM's turn. Watson appreciated the problems involved, the resources required, and what was at stake. He also knew that in the contest he would require the skills and resources available at World Trade.

Tom Watson had come out from under his father's shadow but was about to enter Dick's penumbra and in the process remake IBM in subtle and important ways.

Herman Hollerith, inventor of the first practical census tabulating machine, provided a technological base, leasing practices, and a business tradition which IBM later followed.

Hollerith's machines revolutionized census taking in 1890. Articles and illustrations appeared in popular magazines of the time and stirred thoughts of other applications for these devices.

Charles R. Flint, organizer of CTR, IBM's predecessor, was known as the "father of trusts." His work to advance the automobile and aviation fields is suggested by this 1925 photo of the inauguration of passenger service between Miami and New York.

John Henry Patterson, of National Cash
Register, headed the largest and most successful business machine company of his
day. He trained and indoctrinated scores
of executives—who were fired when they
became a threat, among them Thomas J.
Watson, Sr.

Thomas Watson rose through the sales
ranks of NCR to a management position
second only to Patterson. He appeared to
be the heir apparent, but in April 1914, at
the age of forty, Watson was dismissed.
He is shown here in the mid-1920's.

IBM's chief rival for many years, Powers Accounting Machine Corporation, turned out an impressive line of business products which, during the 1920's, threatened IBM's position in the industry.

Although electric typewriters were used during the 1920's, they had only a small share of the market. IBM attempted to boost sales by introducing a programmed machine, but was unsuccessful.

CTR's largest customer was the Census Bureau. Here is a section of operators processing the 1930 figures.

IBM machines were the mainstay of Social Security record keeping from its inception in 1935. Before file drawers were unpacked, clerks were already feeding information into IBM's devices.

Over the years, IBM has been the target of antitrust litigation. Watson senior is shown testifying in 1940 before a congressional committee investigating monopoly practices.

In 1949, by way of the largest telephone hookup to that date, Watson senior addressed IBM representatives in forty-nine countries on the need to support the United Nations. At his right is IBM President John G. Phillips. On his left, Watson's wife Jeannette, who was rarely photographed.

This 1944 Automatic Sequence Controlled Calculator (ASCC) was among the last of the large electro-mechanical devices. Such five-ton machines had the same calculating power as the hand-held model of today.

The back of this 1945 first-generation computer contained large arrays of vacuum tubes which generated intense heat and were constantly in need of replacement. The machine filled whole rooms.

The world's first electronic computer, the Electronic Numerical Integrator and Calculator (ENIAC), was built at the University of Pennsylvania in 1946, primarily for military use.

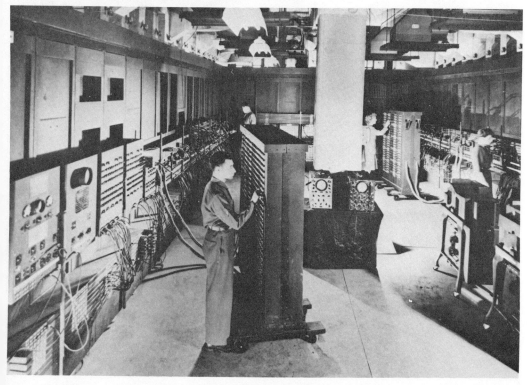

Dr. John W. Mauchly, above, and J. Presper Eckert, below, co-inventors of ENIAC, perfected computer technology in the second half of the 1940's. Their fledgling company was incorporated into Remington Rand, which fashioned their products into the familiar UNIVAC series, providing strong competition for IBM.

The IBM Selective Sequence Electronic Calculator (SSEC) was demonstrated at New York headquarters in 1951. Watson senior was convinced no market existed for such giants. The major task of the SSEC that year was to recalculate the orbits of planets.

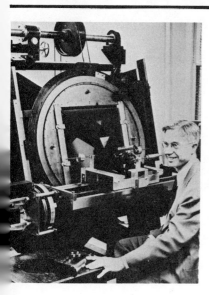

Columbia University professor Wallace J. Eckert had a long and fruitful collaboration with IBM beginning in 1930. He helped develop test-grading devices, as well as the automatic star-position-measuring machine shown in this 1953 photograph.

IBM was a significant factor in the U.S. space program from its inception. IBM machines were used for guiding and tracking virtually all satellite placements from this 1958 Explorer launching onward.

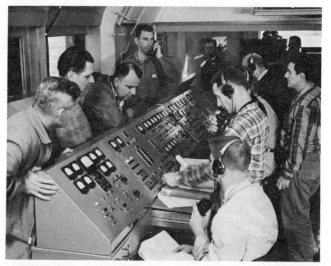

Thomas Watson, Jr., started as a sales trainee in 1939. To the surprise of no one, he filled his 1940 sales quota on January 2 of that same year.

Tom Watson, Jr., photographed above in May of 1956, returned to IBM after World War II and underwent an intensive training period prior to his appointment as chief executive officer.

Arthur "Dick" Watson returned from the war to a position as his father's assistant. By 1957, when this photograph was taken, he was already head of IBM World Trade and was aggressively pursuing foreign markets. In 1970 he left the firm to become ambassador to France.

Continuing the family and company tradition, Tom Watson entertained foreign dignitaries on their U.S. visits. He escorted Nikita Khrushchev in 1959 during a tour of IBM's San Jose, California, manufacturing plant.

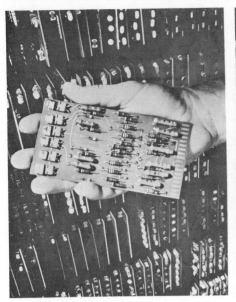

The second-generation computers were constructed around transistors, which replaced the large and trouble-prone vacuum tubes. This printed wiring panel includes transistors, at extreme left, diodes, and resistors. It was used in an experimental IBM unit in 1954.

In the late 1950's, tape replaced the formerly ubiquitous "IBM cards." Information contained in the stack of cards shown has been transferred to a single reel of tape.

This 1966 tape-library corridor at Social Security headquarters in Baltimore, Maryland, contains as much information as a building full of the bulky cards.

Dr. Emanuel R. Piore was the prime scientific mover behind IBM's revolutionary 360 series which shook the computer industry in the mid-1960's. It provided IBM with technological credentials to match those it already had in marketing and services.

IBM's "integrated circuit," heart of the 360's, replaced the transistor and became emblematic of the third-generation machine. This hand-fabricated device, not the true integrated circuit of today, was not at the forefront of technology and represented a compromise for a more assured commercial result.

Tom Watson announces the 360 series in a 1964 televised press conference reminiscent of his father's telephone talks. The 360 was so successful that it dominated the industry from the mid-1960's through the mid-1970's.

IBM's top command in 1960 during the 360 campaign. They are, from left, Dick Watson, chairman of World Trade, Tom Watson, chairman of IBM, T. Vincent Learson, senior vice-president, Albert L. Williams, president.

The silicon "computer on a chip" was developed in the late 1960's. It currently represents the state of the art in computer technology. At left, an early chip is surrounded by the components it replaced. Right, a highly magnified modern chip reveals its complexity.

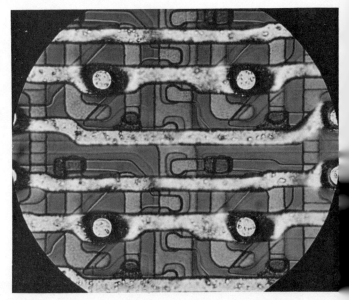

The search for faster, more accessible memory storage led to the development of the floppy disc, seen here in the white case. It contains many times the information of the square tape and is vastly more efficient, but the floppy disc soon will be replaced by bubble memory.

Conventional wisdom at IBM is that top executives won their battlestars during the 360 and 370 campaigns. In large part because of their successes, Vincent Learson, center, became chairman of the board, and Frank I. Cary, left, became president and heir apparent.

T. Vincent Learson, shown with Watson at a 1972 stockholders' meeting in Dallas, Texas, during his tenure as chairman of the board and chief executive officer, 1971–1973.

As IBM chairman succeeding Learson, Frank Cary restructured the corporation, deployed IBM's assets into new technologies, and embarked upon one of the most massive and costly expansion programs in history. He is shown at a 1975 stockholders' meeting explaining IBM's foray into small computers.

IBM workhorse for the 1980's is the 4300 series. Its announcement in 1979 startled the industry with surprisingly large cuts in cost-per-computation.

John R. Opel succeeded Cary as chief executive of IBM on January 1, 1981. At the age of fifty-six, after thirty-two years with the company, he is truly at the helm of a colossus in transition.

PART III

The World According to IBM

9

The Global Entrepreneur

IN 1970, while America was in the midst of a period of self-doubt, hypercriticism, and uncertainty, Columbia University political scientist Zbigniew Brzezinski released a book intended to revive confidence, stir debate, and establish his reputation as one of the nation's foremost strategic thinkers and social critics.

Between Two Ages: America's Role in the Technotronic Era had only a limited impact. It was a derivative work, drawing upon the ideas of such men as Norbert Wiener and John Diebold, while Brzezinski's technotronic era was similar to what Daniel Bell had earlier termed the "post industrial age." Nonetheless, the work was well received by several critics who observed that in it were found a number of interesting notions.

One of these involved the measures Brzezinski employed to gauge national power. At one time, he wrote, one looked to the production of grains. Then it was the turn of industry, measured in statistics for coal and steel. The third stage, which involves "a far-reaching technologically induced revolution," is now upon us. According to Brzezinski, this new America is "symbolized by the new complexes of learning, research, and development that link institutions of higher learning with society and create unprecedented opportunities for innovation and experimentation. . . . Technotronic America is in the electronics laboratories and centers of learning along Route 128 surrounding Boston, it is in the academic-scientific conglomerates around Los Angeles and San Francisco; and it is in the new frontier industries," one of the most important of which was computers. Their production and use, not the statistics for wheat and steel, foretell world leadership.

Brzezinski went on to note that the United States employed some 50,000 to 70,000 computers of all sizes, while among them West Germany, Japan, and Britain had around 15 percent of that amount. According to one computer census taken in 1966, the United States had 386 of the machines in service for every million nonagricultural workers. Switzerland was in second place, with around 125 per million, and so advanced an industrial power as France had only 60 or so. This, concluded Brzezinski, was the most accurate and telling symbol of American pioneering, vitality, and might.

IBM and the other American computer makers appreciated this situation, which for them contained two important implications. First of all, the United States clearly was the world leader in computers and likely to remain so for the foreseeable future. The nature of organization, the asset base, and economies of scale pointed to the foreign markets, and this all but mandated a major effort overseas.

IBM was a familiar trademark in Europe, and even during the interwar period executives there were accustomed to dealing with its agents and using the company's products. The same would hold true for computers. Foreign firms and laboratories would make important contributions in the development of machines and software, but none could match IBM insofar as assets, resources, organization, sales, services, and reputation were concerned. This was as much a matter of tradition as anything else. Later, when the Europeans and the Japanese managed to develop their own computer industries, none made a concerted attempt to sell products in the United States. Just as the foreign calculator and typewriter companies rarely had cultivated Americans prior to World War II, so they remained in their home markets in the area of computers.

There never was a chance that such companies as Olivetti of Italy, Bull of France, Siemens & Halske of West Germany, or Philips of the Netherlands would attempt a major foray across the Atlantic. International Computers & Tabulators, which emerged from what was left after British Tabulating Machine became part of IBM World Trade in 1949, produced computers that might have competed with their American counterparts in terms of price and performance, but the company never seriously considered an invasion of the American market. Several Japanese firms, among them Nippon Electric and Hitachi, were producing computers in the 1960's, but at a time when Sony and Toyota were selling television sets and automobiles in America, the computer makers held back.

Far from developing plans for American subsidiaries or marketing organizations, all these firms feared being squeezed out of their own areas by IBM and the other major American companies. During the 1960's the Americans expanded overseas, while the foreign firms erected tariff barriers and in other ways reacted defensively in attempting to contain the invaders and hold onto whatever they could in their national markets.

Initially each European computer manufacturer sought to meet what French journalist Jean-Jacques Servan-Schreiber called "The American Challenge" by allying itself with governments rather than seeking a common policy. Mergers, if undertaken early enough, might have produced strong firms capable of competing with the Americans. These might have been followed by cross-national arrangements or even the erection of communities of interest. There was some talk of this in the early 1960's, but only in Japan was such an entity created. As for the

European firms, they behaved as though the Americans could be repulsed by a combination of government restrictions and superior machines. This was not to be, and almost all the Continental firms bowed to the Americans, accepting junior positions in their own countries by means of arrangements with an American company.

Machines Bull was one of the first to go. A well-entrenched manufacturer of a wide line of business equipment, Bull was assured of support by President Charles de Gaulle, who was intent on turning it into a showcase for French technology. Bull developed the Gamma series, second-generation computers that were advanced by any standard applied and that were marketed in 1960. The same year Bull entered into an agreement with RCA under the terms of which it would receive patents and be permitted to train its engineers at the American company's facilities, in return for which RCA's computers would be allowed in France. Thus, IBM World Trade, which produced computers in France and so did not require special import licenses, had to face formidable competition.

The French government placed large orders for the Gammas, and the same was true of the nationalized sector of the economy. Privately owned firms were urged to replace their IBMs with Bull counterparts, and there even was talk of government subsidies for those that would make the switch. Bull marketed its machines throughout Western Europe, held discussions with Soviet-bloc governments, and made a foray into Latin America. In 1962 it appeared the Gammas might be introduced into the United States as well, and there were rumors that Bull was seeking to acquire an American firm to distribute its machines throughout North America.

World Trade responded by slashing lease charges, obliging Bull to do the same. Unrestrained by the kind of antitrust considerations that affected the parent firm, it undercut Bull consistently. Thus, although the Gammas were well received, most placements resulted in financial losses, obliging it to cut back in other areas of business. Sales were at record levels, but in 1963 the firm posted a $25 million deficit. Bull was obliged to default on interest payments the following year and entered into what amounted to bankruptcy.

This situation interested Cordiner of General Electric, who was seeking a means of competing against IBM in overseas markets. Since the domestic struggle was straining GE's resources he could not consider the creation of an operation of the size of World Trade. Rather, he would attempt to create partnerships with existing companies and as much as possible integrate their activities across national boundaries. Already GE had an arrangement of sorts with Compagnie Internationale pour l'Informatique et les Techniques Electroniques de Controle, a holding entity the components of which were working on the creation of large computer systems. Now, under the leadership of J. Stanford Smith, head of GE's Information Systems Group, the company lent funds to Bull. This was followed by a capital investment and then by another. After more than $100 million had been invested, the two firms came together to form Bull-General Electric, which, despite the order of the names, was controlled by GE. Smith entered into an arrangement whereby his American computers were imported into France to fill out the line, and Bull's sales force was integrated with that of General Electric. Smith's record on placements was good. Although unable to displace IBM World Trade as leader in the French market, Bull-GE had a third of the market, which placed it far ahead of the rest of the pack. But the price was paid: Bull-GE was a chronic money loser, while World Trade flourished in France.

General Electric entered into a similar arrangement with Olivetti, the leading Italian computer maker. Olivetti was a major office equipment manufacturer with a wide variety of products, and its venture into computers was financed from profits from the sales of its highly popular typewriters, some of which competed successfully in the American market as the Underwood line—Olivetti had taken over that once-powerful firm and was in the process of turning it around. The prospects for typewriters were excellent; Olivetti even entertained notions of displacing IBM as the leader among electrics. But this would not be possible unless capital were diverted from the debt-ridden computer venture, which in any case appeared to have little chance of financial success. Olivetti's Elia computers sold well in Italy because of government intervention, but they couldn't match the Gammas, the IBM 1400's, and the UNIVACs in cost-benefit ratios. Thus, in the autumn of 1964, shortly after GE had engulfed Bull, it purchased the Olivetti computer operation for approximately $20 million, and out of this emerged Olivetti-General Electric. This entity had some 25 percent of the Italian market and was second behind IBM World Trade, which claimed 65 percent of placements. Once again, GE could claim to be a strong competitor (UNIVAC, in third place, had only 8 percent of the market), but as was the case with Bull-GE, the new entity lost money while World Trade continued to have excellent profit margins.

The General Electric approach sounded fine in theory, especially when expounded before management and investment groups in the United States. In practice, however, it failed. "General Electric tried to take the computer operations of three companies with different philosophies and different product lines and blend them into a whole," wrote one industry observer in 1967 as he surveyed the scene, noting that while GE had volume, it had been obtained at the cost of hundreds of millions of dollars. "GE probably would have been better off coming in here on its own," he concluded.

Would that have been any better, considering the domination of IBM World Trade in overseas markets? The real alternative to operating through national firms, which at least had the benefits of political connections, was to remain out of the international area entirely, and given the visions of profits, this hardly was likely. Thus, GE took a 10 percent interest in West Germany's AEG, which not only gained it entry into what had become the world's third largest market for computers but enabled it to use a German sales force to sell and lease the French Gammas there. GE had less success in the Netherlands, where a proposed marketing arrangement with Philips was rejected, and the same happened in Sweden when discussions with Saab broke down. GE sold its machines in Japan through a licensing arrangement with Tokyo Shibaura, but few were ever installed there. Nibbles at the highly protected British market came to next to nothing. Still, insofar as volume was concerned, GE had emerged by the end of the decade as runner-up to IBM World Trade on the Continent.

RCA pursued a similar strategy, but with far less success. While GE was concluding its arrangement with Olivetti, RCA initiated discussions with Siemens & Halske. The German company had a computer line of its own, the 4004's, but the Americans hoped to arrange for some kind of marketing arrangement to introduce its second-generation models there, and it did. Few were placed, however. Toward the end of the 1960's World Trade claimed more than 55 percent of the West German market; Bull-GE and UNIVAC were almost tied for second place, with 9 percent or so apiece. Siemens & Halske, which had made a $150 million commitment to computers—large by European standards—had only 7 percent of the placements, these concentrated in the banking industry. But even there it lagged badly behind World Trade.

RCA entered Japan by licensing its patents to Hitachi for a fee and in this way followed GE's example. Other Americans did the same; Honeywell was associated with Nippon Electric, TRW and Westinghouse went with Mitsubishi Electric for a while, while Sperry Rand worked through Oki Denki. Only World Trade stood alone, rejecting Japanese demands that it affiliate itself with a domestic concern.

Just as the United States had Snow White and the Seven Dwarfs, Japan had the Big Six, which in order of importance were Nippon Electric, Hitachi, Fujitsu, Toshiba, Oki Denki, and Mitsubishi. In 1961, with government support, these firms organized the Japan Electronic Computer Company Ltd., which was initially capitalized at $18 million. Organized to study the prospects for overseas placements, JECC also purchased machines from the Big Six and leased them to end users, thus easing capital strains on the companies. Also, it made certain the Japanese concerns had an inside track on government placements and those in the private sector. Since the parent firms of the Big Six dominated not only big business but the banks and insurance companies as well, this all but closed these markets to the Americans, whose only hope rested in producing machines so superior they couldn't be rejected easily or in relying upon a strong Japanese sales force.

Needless to say, the competition was fierce, but once again World Trade prevailed. Toward the end of the 1960's IBM Japan had about 30 percent of the entire Japanese market for electronic data processing equipment; this meant that it ran neck and neck with Nippon Electric but was far ahead of the others.

Honeywell lagged behind the field, not surprisingly since it was using whatever resources it had in the American contest. After the GE-Saab discussions had ended, Honeywell approached the Swedish firm and concluded a marketing agreement whereby its machines entered Scandinavia. Elsewhere on the Continent, Honeywell relied upon a sales force comprised largely of nationals, who took orders for American-made machines, concentrating upon heavy-goods manufacturers and others that had some experience in dealing with the company in the past. Honeywell expected little from this approach; its European and Japanese ventures were undertaken to establish its presence in those parts of the world, not as a serious challenge to IBM or any local firm.

Britain was perhaps the most interesting area for international competition. Despite that country's many economic problems, it was the fourth largest market in the world, one that was growing at a rapid pace. Like Japan, Britain intended to defend its internal market and discourage outsiders from entering. But while the Japanese lagged in important areas of research and development, Britain had been a leader from the outset, and much of the early work during World War II had been conducted in its universities and laboratories. International Computers & Tabulators, Elliott Automation, and English Electric held many basic patents, some of which had been licensed to American firms, including IBM. Although none of these companies was sufficiently powerful to challenge the leader, each had machines capable of meeting the competition from abroad. ICT in particular had a line of second-generation computers that was well received and that even replaced some of the IBM 1400's in European markets.

In 1964, when there were 251 installations made in the United Kingdom, the British firms accounted for 128, against World Trade's 64. The other firms, all of which were American, trailed badly. Then, as IBM aggressively marketed first the 1400's and 7000's and later the third-generation computers, the gap narrowed. By 1967 the British lead over World Trade had dwindled to 298 to 267, and by then it appeared that Britain, the only country other than Japan where World Trade was in a runner-up position, would soon join the others in trailing the international leader.

In order to prevent this from occurring, the government intervened in the industry. As the Japanese had recognized earlier, no single existing company could defend home markets against World Trade. Given the nature of that country's experience, this all but mandated the formation of JECC. With a different tradition, the British opted for a state-sponsored merger. In March 1968 the leading firms were brought together to form International Computers Ltd., which at the time of its birth was the largest non-American business machine manufacturer and marketer in the world.

ICL was a strong company and a formidable competitor. Although it enjoyed government protection, ICL might have bested World Trade in its home market without this advantage. The firm had some of the world's most experienced and respected computer technicians and scientists, several efficient manufacturing facilities, and a seasoned field operation, which after initial organizational problems performed well. ICL produced several advanced, flexible, and low-priced machines that were a match for the 1400's, especially in the European markets. Its System 4 computers were compatible with, and even more economical to use than, the IBM counterparts. Successes at home and on the Continent emboldened the company. In

1969 it opened an office in Toronto from which an assault was launched on the Canadian market, where IBM had made seven out of every ten installations and no non-American firm had ventured. Meanwhile, ICL was doing well at home. In 1969 the British firm installed 409 machines, against World Trade's 156. With all this, however, ICL still did not have half the market. Moreover, intense competition had resulted in deep losses, the inevitable experience encountered when firms came up against IBM, while World Trade's profit margins on British sales actually expanded.

As had the Americans, the Europeans and Japanese discovered that competition with IBM was likely to result in frustrations and deficits. Perhaps they would have succeeded if, like Control Data, the foreigners had concentrated on special segments of the market, but national pride would not permit such an approach at the time. Superior machines and even government sponsorship did not suffice, as Siemens & Halske, Bull, Olivetti, and later ICL would learn. Abroad, as at home, IBM was a master in the art of providing customers with a sense of well-being as they moved into a new technology. Otto Stitz, UNIVAC's West German manager, summed it up well in 1966, when he observed: "Anyone can make a computer. The trick is putting it in the user's hands, equipped and ready to solve his problems." And this was precisely where World Trade excelled.

More perhaps than anyone else, Tom Watson understood the value of this reputation, and knew how much of an advantage it gave the company in overseas markets. Both he and Dick shared their father's vision of a truly international firm, and there never was any doubt that they would pursue the foreign markets aggressively. Tom Watson even suggested that the overseas demand would be greater than that in the United States. In 1961 he predicted that placements outside the American market would increase at a compounded rate of at least 20 percent during the foreseeable future. Competition was bound to intensify, but World Trade clearly was up to any challenge that might come. In the late 1950's and early 1960's it had grown more rapidly than even the parent company; in 1965 its net revenues topped the billion-dollar mark for the first time, only eight years after IBM Domestic had reached that objective, and its profit margins were much larger. In 1963 *Business Week* suggested that World Trade would surpass Domestic in terms of revenues and earnings within ten years. Tom Watson suspected this was to be; so did Dick, still in polite competition with his brother.

Selected Statistics for IBM Domestic and World Trade, 1956–1967

(millions of dollars)

Year	Domestic		World Trade	
	Revenues	Earnings	Revenues	Earnings
1955	564.0	55.9	132.8	NA
1956	734.0	68.8	157.7	NA
1957	1000.4	89.3	202.1	NA
1958	1171.8	126.2	246.1	NA
1959	1309.8	145.6	296.9	40.2
1960	1436.1	168.2	372.2	48.8
1961	1694.3	207.7	497.6	64.5
1962	1925.2	241.4	653.1	86.7
1963	2059.6	290.5	788.0	104.6
1964	2306.0	307.0	933.0	124.0
1965	2487.3	333.0	1085.5	144.0

NA = Not Available
Sources: IBM 10Ks, 1956–1967

World Trade headquarters, and Dick Watson's office, were in Manhattan, and they remained there for a decade after Domestic moved to Armonk. Then they followed along, to be located in a W-shaped building. But much of the day-to-day work was directed from an edifice on the Place Vendôme in Paris. The staff there was smaller than the one in New York, in part because World Trade was subordinate to Domestic, but also because of the nature of its function within IBM, much of which involved mediation between the parent and the national companies.

Like Domestic, World Trade was basically a holding company, the major responsibility of which consisted of harmonizing efforts of large subsidiaries like IBM Deutschland and IBM

France as well as the smaller ones that operated in comparatively remote parts of Latin America and Africa. World Trade's strategy and finances were coordinated with those of Domestic, but in other ways it functioned as an independent entity, aware, of course, that too great a show of independence might result in less freedom. Dick Watson had less power on his board than Tom had at Domestic, because he clearly was subordinate to his brother and also because of the independence granted national companies.

Each national might develop its own approaches, especially in the areas of marketing and services. While the IBM esprit was strong, it was flexible enough to take account of national sensibilities and sensitivities. Thus, the major subsidiaries would share research and special expertise, usually with headquarters acting as intermediary.

Thus, there were several layers to the structure. At the apex was IBM Domestic, and below it, World Trade. Then came the national firms, some of which were subdivided according to product lines that might be broken down still further into geographic areas. In a large and important market, such as one of the major European capitals, a salesman might work out of a city office, a segment of a central product group which came under a national IBM company, which in turn helped constitute World Trade. Although a separate corporation (as distinct from a division) since 1950, World Trade ultimately was under the control of the American board of directors, most of whom came out of or were allied with IBM Domestic.

All this was familiar enough within the company and the rest of the industry, and insofar as its bare organizational structure was concerned, the IBM model wasn't particularly innovative or unusual. Much of this eluded the unsophisticated, however. World Trade's earnings were not consolidated with those of IBM Domestic until 1963, so that many people who understood that the company was powerful and fast-growing didn't fully appreciate how much of this depended upon World Trade. Nor did they understand the complex financial relationships among the national companies, World Trade, and IBM Domestic.

This growth had to be financed. That meant World Trade had to allocate resources carefully among the national companies, a delicate task that had to take account of pride and nonbusiness rivalries as well as simple economics. The decision on whether a new research facility should be constructed in Japan, Britain, or France was far more difficult to make than one involving the location of a plant in New York, California, or Texas.

Then there was the matter of the financial contribution each would make to World Trade and, if additional capital was required, whether it should come out of New York or the Place Vendôme or be raised locally. Much of the time World Trade permitted each national firm to use banks and insurance companies in its territory; these institutions were prime users of computers, electric typewriters, and other IBM products, so it paid to patronize them as much as and whenever possible. IBM France required capital infusions until 1954, for example, and most of them came from French banks.

This relationship and pattern were repeated in dealings between IBM Domestic and World Trade. What proportion of the corporation's resources should be allocated to the United States, and how much should go to the rest of the world? IBM's cash flow was such that the corporation was never in a financial bind. Short-term loans usually were available at the lowest possible rates not only in the United States but throughout the world. IBM's net working capital expanded by more than 50 percent from 1958 to 1962, and this was accomplished without increasing the long-term debt, as striking a testimony to the company's financial might as any other. In this period World Trade not only financed its own growth but made remittances to the parent organization. In 1967 it reported revenues of $1.6 billion and a net income of $209 million, approximately twice that of only four years earlier. A few years later a prominent IBM executive would remark: "Our business is to convert foreign currencies into dollars." If this indeed were so, then clearly World Trade had succeeded admirably in its mission.

The structures of the two companies were similar, but there were important differences as well. Domestic was a federation of divisions, which changed as the product mix was altered. Each division was involved in the creation and marketing of a group of products, the provision of services, or research. They interacted with one another, shared certain technologies, and competed for funds and power. Personnel transfers in these line operations were possible at the top levels but were rather unusual. The higher one got in the division, the more one came into contact with executives from other parts of the corporation. The staffs at each were in constant communication with the central office in New York, which for the most part was comprised of men who had been promoted from the divisions; Domestic rarely went outside for management talent, preferring instead to develop its own. Virtually all the top staff personnel, at divisional levels or in New York headquarters, were Americans and tended to have similar backgrounds. In the early 1960's this meant they were middle-aged married white Protestant males who had attended top colleges and probably had known one another as they progressed through the organization.

World Trade's structure was more complex. On the surface the corporation seemed a confederation of national companies, the independence of which varied according to size, reach, and relations with the New York staffs of both World Trade and IBM Domestic. For example, IBM Deutschland, which was grossing more than $1 billion a year by the end of the 1960's and in terms of size was one of Germany's top ten industrial companies, not only produced machines for its own market but delivered them to other national companies for lease or sale in their territories. Most of the special machines designed for particular needs came out of Deutschland's research facilities. It was generally known that the IBM Domestic staff felt more at home with the top managers in Stuttgart than with those at any other national company and that on occasion they would disagree openly with the World Trade leaders, argue it out with them before Tom Watson's staff, and come out ahead.

IBM France also was a major power within World Trade. Not only was the operational headquarters in Paris, but Dick Watson was a confirmed Francophile and liked to surround himself with executives who were Frenchmen, often promoted from IBM France. Most prominent among them was Jacques Maisonrouge, an engineer who joined the company in 1948, when it was being organized, and who quickly rose to the point where in 1956 he entered headquarters as manager of market planning and research. Two years later he was placed in charge of virtually all the European operations, and in 1959 he became assistant manager for Europe. By then Maisonrouge was shuttling back and forth between Paris and New York, and there even was talk—especially among those who felt the Germans had become too powerful within the organization—of bringing him into the inner circle at World Trade headquarters. Nor was Maisonrouge the only Frenchman close to Dick Watson. Technician-managers Jean Ghertman and Raymond Pailloux had an important say in product design and resource allocation and during the early years even helped determine the form for IBM Deutschland and select its management.

World Trade's policy was to place its major research and production facilities in nations with stable pro-American or at least neutralist tendencies. Token plants would be established in Latin America, Africa, and parts of Asia, but the main ones would be in North America, Western Europe, and Japan. This meant that the World Trade offices there were primarily involved with placements and services, not manufacture. Moreover, World Trade stressed outright sales rather than leases in countries the political futures of which were clouded and the currencies of which were weak.

As might have been expected, the developed countries of the globe—Western Europe, Japan, and Canada in particular—provided most of World Trade's sales, leases, and earnings. By the late 1960's the Europeans alone accounted for fully two-thirds of revenues. Some within the organization wondered why the corporation bothered to establish offices in the undeveloped countries; certainly it wasn't in the expectation of achieving significant profits. On occasions when such a nation demanded partial ownership of its World Trade company, IBM simply would leave and in so doing often cut losses rather than relinquish a promising market. Yet IBM took pride in the fact that it functioned in about 130 countries. In some, where operations were relatively small, there was hope of future development; this happened in the OPEC countries, for example. But such was not the case with most of them. IBM went there and remained more for reasons of pride and reputation than anything else. The Watsons truly wanted to function in as many countries as possible; the "world" in World Trade would be deceiving if the corporation withdrew from the small, poor nations of Africa, Asia, and Latin America.

Still, World Trade was and is dominated by Americans and Europeans. In addition to Maisonrouge, Ghertman, and Pailloux, the early inner circle included Luigi Castaldi of Italy, Jack Brent of Canada, who was the first executive vice-president, and Thomas Cummins, an American. For a while, in the 1950's and early 1960's, it appeared that World Trade would have truly international—or at least Western—management. It was in this period that some business philosophers wrote of the emerging transnational corporation, the leaders of which would owe their allegiance to the firm, not to their countries. World Trade often was cited as the prime example of this. Arabs and Israelis worked together there even while their countries were at war, and the reason was simple, or so it was supposed: They were IBM men, having transcended national limitations. Maisonrouge, the most visible and prominent of the foreigners in the organization, was singled out as the symbol for this new kind of loyalty. He continued to move up in the company and in 1967 became president and chief operating officer, as well as a vice-president at Domestic. There was much talk at the time of his becoming chairman once Dick Watson retired.

All this was much overdone. National differences remained;

The Global Entrepreneur

Arabs and Israeli managers rarely met, while salesmen came together only during brief conventions and at schools. The genteel rivalry between IBM Deutschland and IBM France continued. More to the point, Tom Watson wasn't going to permit any further Europeanization of World Trade. In the first place, he insisted that the top staff be American; like his father, he was a strong nationalist and unwilling to see any real measure of central power migrate overseas. More important, however, Watson understood that the intense nationalism within the foreign computer industry militated against not only an American company but also any other one that seemed transnational as distinct from national. There was nothing to be gained from having a European staff; it was more important for each individual national company to be as strong, and give the appearance of being as independent, as was possible.

The organizational team that Dick Watson had put together in the late 1950's was slowly disbanded, and in its place came Americans from IBM Domestic. Brent returned to Toronto, and his place as executive vice-president was taken by Gilbert Jones, who came out of Domestic and brought with him a staff comprised of other Americans. Castaldi was shifted to a major post at IBM Italy, and some of his responsibilities were given to Charles Smith, also from Domestic, who soon began to function as Jones's chief of staff.

Increasingly Dick Watson felt out of place, and he traveled more than ever before, visiting national company headquarters, engaging in high-level corporate diplomacy, and leaving much of the actual executive work to Jones. In 1970 Dick Watson was named ambassador to France by President Nixon and left the firm. As expected, Jones succeeded him as chairman, but Maisonrouge was mollified, being told in effect that his time would come, that the time simply wasn't right for a foreigner to take command. Two years later, in a gesture to reward Maisonrouge further, he was given the powers of the chief executive officer, even though for the time being Jones retained the title of chairman.

Jones now spent much of his time helping restructure

World Trade, which was on the brink of surpassing Domestic in terms of revenues. For several years Domestic had been aware that it had become too large, its problems too diverse, to be managed as it had in Dick Watson's time. Thus, it was divided into three segments, Europe/Middle East/Africa, Asia/Pacific, and Latin America (the last was short-lived and soon was united with Asia/Pacific to form Americas/Far East). Gordon Williamson, a veteran Asia hand, became chairman of Americas/Far East, and Maisonrouge was given the same post at Europe/Middle East/Africa. Jones continued as chairman, but under the new structure Maisonrouge was in fact the operating chief of a company which was grossing more than $3.5 billion.

On the surface it appeared that the second largest segment of IBM had come under foreign domination. Such was not the case, as the individual national companies quickly realized. Many of Maisonrouge's top staff were Americans, who now were operating from Paris, controlling the nationals to a greater extent than had been the case with direction emanating from Manhattan and Armonk. Maisonrouge had been granted major power at IBM—but not before he had been transformed into what for all intents and purposes was an American. As one former leader at IBM France said, "The only thing about Maisonrouge that remained French was his accent."

The gradual Americanization of World Trade's hierarchy had minimal effect on the ways the nationals conducted business during the early 1960's, and so diplomatically was it carried out that even later there were no disruptions of any importance at the line companies. Much of this was due to managerial skill and tact. In addition, the changes were carried out with the active cooperation of and with regard for the sensibilities of top executives at the national companies. As a result of IBM's tradition of promotion from within, many of these men had come into their organizations prior to World War II and had worked under Watson senior. In those days their offices were little more than marketing arms of the parent corporation. These men belonged to organizations that had a specific territory, in which they competed against domestic firms. Their situations were similar to those that existed in the United States, in which salesmen were given exclusive territories and were measured against quotas and in terms of shares of market. Naturally, there was some measure of rivalry, but never in the field, since exclusivity was rarely breached. Leaders at the national companies by and large were former salesmen, accustomed to independence in the field and to taking directions from Americans or from headquarters; therefore, the emerging pattern and structure of the late 1960's was familiar and, for the most part, acceptable.

The major difference between the situation then and that of the earlier period, when they were young men, lay in areas of production and research. Prior to the war little of either had been done in Europe. This changed after the war, as business expanded during the boom years, matters of national pride became more important, and economics dictated a greater degree of overseas production. By the early 1960's IBM had plenty of research and development money to invest, and both Watsons were eager to expand operations in Europe and Japan. Similarly, new manufacturing facilities were established at a rapid rate, especially in Europe.

While the research arms tended to operate independently, some of the plants cooperated with one another, and it was on this level that contacts between the nationals was highest in the early years, from which the concept of commonality percolated upward. An IBM typewriter produced in Europe might have contained components contributed by plants in six countries, and the same was true for other machines and supplies, up to and including the 1400 computers.

Confidence and pride grew in Europe, to the point where World Trade asked for permission to develop its own machines, nominally in order to compete with small computers then in great demand that were being turned out by competitors. Since Domestic had no such product and Tom Watson didn't believe there was a large market for such machines in the United States, permission was granted. Design work on what was to become the 3000 series was initiated at IBM Deutschland, while components would be produced at several European factories. The 3000's were simple, nonelectronic machines that might be purchased for less than $18,000 and leased for as little as $350 a month. The line was a huge success in Europe, and demand was high in the rest of World Trade. Machines were shipped to Africa, Latin America, and the Far East; facilities in Japan were converted to their fabrication. Dick Watson was elated and suggested the 3000's be brought to the United States as well.

Serious matters of pride and economics, as well as tradition, were involved. Dick's suggestion not only contravened the arrangements between the two companies but was seen as a sign of arrogance. What no foreign computer manufacturer had dared do was now being recommended by World Trade—no less than an invasion of the American market. This was not to be tolerated, even though the idea was eminently reasonable from a marketing point of view. That there was a demand for small, simple, inexpensive computers was becoming increasingly obvious, and already several companies, among them Digital Equipment and Hewlett-Packard, had started to capitalize upon it. IBM held back, preferring instead to fill out its second-generation lines and prepare for the third. Importation or production of the 3000's would enable the company to enter this part of the market at a low cost and probably come to dominate it within a short period. Yet Domestic's leaders argued against such a move. Because of cost differentials between Europe and the United States, they argued, the 3000's would be priced out of the market for most American users and so should not be produced domestically. Nor could they recommend importation, although no convincing reasons could be marshaled to support their opposition. Dick understood the situation and backed down, diplomatically suggesting that in any case, World Trade lacked the resources to initiate production for the American market. The issue was allowed to die.

The episode did have an important effect on Tom Watson's thinking, however. He was already deeply involved in planning the third generation. Not only would the new machines require enormous amounts of capital, but they would strain Domestic's human and physical resources as well. Because World Trade had demonstrated its abilities at research and production, it might be called upon for assistance and cooperation. That way potential rivalries would be dissolved, new ties created, and a truly international corporation formed, one that possessed the benefits of both unity and diversity. This was to be one of the side effects of the third generation. By the mid-1960's World Trade was the equal of Domestic, but it was far less independent than had been the case in the 1950's and earlier in the decade. Thomas Watson may have divided the world between his two sons, but now his elder son was drawing the pieces together again.

10

The Incomparable 360

DURING the late spring and early summer of 1966 IBMers at the Armonk headquarters might have encountered someone who clearly was out of place. Tom Wise, a tall, hulking southerner, often appeared in wrinkled suits that didn't quite fit. His ties weren't of the proper hue and tended to go awry. Wise's hair wasn't trimmed or as carefully combed as it might have been; this alone would have marked him as an outsider, even at a time when discipline had relaxed somewhat.

Security was tight at Armonk. One could scarcely get on the grounds without a pass, much less go through the offices, speak with anyone around, and explore recesses closed to all but top management. Yet Wise did and saw all he wanted.

The reason for this was made known to everyone he met. Wise was an editor at *Fortune* magazine, at the firm to write a story about recent developments there. In itself this was nothing special; articles on IBM had become a staple for such magazines as *Forbes, Business Week, Dun's,* and *Fortune.* Generally speaking, the company had always received a good press, and on the basis of experience, there was no reason to assume it would be any different this time. Thus, for the first time in its history IBM allowed the curtain usually drawn over its internal workings to be parted a trifle. Wise was permitted to prowl the hallways and offices, usually accompanied by several public relations men, who would also audit his interviews. Otherwise, he had a free hand, and of course, IBM could have no control over what he wrote.

The result of Wise's research was two articles that appeared that autumn, both of which dealt with the development of IBM's 360 line of computers. The titles are an indication of Wise's message: In September it was: "I.B.M.'s $5,000,000,000 Gamble," and the following month's *Fortune* featured an article entitled "The Rocky Road to the Marketplace." In each was found a record of personality clashes, errors in judgment, and what appeared a somewhat reckless method of confronting problems. Bob Evans, a major figure in the 360 enterprise, was quoted as saying, "We called this project, 'You bet your company,'" and the author showed how the wagers were placed. It was a dramatic story, one well told. Wise concluded that the difficulties in the project would probably harm the company. The nature of the 360 experience thus far had "done something to that extraordinary I.B.M. mystique of success. The mystique is probably gone for good—though the success may just go on becoming greater and greater."

IBM's management was furious about the article; never again would the firm open itself in this way to an outsider. Wise's articles became a touchstone of sorts for all who hoped to understand how the company operated, and for several years they shaped the industry's perception of IBM. But as accurate in details of fact and as vivid in description as they were, they suffered from a lack of perspective, which, of course, couldn't have been recognized at the time but became evident later. In retrospect the decision to go ahead with the 360's appears to have been more sensible and studied than it did in 1966. It was a logical step; although there were problems, blunders, and dangers along the way, it ended successfully. As for IBM's "mystique," rather than shattered, it was strengthened. The machines were enormously profitable, even more than the 1400's had been. In fact, they remade the industry. Moreover, the 360's provided IBM with a reputation in technology akin to what it previously had enjoyed in sales. The episode also demonstrated that Tom Watson was every bit as bold and resourceful as his father had been.

By 1961 data processing dominated thinking at IBM. Approximately three out of every four sales and rental dollars ($1.7 billion that year) were derived from computers and related services and products, and the same held true for profits ($167.5 million). Watson was proposing that sometime in the near future this part of the corporation should dedicate itself to a single line of machines. The risks were such that in case of failure IBM's share of the market could be sliced by half. Given the economies of scale and the nature of the industry, this could mean a great deal of red ink on the ledgers. The corporation would survive, but as the first among equals, not the undisputed leader of the data processing industry. Watson hadn't gone so far as to wager his company on the outcome of the venture, but at stake were his own reputation and position at the firm. In such dire circumstances—with earnings down and dividends cut—he would have been obliged to step down from the chairmanship, taking with him many of those executives involved in the project and leaving a vacuum at the top and a company in disarray. Thus, more was involved than "mystique." Prior to making the initial commitment, Watson had to make certain that some kind of decision was necessary, that it was the best course available, and that the odds were in his favor.

That a third generation of computers soon would be on the way became evident in the late 1950's and early 1960's. This was due to the same forces that had created the second generation: the technological imperative and the nature of competition within the industry. The impetus came from the laboratories and was then taken up by businessmen. The new technology and product involved this time was the integrated circuit, an extremely small and delicately etched component on which several functions previously performed by groups of transistors could be contained. Just as a foot-long array of transistors might have replaced a large bank of electronic tubes, so a single integrated circuit might accomplish the same functions as the transistors and do them faster and with less expense. In time developments in integrated circuitry would result in what amounted to "a computer on a chip" and in hand-held models more powerful than some of the early computers that filled a room and required extensive plumbing to cool down the tubes. All this was in the future, of course; in the late 1950's the integrated circuit was still exotic, a device created to serve the needs of the military and space programs.

As was the case with many electronic products developed in this period, research was simultaneously conducted at several laboratories, so that no single firm or individual can claim credit for the entire invention. The diffusion technique for placing several components on a single chip came out of the Bell Laboratories in 1955. Texas Instruments created a crude version of the integrated circuit in 1958 and three years later demonstrated how it might be used in small computers. Meanwhile, the armed services funded several research projects, most of which were connected in one way or another with computers. Specifically, they wanted small devices that might be carried on and direct weapons or, in the case of the space program, satellites. Multimillion-dollar grants were received by Westinghouse and RCA; IBM had one from the Navy. Working independently, Fairchild Camera organized a subsidiary, Fairchild Semiconductor, which in 1959 developed the planer technique for connecting components on the chip. Other advances followed in rapid order.

By 1963 integrated circuits were being used in the creation of the Apollo guidance system and the Minuteman missile program. Only a few firms, notably Texas Instruments and Fairchild Camera, produced the expensive components. Quality control was a problem, and so, of course, was cost. Still, by then it was evident that once both these were overcome, integrated circuits would be used in computers.

Already several companies were at work on this. The arrival of the integrated circuit would mean the end of the second-generation machines. Only two years earlier it had appeared they would remain in production through the end of the decade. In 1962 several companies were still producing vacuum-tube models. Some 626 million transistors and diodes were turned out in 1963, at an average cost of only 29 cents. Yet such were the dynamics of the industry that even then leading companies knew they soon would have to convert to the production of integrated circuits. Computers based on chips rather than on transistors were the next logical development in the technology. IBM could not afford to be a laggard in this area, so it proceeded at a rapid pace, exploring several methods of approaching the technology.

The company might have been obliged to create a new line of machines even had integrated circuits not existed. As has been indicated, Honeywell had prepared a group of computers to compete head-on with the 1400's. The industry had wind of them in 1961. Two years later Honeywell started taking orders for the H-200, a machine capable of using 1400 software which was faster, more powerful, and less expensive than the 1401. IBM had known this was coming, and its salesmen were prepared. They informed customers that IBM shortly would present a new family of machines, far in advance of the H-200's, and urged them to defer placing orders. By offering discounts and special trade-in deals, they were able to maintain most installations. Still, it was evident that the 1400's had peaked, having reached the end of their product cycles, and that after a while even deep discounts would not serve to maintain old loyalties. Furthermore, IBM was risking charges of unfair competition by making such assertions; unless a new line indeed was on the way, complaints against the firm might be lodged with the Federal Trade Commission and the Justice Department.

Related to the counterattack against Honeywell was an attempt to enter a market it appeared IBM had abandoned—namely, that for giant computers. As has been shown, the company had suffered losses on the STRETCH machines and had decided there was no substantial market for such products, at least not one that merited any special attention. But if the third-generation constellation could be made sufficiently flexible to replace both the 1400's and the 7000's, might it not be expanded to include one or more models to compete with Control Data's large machines?

In 1961 the industry learned of the forthcoming CDC 3600, a system that could easily surpass the IBM 7090, while plans were being made for the 6600, with a capacity far in excess of that promised by STRETCH, but for which chairman William Norris had only limited hopes. The initial 3600's were placed in 1963, and as orders came in at a rapid rate, IBM and the other manufacturers began reassessing their sentiments regarding the size of the market for such machines. Then CDC opened the order books for the 6600's, and interest was so great that Norris was obliged to embark upon an unexpected expansion program. For the first time CDC entered the long-term capital markets. The company's debt, which had been practically nothing in 1962, went to almost $20 million the following year and then doubled and redoubled in 1964 and 1965. While Wise and others talked and spoke of the Watson gambles, Norris truly had become a high roller; having taken the lead in a rapidly growing segment of the market, he meant to hold it in the face of competition from anyone, Watson included.

How long could this last? In 1963, while discussing the 360's, IBM indicated that none of the machines would be large enough to compete with the proposed 6600's. But at the same time some salesmen told customers that they might do well to hold back on purchases or leases of Control Data machines, that IBM indeed was preparing to enter the field with its own giants. Thus, the nature of the competition not only mandated the new third-generation family but dictated its scope. If IBM could capture a few dozen or more sales that might have gone to CDC, it could lessen the risks involved in financing its major venture. As had been the case when it competed against the Honeywell 200's, IBM was almost inviting legal actions by permitting its salesmen to speak as they did to potential customers. At the time the risks seemed worth taking.

IBM might have been obliged to create a third generation even had there been no technological advances or to meet competition on the part of Honeywell, Control Data, and the others. This was so because there was a growing dissension within the corporation itself, which might be resolved by focusing attention and resources on competitors instead of on one another. The company was in the midst of an internal reorganization in the early 1960's, and Watson hoped to eliminate some of his problems by creating a new series.

As has been indicated, there was concern at headquarters about the way World Trade had demonstrated its independence. Several Domestic executives interpreted the creation and marketing of the 3000 series as an implied challenge to their domination. Tom Watson had another view of the situation. If this was allowed to continue, he thought, there would be wasteful duplication of effort. Proliferation of product lines made little sense, and he called for a unified effort on the part of both corporations to design and produce a third-generation family that would be sold throughout the world. Thus, Domestic would join with IBM Deutschland, IBM France, and other major national entities, and in this way the lines between the two segments would be partially eliminated, as would be the rivalries. This was one of the reasons Dick Watson's original internationally minded team was broken up and replaced by Gilbert Jones and his Americans and why Dick started to devote more time to his duties on Domestic's board than to those of chief executive for World Trade. Maisonrouge was in Europe to help coordinate the efforts, and he became an important link between the two firms, which were coming together to create and market the 360's. It was a clear case of the product's helping to dictate organization—and at the same time to unite two potentially antagonistic forces to meet the common enemy.

The Incomparable 360

A somewhat different situation existed within Domestic itself, where an altered perception of the nature of the industry and product line also resulted in a major shake-up. In the 1950's it was believed that there were two separate markets for computers. Medium-sized machines would be leased or sold to many large and small corporations, while large computers would find their ways into government, agencies, and some corporate headquarters. That there would be overlaps in the market appeared unavoidable, but initially this was not an important problem.

For this reason Watson had supported separate funding, research, development, and production programs for his two major second-generation lines. Each was to be handled by a different sales force, and the same would be true for services. T. Vincent Learson was in charge of both programs, and he, too, couldn't foresee any difficulties.

These soon developed. The 1400 medium-sized machines came out of General Products, while the Data Systems Division turned out the 7000's at a different plant. All went smoothly in 1959 and 1960, and there were few difficulties in 1961, when both series were well received. Then, as additional versions of each were produced and prices started coming down, the lower end of the 7000's came head-on against augmented 1400's. Often it would be learned that one IBM division had placed its machines at the expense of the other, not by beating out Honeywell, GE, or UNIVAC. By 1962 there had developed a rivalry between General Products and Data Systems that rather than sharpening skills was sapping strengths and was more damaging than any frictions that might have developed between Domestic and World Trade. The creation of a single line of machines by the two divisions could bring this to an end.

What Watson had in mind, then, was an all-company effort, coordinated by Domestic's board of directors and led by Learson, in which each major segment of the computer business would have a say and make a contribution. At first there was to be a competition of ideas, but after the decision was made, all would join to produce and market the new line. At a time when most companies its size were thinking in terms of decentralization, Watson was gathering power to the board, in preparation for the new effort. This was to be the critical phase, that of organization for the assault, and in it Learson emerged as the central figure.

Vin Learson, who was fifty years old in 1961, had been at the corporation for half his life. Then and now, he was considered the quintessential IBM man, one devoted to the company, shrewd, tough, and energetic. Learson was over six and a half feet tall, a bulky man who looked like an Ivy League fullback who kept himself in shape. Indeed, he was a Harvard graduate who went from college to the corporation, and like most top executives of his era, he began in sales. After a highly successful stint in the Boston area he was transferred to Washington, the key office during World War II. Afterward Learson became a corporate troubleshooter, a gypsy who put in time in New York, Philadelphia, and Detroit, and with each shift he moved higher in the corporate pyramid.

Along the way he earned a reputation as a tough taskmaster and a brutal opponent, a person who whipped his staff into shape, was merciless in dealing with less than outstanding performers, and was capable of destroying an opponent. Even Tom Watson stood in awe of Learson, one of the few men willing to contest him at an open meeting. Of all the men in the executive suites, Learson was the only true "wild duck" who seemed incapable of being tamed. Yet with all this he clearly was an IBM product, proud of the company, knowledgeable about its inner workings, and willing to accept its discipline.

Learson became a vice-president in the 1950's and, as has been indicated, joined Tom Watson in urging Watson senior to make a major effort in computers. He took a seat on the board in 1961, at the start of the third-generation campaign, and also was a group executive in charge of data processing, which in corporate terms meant he was to be in command of the operation. Learson would serve Watson as Grant and Eisenhower had Lincoln and Roosevelt. As had been the case with the generals, he had reason to believe that success would mean promotion to a top post at the corporation. There would be a long wait for the chairmanship, however; Tom Watson was only forty-seven years old in 1961 and had no intention of stepping down, while Dick was known to have ambitions for the top post.

Initially it seemed that IBM would accelerate research for an ongoing program at Data Systems. When it had appeared that the STRETCH computers had failed, technicians there had begun work on a new series of transistorized machines, known as the 8000's. By downgrading and expansion these might replace both the 1400's and 7000's. Costs would decline sharply if the machines were produced on a worldwide basis, and conversions would be relatively simple since the 8000's could use software design for the earlier models. Moreover, they could be brought to market rapidly, with orders being taken in late 1961 for delivery a few months later.

Learson was unconvinced. In the first place, the 8000's clearly gave the appearance of being stopgap machines, based upon what soon would be an outmoded technology. Data Systems thought the line could carry the company through until 1968. Learson believed other firms would have integrated-circuit machines with larger memory banks on the market long before then, and although IBM might compete on a cost basis, profit margins would be cut severely. Moreover, Watson had mandated management to place IBM in the forefront of technology, and the 8000's would be a step backward in this respect. Also, there wouldn't be sufficient incentive for users to switch from their old machines, and this would harm the new line. The idea was to end proliferation; the 8000's might worsen the situation. In all, this was not the kind of program upon which to stake the future of so large an enterprise. Thus, the 8000's were scrapped. Similarly Learson rejected a plan to expand the 7000's in both directions—to produce larger and smaller versions. A fresh approach was required. Scientists and technicians who had worked on both ideas were reassigned, with most going to a project at Data Systems, which Learson called, appropriately, the New Product Line, or NPL.

The NPL ran into difficulties from the start. Gerrit

Blaauw, who had been a major force in the 8000 venture, attempted to introduce some of its concepts into the NPL. Gene Amdahl, who had been involved in other programs at the time, took a different approach and attempted to design an all-integrated circuit line that was truly revolutionary in concept. The two men clashed, the research teams divided, and for a while the project foundered.

Meanwhile, Learson set about establishing an organization to manage the technologies, decide upon formulations, create the machines, and then market and service them. Ideally this would have involved the creation of an entire new division and the elimination or merger of the old ones, but such was out of the question, given intracompany rivalries and easily bruised egos. Instead, in the autumn of 1961 he set up a special committee on which would be represented each major segment of the corporation involved with the New Product Line. The Systems Programming, Research, Engineering, and Development Committee—which naturally was known as SPREAD—brought together men who previously had been involved in the 1400, 7000, and 8000 series, and as should have been expected, each was wary of the others. General Products, the most reluctant of the divisions to cooperate because of its pride in the 1400's, was mollified by having its vice-president, John Haanstra, named committee chairman.

It didn't work out well. As had happened in the labs, there was little progress, the result in part of Haanstra's lack of commitment to the idea. Unhappy with the situation, Learson had Haanstra promoted to the presidency of General Products and out of SPREAD's chairmanship. His place there was taken by Robert Evans, who was in charge of General Products' planning and development operations. He arrived with a reputation for toughness, a strong loyalty to Learson, and a commitment to a new line. Evans prodded SPREAD into action, and out of this, in December 1961, came the strategy for what was then the NPL and soon became known as the 360's.

The SPREAD report recommended a completely new family of computers, based upon current technology—that is to say, the use of integrated circuits. There would be models less powerful than the 1400's, and some larger than the 7000's. Each would be compatible with the others; in the jargon of the time, interfacing was deemed crucial. As had been industry practice, there would be a full line initially, while different 360 configurations would be brought out over a period of several years; variants would be manufactured and marketed as demand developed. Most important, the report implied that the 360's might not be compatible with the 1400's and 7000's. This meant that software and ancillary equipment then being used on the second-generation machines could not be switched to the new ones. Upgrading would be impossible.

If the plan were followed, IBM's second-generation equipment would become obsolete as soon as the third generation appeared. Those who owned or already had leased the old machines might hold onto them, but the number of new placements would decline precipitously, and leasing rates would have to be revised sharply.

On the face of it, this seemed almost suicidal. The first of the popular 1401's had been installed less than a year and a half earlier, and the 7070's weren't much older. It would be several years before they would return their costs, after which time profits could be extremely high, even in the face of competition from UNIVAC and the knowledge that Honeywell was preparing its H-200's. Yet Learson and Evans were suggesting that IBM play a role in killing off its two most promising lines. Still, if all went as planned, the company not only would have solidified and even expanded its industry position but also would have both a group of machines that could be marketed for perhaps a decade or even more and a corporate reorganization that could serve it well during the Watson era and beyond.

All this would cost enormous amounts of money. When finally completed, the research and development program alone came to more than half a billion dollars. New manufacturing facilities would have to be planned and constructed, and tens of thousands of additional workers taken on and trained. As has been seen, the changeover deeply affected World Trade. Scores of executives and scientists would be shifted into new posts, and those who performed well knew that they probably would emerge as IBM's next generation of leaders. For example, at New Products it was generally thought that Gene Amdahl, who had won his fight against Gerrit Blaauw, would rise to a top management post if all went well.

The report also meant that IBM would have to marry itself to its bankers. Although it was true that the corporation was generating large and ever-increasing revenues, they would not suffice to fund the program. It had happened before, when Tom Watson had talked his father into taking on a large amount of debt in order to get into computers. On that occasion he had relied upon Albert Williams for support and expertise, and once again he was to fill that role. Along with Learson and Amdahl, Williams was to be a key figure in the operation. To signal this, he was named president of the corporation in 1961, a move designed more than anything else to impress Wall Street and enhance his stature there.

Learson understood this and didn't view Williams's new prominence as a threat to his position at the company. As the project developed, it became evident that Learson was moving into the position of heir apparent and that Williams, who might have challenged him, wasn't even considering such a move. He was content to serve Tom Watson in much the same way as John Phillips had his father—namely, as a loyal aide whose personality enabled him to subordinate his own career to that of others. By so doing—by posing no threat to apparent rivals—he had risen rapidly at the corporation and in his own way had achieved power.

Williams's career to that point had been truly impressive. An accountant by training and vocation, he had joined IBM in 1936 and, along with other future executives, started as a salesman. Williams had a good, if not outstanding, record, but from the first he had other objectives in mind. Soon he was shifted to headquarters, where he was assigned to work in the treasurer's office. John Phillips was impressed with his intelligence and abilities and made Williams his protégé. In 1942, after having been with the firm for only six years, Williams was named comptroller and so became one of the corporation's officers. By then he had become close to Watson senior and served him not only as a financial adviser but also as a surrogate son while Tom and Dick were away. When Tom arrived at headquarters, Williams was one of those entrusted with his orientation, and on occasion he served as intermediary when father and son squabbled. In 1947 he became IBM's treasurer, and the following year a vice-president as well. Williams was placed on the board in 1951 and at that time was considered Phillips's likely successor as executive vice-president, a position he occupied in 1954.

At some companies the executive vice-president plays an important role in day-to-day operations, and to an extent this was the case at IBM. But Williams had another, even more important set of tasks. During the next seven years the corporation's lease base expanded rapidly, and this was his primary concern. Williams had a dominant voice in the establishment of leasing terms, and he acted as liaison for IBM with the financial community. By the late 1950's some financial publications observed that in order to understand IBM, one had to think of it as a bank with a manufacturing subsidiary, that the corporation made more money from leasing charges than outright sales. If this were truly so—and a strong case might be made for this view—Williams was one of the handful of key men at headquarters. Now he was to have responsibility for the financing of an enterprise which, as Tom Wise noted, would cost more than twice as much as the Manhattan Project—which had produced the atomic bomb—and would be the largest privately funded venture in history.

In no year of the 1950's did IBM report capital expenditures of more than $340 million. In 1963, as the corporation tooled up for production, expenditures totaled $570 million and were rising rapidly. They were more than $1 billion in 1965 and $1.6 billion the following year. Most of this would be paid by earnings and depreciation, but a great majority of the new machines, like the old, would be leased rather than purchased outright and so would have to be financed. The combination of large capital expenditures and increased leasing strained IBM's resources, making Williams's tasks all the more delicate and thus enhancing his position within the corporate hierarchy.

IBM was in a highly liquid situation when the 360 program began. Current assets were more than four times current liabilities, and cash items alone were twice the latter figure. Thus, Williams was in a good position to start spending money, and he went into the financial markets for both long- and short-term loans and credits. IBM's long-term debt rose from $425 million in 1961 to $522 million in 1967, and during the same period current liabilities went from $158 million to $1.16 billion; the asset-to-liability ratio was now 1.18 to 1, and cash items were $347 below current liabilities, fairly normal for some companies but unusually thin for IBM.

As striking as the financial turnabout was, the increase in the corporation's size was even more impressive. Six large new plants—one apiece in France and Germany, the others in the United States—were constructed for the production of 360 components; from having been the world's leading purchaser of electronic parts, IBM became its major manufacturer, surpassing Texas Instruments and Fairchild, and all its units were used in the company's own products. In five years the company expanded its work force by more than 50,000 worldwide, thus increasing its payroll by a third. In 1961 IBM carried its plant and property at less than $2 billion; in 1967 these were on the books at more than $6.6 billion.

With Learson's leadership, Amdahl's technology, and Williams's financial acumen, Watson didn't wager the company so much as rebuild it. Industry insiders and a few technical journals appreciated what was happening years before the story became a feature in the business magazines. Some compared it with the massing of troops and equipment for the D-Day invasion of France during World War II; others put it in the same class as the space program. And competitors sought rumors and sifted evidence on what was occurring within the corporation for information on the progress or lack of it on the 360's, when the machines would be ready, and, of course, how they would affect their own fortunes.

Some of the talk was fantasy, such as an assertion that Dr. Emanuel Piore, who remained in charge of research, had come up with a radically different memory system by which the contents of the Library of Congress could be fitted into a shoebox. There was much talk of personality clashes within the organization, impending departures, mixups, financial blunders, and at one point a rumor that Dick Watson had given his brother an ultimatum: that Learson or he would have to go. But the most persistent rumor—one that contained a certain amount of truth —was that the 360 systems would resemble a multiheaded missile insofar as marketing was concerned. One group of machines, the largest, would take aim at the Control Data 6600's, while smaller versions would eclipse the Honeywell 200's. According to one such rumor, IBM was preparing 360 variants to meet every challenge, to offer more processing power for the lease or sales dollar and at more attractive terms than could be afforded by any other firm.

This, then, was the talk of the industry in 1962 and 1963. Most of the speculation revolved around future market strategy and legal implications—whether or not IBM would risk such an assault in the light of possible antitrust actions and, if so, what it might do to the Seven Dwarfs and others in the industry. That their situations and positions would be altered was obvious; several might be obliged to discontinue operations, enter into mergers, or cut back drastically.

The larger firms prepared themselves for the 360's in two ways. They would intensify work on their own third-generation machines, and in addition, law firms employed by competitors were alerted and asked to prepare the groundwork for appeals to the Justice Department and the courts. In early 1964 one industry observer quipped that the 360 program had caused shortages in three professions—IBM was cornering the market in scientists and technicians, while Control Data, Honeywell, RCA, and the rest were taking on antitrust lawyers by the score.

By then it seemed evident that the 360's would not only transform the industry but open the way for what might be a generation of litigation.

Watson appreciated the risks, and he, too, started to assemble a strong legal team, one that would go along with his revamped management and market approach. A key role would be played by the firm of Cravath, Swaine & Moore, the most experienced in the field, for which IBM had already become a major source of litigation fees and which was expanded in preparation for new attacks. IBM also took on its own legal staff and in time would acquire Burke Marshall, formerly head of the antitrust division of the Justice Department during the Kennedy years, and Kennedy's attorney general, Nicholas de B. Katzenbach. Once litigation began, competitors complained that the very same individuals who had prepared the case for the government were now in IBM's employ. Norris of Control Data was furious at what he deemed an unfair attempt to outflank and subvert justice. Whatever he might win on the marketing front, so he believed, could be lost in the courts, and to platoons of lawyers, not technicians or even salesmen. On one occasion he and an associate were looking out the window at a long line of black limousines. "Someone important must have died," said the friend. "No," snapped Norris. "That's just the IBM lawyers going out to lunch."

Although most of the talk within the industry revolved around marketing, financing, and possible antitrust actions, there was relatively little hard information on technology. The large capital expenses and the pattern of hiring indicated that IBM was planning to mass-produce the 360's on scales previously unknown, that for the first time in the computer industry, true assembly-line techniques would be employed. Furthermore, the operation would be as self-contained within the company as possible: IBM would place fewer orders with vendors and subcontractors than previously had been the case. What the Ford River Rouge plant complex had been for automobiles in the 1920's, the IBM worldwide network would be for computers in the 1960's.

The Incomparable 360

It was no secret, either, that IBM was going to create a new line of software—programs—to go with the machines. Since there would be no compatibility with the 1400's and 8000's, the company had to start fresh. In addition, the demands on the part of users had changed, becoming more complex and specialized. Those who required special software had to be accommodated, and in some cases the state of the software would determine which computer a user would lease. It was, then, part of a package, and in fact, hardware and software were marketed together; one could not have the IBM software unless one had an IBM computer. And if IBM were the only purveyor of the kind of software required, the user by necessity would have to take an IBM machine. It was tantamount to a situation in which General Motors produced not only automobiles but fuel as well, and in order to have access to the fuel, one would have to buy a GM car.

This complicated the tasks for those who hoped to compete with IBM by turning out plug-compatible machines, as Honeywell had done with its early models and would profit on with the 200's. Watson was as certain that third-generation compatibles would appear as he was of antitrust actions. But he also believed his rivals would be unable to come up with the quality and quantity of his software; the leasers of the CDC 6600's, for example, would have to make do with what the industry considered inadequate prepackaged programs or develop their own. Norris had never made an important effort in this area, believing that users who wanted and understood his machines tended to be sophisticated in matters of this kind and would rather create their own programs than pay for software they really didn't need. Watson thought otherwise; he believed some of them at least would prefer the large 360's rather than the 6600's for software reasons and so would enable IBM to cut into a market in which it previously had been an also-ran.

What was to prevent some of the other companies from copying the new software, just as they had the second-generation hardware? Of course, they might make the attempt, but the legal implications of the two actions were quite different. In the nature of things there was little that was unique about any of the second-generation machines. Companies conducted research along parallel paths, so infringements of patents would have been difficult, if not impossible, to prove. Software was a different matter; programs were unique and probably came under the copyright law. Thus, lawsuits might be entered against firms the programs of which closely resembled those created at IBM. Of course, as the capabilities of computers usually increased regularly and new programs had to be created, some old ones would have become obsolete by the time they were copied.

There was no indication that the Justice Department would prosecute IBM for dominating this segment of the industry, any more than it would a publishing house the novels of which became best sellers. Since IBM planned to offer both hardware and software as a package, customers wouldn't know how much each might have cost individually. Some within the industry suspected that the larger portion of profits derived from software, that a pattern was emerging similar to that which had existed with the tabulators of the 1920's and 1930's, by which the machines themselves cost relatively little and IBM made most of its profits from the sale of cards. There were differences, of course, but the principles seemed strikingly alike in the early 1960's. Some competitors spoke of antitrust actions forcing IBM to sell and lease hardware and software separately, so that the rival machines could be adapted to the IBM software and challenge the 360's, which they felt were vulnerable.

One major reason for this hope derived from a decision made by IBM's Logic Committee in 1961. This group, responsible for decisions on what would become the hearts of the new machines, was reluctant to come out in favor of the new and yet unproved integrated circuits. Design had not yet proceeded to the point where testing and early production were possible. In addition, the integrated circuits were to be mass-produced by computer-directed assembly lines, itself an evolving technique. Thus, it would be risky to base the entire project upon such a weak foundation. The 360's would be stalled should any foul-ups develop, and losses in areas of credibility and reputation could damage future leases and sales. Then, too, flaws in the designs might show up later, resulting in call-backs and modifications that would cast doubt on the reliability of the entire series.

For these reasons the Logic Committee opted for devices more advanced than transistors but not quite as complex as integrated circuits of the kind being turned out by Texas Instruments and Fairchild, something the company referred to as solid logic technology. Transistors and diodes would be produced individually and then soldered into place on a chip. The resulting component was reliable and worked as well as integrated circuits, but were not as inexpensive as the latter would be once full-scale operations commenced. This implied that third-generation machines produced later by competitors might be able to undercut IBM in matters of price, although at the time this was not certain.

Once this decision was made and design plans were completed, Evans assigned the production tasks to different units within the organization. The 360/30, which was to replace the 1401, would come out of the central plant at Poughkeepsie, New York, while the more powerful 360/40's were to be manufactured at the Hursley installation in Great Britain. Other variants were to be produced at the new facilities once they were completed. All was proceeding according to plan, and the corporation's cash flow was so favorable that in early 1963 Williams approved the accelerated repayment of a $160 million loan from Prudential Insurance.

Then problems developed. There were snags in the design and assembly processes; rivalries Watson and Learson had believed resolved flared up once again. Amdahl became the center of a controversy about the use of hybrid integrated circuits; he was not happy with them. The company had to return to the money markets and borrow additional funds at unfavorable rates. To top it all, there were rumblings out of Honeywell and Control Data. The H-200's, announced in late 1963, made their first placements the following March, and the reception was so good as to take some of the shine away from the upcoming 360/30's. Apparently some IBM salesmen, fearful of losing placements, were urging clients to hold back on Honeywell orders, doing so in such a way as not only to violate corporate policy but also to open IBM to antitrust charges.

Then, in August 1963, Control Data announced its 6600's, which were to be ready for delivery the following year. At the time the 360 series was stalled, in large part because of shortages of components and lack of proper coordination between internal suppliers. Watson was irate. The largest and supposedly most efficient firm in the industry was being bested by this small relative newcomer. In a blistering memo to those involved, he observed that in the Control Data laboratory where the 6600's were developed "there are only 34 people, 'including the janitor.' Of these, 14 are engineers and 4 are programmers, and only one person has a Ph.D., a relatively junior programmer. To the outsider, the laboratory appeared to be cost conscious, hard working, and highly motivated"; Watson clearly didn't think the same could be said for those who worked on the 360 project. "Contrasting this modest effort with our own vast development activities, I fail to understand why we have lost our industry leadership position by letting someone else offer the world's most powerful computer." Implied in this was a promise to reshuffle the management if conditions did not improve markedly.

In 1962 Watson had told a group of IBM customers that he hoped to have a full line of machines ready for sale and lease by April 1964. In March 1964 he conceded that the pledge had been "ill-advised," that most of the machines were still in the process of being completed. But he couldn't wait—not if IBM were to undercut Honeywell and Control Data. So on April 7, at simultaneous press conferences in sixty-two American cities and fourteen overseas, IBM unveiled the 360's and announced that orders would be taken.

Almost immediately competitors claimed that this was a deception, a ploy aimed at taking placements from them under false pretenses, since Watson wasn't prepared to make deliveries within a reasonable amount of time. The charges struck a familiar chord for those with long memories; just as John Patterson had had his phantom cash registers when Watson senior was in his employ, so Watson junior seemed to have fabricated an entire line of phantom computers. This, indeed, was close to the truth; IBM conceded that it was running into production snags and that costs were mounting. For the first time in more than a generation, the company was obliged to raise capital by selling equity; its shareholders purchased $371 million worth of stock in a new underwriting, all of which was to go into the 360 project.

Problems continued to dog the company, and now Watson carried out his threat and shifted his management team. Dr. Piore was released from all operational duties so he could go into the field as a technological troubleshooter. In an unusual move for IBM, his place was taken by an outsider, Eugene Fubini, a former assistant secretary of defense who had also served as director of research and engineering at the Pentagon. Fubini became a group vice-president, a post usually reserved for those who had come through the ranks. Then Tom and Dick Watson, Learson, and Williams constituted themselves the Management Review Committee, a group executive to make future decisions regarding the 360 project.

Both Williams and Learson were to pay for errors, although it wasn't realized at the time. Williams moved out of the presidency to take a place as chairman of the executive committee, and Learson became the new president and, as such, Watson's heir apparent, eclipsing both Williams and Dick Watson. Learson was a year older than Tom Watson, however, and so might be prevented from occupying the top place by the simple unraveling of time—since he would retire first. In the mid-1960's the succession remained in doubt.

As it happened, the 360 line proved a huge success. The first of the 360/40's were installed in April 1965, at which time there was a record order backlog for the machines. Before the end of the year the initial 30's, 50's, and 65's made their appearances, to as great an acclaim. By then the production problems

229

had been worked out; all was proceeding smoothly. The transition at IBM from the second to the third generation was taking place with fewer problems than might have been anticipated given the early tangles in production. Within two years the 360 line accounted for almost half the total value of IBM installations in the United States, and the company's share of the domestic market actually increased slightly. The same happened overseas, where the 360's swamped the competition.

This massive venture, the centerpiece of the third generation, created problems, too, in that it reshaped the industry. So great were the economies realized, in both production and use, that placements on the part of almost all manufacturers increased more rapidly than anyone had expected. In 1963 there were approximately 11,700 machines in use in the United States. This figure doubled by 1965 and redoubled by 1969. But although production and placements increased, they did not bring anticipated profits for all companies. Like IBM, they made the transition to the third generation; but in some cases the costs were too great to bear, and several had to give up and leave the field.

Then, too, the manner by which IBM had introduced—and then failed to produce within a reasonable time—its third-generation machine variants prompted a new wave of legal activity. As anticipated, Control Data proved central to this phase of activity.

In August 1964, as CDC prepared to make its initial 6600 delivery, IBM made a formal announcement of what its salesmen had talked about for close to a year: It announced the 360/91, which, according to specifications, would be a large machine, more flexible than the 6600, with superior software and lower lease prices. Conceding that the machines weren't ready for installations, IBM accepted orders and made pledges of delivery. This naturally cut into CDC's sales and leases, and in order to keep orders already booked, the company was obliged to revise its prices downward and make other adjustments. CDC's profits, which had soared early in the decade, now

The Incomparable 360

leveled off, and in 1966 the company actually showed a net loss, attributed in large part to the manner of IBM's competition.

As for IBM, it kept pushing back the delivery dates for the 91's and in early 1967 discontinued its sales and lease efforts, while it promised to fill those orders already accepted.

Norris was irate. He had suspected from the start that the 91's had been priced so low as all but to ensure future losses. The machine was never meant to be viable, but instead was a phantom computer put forward to deter customers from taking delivery on the 6600's. In other words, IBM was trying to push Control Data out of the industry by using unfair and clearly illegal tactics. The company complained to the Justice Department about this in 1966, and again the following year, to no avail. In 1968 the antitrust division told Norris (falsely, as it turned out) that no prosecution of IBM was being considered. Disgusted and half-convinced that collusion had taken place, Norris decided to act on his own, and in early December 1968, Control Data filed antitrust complaints against IBM. Stirred, the government a month later filed its own suit, one that was parallel to CDC's. Thus began what would turn out to be a prolonged period of antitrust litigation in the computer industry.

Finally, the advent of the 360's helped accelerate the growth of several subindustries, most of which were satellites of the new series. Leasing companies proliferated, purchasing the 360's and then renting them out on terms better than those offered by IBM. Service firms, which purchased or leased the 360's and then sold data to users who didn't want to lease or rent, sprouted in all parts of the country and often were founded and operated by former IBMers. Manufacturers of small machines not covered by the 360 spectrum enjoyed major increases in sales and profits. There was a large business in used second-generation computers, the low prices of which made them attractive to many small and medium-sized firms. The 360's, then, resembled a school of whales, which attracted pilot fish and scores of parasites—as well as hunters.

The World According to IBM

The great gamble had paid off, but in ways that couldn't have been anticipated when the machines were first planned. What Tom Watson had in mind was a family of technologically advanced computers that would provide IBM with a lead in technology, expand its markets, ward off competitors, and unite his company. He had success in most of these areas. But at the same time he had reshaped the industry; in the history of computers, everything is either pre-360 or post-360. Without meaning to do so, Watson had opened his own Pandora's box.

11

On the Periphery

TO THE CASUAL OBSERVER it might have appeared that the computer industry had achieved a measure of institutional stability by the mid-1960's. Certainly it was true that each of the Seven Dwarfs was preparing its response to the 360 challenge, but no new company seemed ready to enter the arena, as Control Data had done during the second generation. This perception resulted from what had become the conventional view of the industry—that is, it appeared to be dominated by manufacturers of hardware, companies that had had their starts in business machines, electrical supplies, and military electronics. All were taking aim at IBM, hoping to snare part of its customer base. The feeling was that some would not survive, that there would be fewer rather than more companies in the field within a decade or so. Such seemed to have been the rule for many industries, from cigarettes to radio, soap to motion pictures. Just as the dozens of automobile companies of the 1920's had been whittled down to the big three plus one of 1965, so the same would happen with computers. Or at least that is how it appeared at the time.

This was not to be. Although it was true that two of the dwarfs abandoned their efforts and the other five became stronger, one new entry appeared: Xerox, which for a few years looked as though it might become a formidable competitor, since it possessed not only good equipment but a sales force second only to IBM's within the industry. More important, however, was the rise of several companies deemed minor factors during the second generation since they survived by taking the leavings—by exploiting markets either ignored or paid short shrift by the industry leaders. Of these the more prominent were Digital Equipment, Hewlett-Packard, Varian Associates, and later Data General, though, of course, there were dozens of other firms which either failed to make the grade and dropped out, merged out of existence, or remained small.

A second group of companies made no attempt to produce complete computers but concentrated instead upon what became known as peripheral equipment, or one or more segments of the system. The modern computer consisted of three basic building blocks: the central processor, the memory bank, and the printer. The peripheral equipment manufacturers concentrated on the memories and printers, turning out equipment that was compatible with the processors manufactured by IBM and the Seven Dwarfs. Their products would have to be either more advanced or much less expensive than those of the major companies, and in some cases both features were necessary. On occasion these companies would cooperate with manufacturers of central processors. For example, during the second generation both Honeywell and RCA purchased disk-drive mechanisms from Bryant Computer Products, in this way saving themselves both time and research funds. More often, however, the peripheral equipment manufacturers competed directly with the major firms, and this intensified during the third generation. The leading firms at the time were Potter Instruments, Data Processing Financial & General, Telex, Memorex, Marshall Laboratories, Mid Western Instruments, and Ampex, while Management Assistance, Inc., specialized in the marketing of its products to both manufacturers and users.

As a result of the leasing schedules established by IBM during the second generation, there appeared on the scene firms which found it profitable to purchase 1400's and 7000's and then to lease them out to users at competitive rates, and this practice intensified when the 360's made their appearances. In so doing, the leasing firms uncovered a major flaw in IBM's façade.

Their basic concept was quite simple and depended more upon bookkeeping and generally accepted accounting procedures than on technology or marketing expertise. Typically IBM would draw up leases on the basis of five-year writedowns; that is to say, the cost of the processor was at least in theory to be recovered at an average rate of approximately 20 percent per annum plus charges. At the end of this period because IBM would have been paid the entire sales price of the machine, it would be carried on the books at zero value. Yet it would remain in service, churning out revenues, all of which, after expenses, would be pure profit.

The leasing companies were wagering that IBM wouldn't come out with an important new series for approximately a decade. This conclusion seemed reasonable, given the enormous costs for the 360 project, the advanced nature of the technologies involved, and IBM's corporate restructuring around the new line. The company also had made a major investment in software, and it appeared hardly likely that the next computer generation, if and when one came, would require wholly new programs; it seemed more likely that it would rely instead on those developed for the 360's. Unlike the 1400's and 7000's, then, these machines would be long-lived, and although leasing charges might be dropped, the 360's would remain on the market for many years.

It did not appear imprudent, therefore, for a leasing company to make an outright purchase of a 360 configuration and then to offer it for rental on the basis of a ten-year write-down; this meant that a placement made in 1966 would recover all its costs plus charges by 1976 instead of 1971 if the rental fees were the same as those charged by IBM. But of course, they would not be. Rather, a placement made by a leasing company might cost around 80 to 90 percent of IBM's charge, thus ensuring the company a fine profit and the user important savings. Servicing would be taken care of by IBM, of course, and all the necessary software would be available as well.

The leasing companies came on in a rush in 1965, and since all that was required was a middleman's talents and cash, they soon proliferated. Large industrial firms entered the field, as did banks and finance companies. The competition was keen, so rates soon were cut, further accelerating the growth of this new subindustry. Among the leaders were GC Corporation (controlled by Greyhound), Leasco Data Processing, Levin-Townsend Computer, Randolph Computer, and Data Processing Financial & General, the last of which, as has been noted, was also a factor in the peripheral equipment industry.

Finally, the 360 revolution stimulated the development of firms that sold services rather than products and that specialized in software instead of hardware. Doubtless this segment of the industry would have grown rapidly without the 360's, but the new generation influenced those firms that needed data processing to seek their services.

By the mid-1960's many medium-sized companies had learned they really didn't require the full-time services of a computer. Others saw no need to maintain a staff of programmers and other personnel for their limited requirements, and a growing amount simply didn't know how to make effective use of the machines. A number of firms which were using the equipment effectively found themselves in need of additional services, which under ordinary circumstances might have called for the purchase or lease of several new or used machines that wouldn't be used much of the time. Some of these experimented with time-sharing, while others went to one or more of the companies that constituted the service industry. This hardly was an unusual development, and it was one easily anticipated as early as the advent of the second generation.

IBM helped show the way. Service Bureau Corporation was the leader, and although statistics weren't kept in the late 1950's, it generally was conceded to have captured more than 70 percent of the business. The Corporation for Economic & Industrial Research—more familiarly known as C-E-I-R—was a runner-up which in 1965 was acquired by Control Data as its vehicle in the subindustry. Computer Sciences Corporation, which appeared later, quickly became a major factor, along with Electric Data Systems and University Computing.

For a while one heard much of a computing utility, which would offer to take care of a client's inventory, payroll, and related needs and any other needs that might develop. There were visions of service bureau companies with a central core of computers in one location, bouncing data off satellites to all parts of the world, as the business of information transcended national boundaries. But more important insofar as the future of the computer industry was concerned, this kind of utility would employ the machines more efficiently than was the case with most users, and fewer of them might be required. Leaders of service companies spoke knowingly of keeping their computers working around the clock, seven days a week, thus enabling them to lower costs while still realizing great profits. In addition, the service companies might develop their own software— this was their specialty, after all—and undercut the mainframe manufacturers in this area as well.

The advent of the 360's, then, helped reshape the industry. In the shake-out dozens of small firms grew, and still more of them were organized, often by former IBMers out to make it on their own. Electronic Data Systems and University Computing were founded by men who once were IBM salesmen; Comma Corporation, which offered service contracts at prices below those set by IBM, was run by a group of engineers who had been trained in Armonk. Because these companies were out to take special parts of the business away from the industry leader, they posed a major problem for Watson, Learson, and the others at headquarters. IBM was still in the process of funding the 360 program, of filling out the line. It lacked the resources, time, energy, and will in mid-decade to meet each of these challenges head-on. For a while at least, the challenges went unmet, and by the time IBM was able to turn its attention to them several of the new firms had become so well entrenched that uprooting them wasn't possible. The 360's were meant to assure IBM's domination of the industry for at least a decade, and initially this ambition appeared realizable. Later, however, it became evident that in reformulating its product mix, IBM had helped accelerate the movement of forces which would soon alter the shape of the industry, so that it bore as little resemblance to that of the first and second generations as these did to the mature calculator/accounting machine/tabulator-based industry of the early 1950's. It was familiar to those who had lived through the earlier period. As though to add to the similarities, the Justice Department decided to prosecute the firm under the antitrust statutes and, as had been the case during the last such action, did so by utilizing an obsolete and outmoded definition of what constituted the computer industry.

In 1965, when IBM was making its initial placements of the 360's and the Justice Department was pondering the antitrust implications of the third generation, Digital Equipment Corporation shipped the first of the PDP-8's. Few outside the industry knew much about Digital Equipment, at the time a small operation, run by a handful of scientists and technicians, that had been organized eight years earlier and only recently had emerged from its initial home in a barely refurbished woolen mill in the Boston suburb of Maynard. This was a period when large numbers of high-technology-based firms were being set up by academic scientists, many of whom had some affiliation with Harvard and the Massachusetts Institute of Technology. Their survival rate was not high; most went out of business after a few months or were merged into a larger entity. The fact that DEC had lasted as long as it had was one of the few remarkable aspects of the firm.

DEC's principal organizers were Kenneth Olsen and Har-

On the Periphery

lan Anderson, both of whom had been researchers at MIT, where they had worked with and on small computers. Olsen had become convinced that there was a market for such machines in laboratories and other research organizations and perhaps, later, in offices as well. The initial outlook wasn't particularly promising. The major firms had decided that the future rested with large and medium-sized machines. Individuals and firms with simple data processing needs might turn to time-sharing, and even then the service companies were organizing to take care of their needs. The firms which had produced small computers found the pickings lean, and the leader in the field, Bendix, was considering closing down this side of its operations.

Olsen and Anderson put their own savings and those of some associates into DEC; but the money soon ran out, and Olsen sought additional financing. Initially he failed, but then he was introduced to General Georges F. Doriot, who, in addition to running an investment company called American Research & Development, was affiliated with the Harvard Business School. AR&D specialized in making long-term investments in fledgling high-technology companies and, after several meetings with an increasingly desperate Olsen, paid $70,000 for what amounted to approximately 60 percent of DEC's stock.

Olsen thought the two major drawbacks in the area of small computers were price and complexity. These machines usually were sold rather than leased and went for around $100,000 each. Potential purchasers soon found that they probably would be better off renting a medium-sized machine from one of the major companies. By so doing, they would receive backup support, the education of operators, and whatever else was needed for efficient operation. Given this situation, it was little wonder that IBM and other firms ignored this segment of the market.

DEC's strategy was to bring in low-priced, simple computers, the rudiments of which might be mastered within a few days.

Olsen released the PDP-1 in 1960, which was followed by the PDP-4 two years later, while the PDP-5 was marketed in

1963. Each was more powerful, had additional features, was simpler to operate and lower in cost than its predecessor. All enjoyed a modest success, but since they were sold outright rather than leased, DEC was able to recover costs quickly and so fund research and development for its next products. The PDP-8, which sold for around $20,000, enjoyed an enormous popularity, in part because users had become more familiar with the products, but also because it had one of the highest levels of performance to price then available.

DEC provided its customers with little in the way of software and services, and its sales force was both small and mediocre compared with those of the major firms. Insofar as the PDP-8 was concerned, the product sold itself; scientists and engineers who had learned of the machine by word of mouth or through articles in specialized magazines often called Olsen at the factory to place orders. Within a year of its introduction DEC was able to boast that placements of the PDP-8 were outrunning those for the IBM 360's. By the end of the decade the company was producing more computers than IBM, though, of course, by any other measure it was a much smaller company.

DEC's growth was phenomenal. For fiscal 1968 sales came to $57 million and earnings were $6.8 million; both figures were more than doubled within two years, by which time the PDP-8 had become ubiquitous in factories, power stations, and print shops as well as in laboratories. Olsen was also able to pierce the business market, with machines that sold for as low as $8,500 and at a top price of $20,000. Most were taken by either small businesses or large offices, where they were used to handle tasks not given to the major machines. Several DECs were capable of functioning in tandem with larger machines, processing information generated in them, and it was possible to hook together two or more of the DECs, thus obtaining some of the capacity and power available in medium-sized units. Indeed, the flexibility and simplicity of the DECs provided them with advantages in competition with products turned out by the older and bigger firms.

On the Periphery

In speaking of problems involved in doing missionary work in the field, Olsen observed: "The idea was surprisingly difficult to sell. Most people thought the day of the large IBM computer had arrived." Nick Mazzarese, his vice-president in charge of small computers, thought DEC would dominate that market in much the same way IBM held the lead in medium-sized and large machines, and like Olsen, he kept a weather eye on developments in Armonk, feeling that someday IBM would enter his area. DEC would continue to do well if and when that happened, said Mazzarese, not only because of its head start and firm customer base, but also because the demand for small machines would outstrip that for all others combined.

Furthermore, DEC was prepared to take the offensive against the industry giants. The PDP-6, a medium-sized computer with time-sharing capabilities, was released in 1964 and, though a slow seller, did take some placements from the IBM 1401, then about to be replaced by the 360's. More important, it provided the technical experience needed to produce the PDP-10, deliveries of which began in 1970. This machine, which with different add-ons, could cost from $300,000 to $400,000, competed directly with the lower end of the 360 line. In many ways it was a superior machine, and the DEC salesmen had little trouble placing it in scientific installations and among experienced users of computers. They had a more difficult time of it in the office market, where IBM's salesmen continued their domination of the field.

In this respect and others DEC bore a striking resemblance to Control Data. Each had been organized by scientists rather than businessmen, neither was weighted down with obsolete ideas and individuals, and both had a strong position in a specialized segment of the industry; from different directions they were moving into the medium-sized computer market, Control Data in a more aggressive fashion, of course, but this was to be expected in view of its larger size and the nature of its technology. The products of both CDC and DEC appealed more to scientists and sophisticated users than to businessmen; each firm possessed superior machines but an inferior sales force. For a while it seemed that acquisition-minded CDC would make a play for DEC, producing a strong company with a wider range of products than even IBM. But neither Doriot nor Olsen was particularly interested in a merger, and the top management at DEC made it clear they would continue to specialize in the lower end of the spectrum; they would stay away from IBM's major area of interest and hoped Watson would do the same for them.

This somewhat benign attitude toward expansion troubled several ambitious young men at DEC. While agreeing that the company should continue to specialize in small machines, they urged Olsen to mount a major sales effort, imitate IBM's approach in this area, and so be better entrenched once Armonk decided to come out with its own small systems. In addition, they were concerned with the office market and foreign sales, neither of which had a top priority at DEC. Finally, they realized they had little chance to rise to the top, given the relatively young management team then in control. After much grumbling but little planning they decided to go their own way. Obtaining $50,000 from a stock underwriting in 1968, they opened operations as Data General Corporation.

An additional $21 million was raised through equity offerings in the next three years, by which time Data General's initial machines were not only on the market but making inroads into DEC's sales. Within less than a decade Data General had become the runner-up in this subindustry, where a small amount of seed capital, sales rather than leases, and an aggressive sales force more than compensated for a lack of large research and development budgets and an established client base. Other firms followed, many founded by scientists and technicians from the older firms. Proliferation rather than concentration was the rule at the lower end of the industry spectrum.

Control Data entered the small computer market on its own, acquiring Librascope and Bendix's computer subsidiary and eventually producing the 160 line of machines. Scientific Data Systems, another rapidly growing firm, also produced such computers, as did Honeywell, which remained intent on becoming the second largest factor in data processing.

But not IBM, at least for the time being. The 360 experience had been scarring and had given the men in Armonk a sort of tunnel vision when it came to computers. Their concept of the industry had hardened; the flexibility which had marked thinking during the late 1950's was by now gone. Having successfully piloted the 360's into the marketplace, Watson, Learson, and the others had come to believe that this was the way innovation was managed and that computer families were to be the norm in the future. Of course, there always would be special computers for particular markets, but the road ahead, insofar as product introduction was concerned, appeared clear enough. The upcoming generation of machines would feature exotic memory systems, rapid disk drives, and fully integrated circuits. The company's scientists and technicians were already at work on such projects. In other words, the next family of IBM machines would offer more capacity and flexibility for the data processing dollar and in this respect be in direct succession to the 360's, displacing them in somewhat the same way as they had displaced the 1400's and 7000's. The 360 software would be maintained, but all else would follow on track.

During the postwar period Tom Watson and his father had argued about the relative roles of salesmen and scientists in the organization. Tom, who had maintained that IBM had to stress technology, had achieved a major part of his objective. By the late 1960's the company was in the forefront in several areas of research and was involved more in pioneering than had been the case a generation earlier. In the process, however, the influence of salesmen had weakened somewhat. This is not to suggest sales no longer were an important part of the process or that the path to the executive suites began in the laboratories instead of the field. Rather, technological innovation played a greater role in the late 1960's than it had a generation earlier.

The change was subtle and unplanned and, in fact, was not perceived as a shift by the men involved. But in Watson senior's time, when a salesman would report that customers would require a new kind of data processing capability, the managers would consult the technicians on how the request might be met. After the 360 experience, Watson and Learson would learn of an innovative technology and then plan to introduce it into the next group of machines, adapting them to customer requirements as expressed by sales personnel. Perhaps this was to have been expected, given the different kinds of business and technological atmospheres occupied by father and son in their primes. Still, IBM was less customer-oriented by the late ˙960's than it had been in earlier periods.

This helps explain why Watson failed to move promptly into the minicomputer field. His salesmen reported that clients were turning toward them and told of lost opportunities in placements. DEC's growth was no secret, but because it was taking place outside IBM's historic markets, it was permitted to continue without a direct challenge. Already there was talk of distributed data processing in which small systems would be featured, but IBM tended to dismiss this as a variant of the familiar time-sharing. Had Watson mounted a campaign in this field in the late 1960's, he doubtless could have assumed leadership within a few years, and DEC, Data General, Honeywell, and the others would have had to fight over the leavings. By remaining on the sidelines as long as he did, Watson permitted these firms to establish themselves in such ways as to be almost impervious to future challenges. As it was, Digital Equipment became "the IBM of minicomputers," which may turn out to be a larger and more attractive area than that for major systems. In retrospect, the failure to act more promptly in this area may turn out to have been Tom Watson's greatest error in business judgment.

At the time, however, it appeared otherwise, for a great deal of attention was focused on Xerox, larger and more glamorous than DEC and to some the next great challenger for leadership in the industry. Xerox, which in the late 1960's dominated office copying machines to a greater extent than IBM did data processing equipment, had become the second largest company in the overall business machine market. From almost nowhere

($27 million in sales in 1958) it had expanded to enter the ranks of the billion-dollar corporations by the close of the 1960's. At one point in the early postwar period IBM had had an opportunity to purchase the then-named Haloid Xerox Corporation for a nominal price. Not having done so proved an error of historic proportions. Yet the Watsons might have been forgiven for their failure to perceive the magnitude of demand for dry copiers; they were not alone in this, for others also rejected the firm. Tom Watson's reactions to the DEC challenge were less understandable, as were his failures to rectify mistakes. Afterward several corporate insiders attributed this to fears of anti-trust prosecutions, while others spoke of exhaustion of will after the 360 gambit. Whatever the reasons, IBM's responses to challenges in this period were defensive, halfhearted, and sluggish.

IBM didn't introduce its own small-computer line, the System/3, until the late summer of 1969, and initial deliveries were made the following year. These machines not only were inferior to, but carried higher price tags, than their DEC counterparts. IBM mounted a strong sales effort and offered greater product support than did DEC, Data General, Varian, and the others. Its machines might be leased, while Olsen continued his sales-only policy.

It didn't work this time. Customers were prepared to line up for deliveries of DECs at a time when System/3's were available for immediate placement. Clearly Watson had misjudged the market in 1969 and 1970. In commenting upon this, industry insiders agreed that it was only a matter of time before IBM regrouped and then assumed leadership in the field, that once the company made a commitment, it became unstoppable. Even Olsen was prepared to concede a large share of the market to the industry leader, although he told the press that DEC was well prepared for the onslaught. Yet it didn't come. IBM was to make an important effort in small computers a decade later, but DEC was able to maintain leadership and continue to grow at a more rapid rate. In addition, IBM was bested in contests with a score of other manufacturers of small computers, firms that made their initial placements in the 1960's and 1970's. Tom

Wise had claimed that IBM's mystique had been dealt a major blow by the 360 experience, an exaggerated and unfair judgment. He might better have claimed that the company's aura of infallibility had been dissipated by its inability to take command of the small-computer market.

IBM was more successful in turning back a challenge from Xerox, but this was due more to that company's blunders than to strategies devised in Armonk.

Xerox piled success upon success in the 1960's, so that by the end of the decade it appeared impregnable in its area of expertise. Not only were machine placements accelerating, but also the potential competition was kept at bay by a wall of patents. There was some talk of major new competition from Polaroid and IBM. Each of these three companies dominated its special field, and all had difficulties when they attempted to move into that of the others. Polaroid was the only producer of instant photography cameras and was said to be readying a copier based upon its special technologies. Several pilot projects resulted in models which might have offered Xerox severe competition. But Polaroid's chairman, Edward Land, decided that the marketing risks were too great in this area and that the firm would do better in others. So the machines weren't produced and marketed. Meanwhile, IBM's scientists worked on a machine that would parallel the Xerox machines in design and performance and so clearly would invite litigation. In order to avoid this, IBM committed energy and money to finding an alternate technology and failed. This also necessitated an expenditure of time, during which Xerox consolidated its position and other strong companies entered the field. By the time IBM was able to come up with viable copiers of its own it was too late to make much of an impact upon the market. The industry had matured, and placements were difficult to obtain. Thus, the foray into copiers wasn't as profitable as had been expected in the early 1970's.

IBM didn't regret having made the effort. By then there was much talk within the industry of "the office of the future," in which data processing machines, word processors, computer consoles, telephones, and copiers would be integrated into a total information network. Because any company hoping to compete here would have to develop expertise in all these areas, IBM was able to utilize its copier experience elsewhere. In addition, copiers were similar to computer readout equipment, and here, too, IBM was to benefit by producing superior machines.

In discussing forays by his company into new areas, Xerox president Peter McColough observed: "A lot of computer peripheral gear is going to depend on graphics, putting images on paper," which was precisely where Xerox excelled. He saw no way of avoiding a head-on confrontation with IBM; each firm was destined to expand into the other's territory. "Xerox and IBM are the two big companies exclusively in the information business," he said somewhat disingenuously. "IBM owns the manipulative data processing part, and we own the part that puts things on paper. But the lines of separation are getting blurred, and it will be harder and harder to distinguish them. Sometime in the 1970s, we intend to be able to say to any big company, 'We can handle all your information needs.' " That was to say, Xerox would become a producer of computers— mainframes and all. Joseph Flavin, a former IBMer lured to Xerox, where he became McColough's head of planning and finance, agreed and echoed his chief. "There's talk about a time when there'll be terminals in most executive offices," said Flavin to a Wall Street investment seminar. "I can see a time—maybe ten years away—when you look at the information on your terminal, you push a button, and you make a piece of paper out of it. Well, that's Xerox, that piece of paper." He went on to observe that Xerox had a reputation equal to that of IBM and, like the Armonk giant, leased rather than sold its machines, giving it a powerful cash flow, sufficient to sustain a prolonged effort.

McColough wanted to make certain that at least some of the buttons described by Flavin belonged to Xerox, and as soon as possible. In other words, to be credible, Xerox would have to mount an immediate effort in computers. This could be done either by starting from scratch or through acquisitions. In 1968

Xerox was in an unusually strong cash position and its stock was selling for a high price. McColough could afford to be lavish, and he was. In return for stock worth $908 million he purchased Scientific Data Systems, a medium-sized entity which at the time had assets of approximately $113 million. Other acquisitions followed, most notably Diablo Systems, a small manufacturer of peripheral equipment with little in the way of assets and a series of losses, which nonetheless cost Xerox $29 million in stock in 1972.

These were promising companies, with fine technological bases and reputations for excellence in design and production. Scientific Data's founder, Max Palevsky, was deemed one of the most brilliant innovators in the industry and had been one of the first to utilize transistors in computers, having done so with the SDS-910 in 1962. Since then Palevsky had cultivated the market for scientific machines which for the most part were placed in laboratories and other research-oriented locations. SDS had several important government contracts as well and designed guidance systems for both the military missile and the space programs. Palevsky was content to remain in this market; he had no desire to challenge IBM and the others in business offices, realizing that he lacked the resources and the experience to do so. McColough expected to provide both. Similarly, Diablo's major product was a printer that was much faster and more efficient than the "golf ball" component found on IBM typewriters and computer printers. Diablo had the product, but not the finances to challenge the leaders in this area. It and other small companies would be integrated into the SDS operation, which, provided with funds and the large Xerox sales force, would develop machines to win placements in the office equipment area.

Palevsky believed the newly renamed Xerox Data Systems would be able to match IBM and the others on a purely technological basis, but he doubted that even Xerox's resources would suffice to establish it firmly in the business machine market. At the time of the acquisition he told reporters that it would take "at least five years" before XDS had a significant niche in the area, and he spoke optimistically of the possibility of producing peripheral and special equipment for other, strongly entrenched companies. McColough would have none of this and instead embarked upon a major restructuring of his company. Xerox's major business would continue to be in copiers, but money earned in this part of the operation would be plowed into XDS. The cash drain was significant. During the next three years XDS lost more than $100 million—in its last full year prior to the acquisition SDS had earned $10 million on revenues of $100 million. McColough conceded that the losses had scarred Xerox. "I didn't anticipate losing money," he said in 1972, but at the same time he expressed a determination to press on. This McColough did, but only for another three years. In 1975 Xerox announced its abandonment of the data processing field, thus wiping out its huge investments in SDS and the other companies acquired in the late 1960's and early 1970's.

For all its resources and reputation, Xerox hadn't been able to crack the market for major systems, and the reason for the failure was obvious: The core of the data processing industry had matured, especially after the introduction of the 360's. All the major players were in the field, and from that time onward their numbers would decline, not expand. The situation in peripheral and allied subindustries was different. In these areas, where capital needs were relatively low, product loyalties unformed, and entrepreneurship a prized commodity, entry was not only possible but relatively easy. Thus, Digital Equipment, Data General, and their ilk could not only survive but actually prosper, doing so in their first few years of existence, not—as was the case with first the Seven Dwarfs and later Xerox—after several years of losses and frustration. In time they would be joined by such firms as Tandem, Data Products, Datapoint, Cray, Amdahl, Floating Point, and a slew of others.

Success was to be found on the periphery, then, not in the main arena.

Of the other peripheral subindustries, the one with the greatest profit potential in the late 1960's and early 1970's was leasing. As was the case with the minicomputer manufacturers, the growth in both revenues and earnings was more rapid even than IBM's. The Armonk leadership might have reflected that the DECs and Data Generals of the industry might have merited their successes; after all, they clearly had designed and marketed fine machines, or in other words, they were "legitimate computer people." IBM took a different attitude toward the leasing companies, the founders and executives of which often were outsiders—not scientists or technicians, but lawyers and accountants—or defectors from one or another large company. In the eyes of men like Watson and Learson, they were wheeler-dealers who seemed more at home on Wall Street than in the field, parasites living off the concrete accomplishments of others.

While it was doubtless overstated, there was a basis for this assessment. Harvey Goodman, the president of Data Processing Financial & General, was a lawyer and accountant who founded his company in 1961 with the assistance of the investment banking house of Allen & Company. Two years later Howard Levin, a consultant, joined with business executive James Townsend to form Levin-Townsend, with backing from Greyhound, the bus transportation company. Later the agreement was terminated, and Greyhound entered the field on its own. Sam and Charles Wyly, both of whom were computer salesmen, organized the University Computing Company that same year, 1963, and declared they would concentrate on providing services. A flamboyant Texan, Sam had his unique way of formulating the peripheral approach: "You find a little bitty thing you can do, and you keep on doing it." He didn't follow this dictum, however. University acquired an insurance company and then used part of its assets to lease computers, which by 1968 were providing University with approximately a third of its revenues and profits.

Saul Steinberg, the founder-president of Leasco Data Processing, was both the most ingenious and the most ambitious individual in the subindustry. Reared in Brooklyn and Long Island, Steinberg attended the Wharton School of Finance, where he had his first in-depth confrontation with IBM. An instructor there suggested he write a thesis on "The Decline and

Fall of IBM." As Steinberg later recalled, "I was the kind of student who was prepared to believe anything was bad, so I accepted the assignment." In the process of conducting research he arrived at an opposite conclusion. In his view, "IBM was an incredible, fantastic, brilliantly conceived company with a very rosy future." Although he wound up writing on another subject, Steinberg had become an inveterate IBM watcher and admirer, and that was the way he arrived in computer leasing.

Steinberg spotted the previously mentioned flaw in IBM's method of depreciating its machines, and he quickly realized that large profits could be made simply by using different methods of calculation. Instead of minimizing profits (to assure a steady cash flow and for tax reasons), he would maximize them (to be able to report sharp and spectacular increases in earnings and profit margins, which would then cause his company's stock to rise, providing him with instant wealth and a vehicle with which to make acquisitions).

Steinberg went to work for his father after graduation and used his spare time to perfect his concepts. In 1961, with $25,000 in borrowed funds, he organized Ideal Leasing, placed his initial orders, and declared his intention to challenge IBM. At the time Steinberg was twenty years old.

The company was an immediate success. In 1962 Ideal reported revenues of $1.8 million and earnings of $55,000; two years later revenues came to $8 million and earnings were $225,000. Steinberg changed the name to Leasco Data Processing Equipment in 1965 and made his initial public offering of stock.

Leasco and the other leasing companies were prepared for the 360's, and along with the rest of the industry they knew the machines would employ software different from that used in the second-generation models. Forewarned, they took on relatively few 1400's and 7000's and piled up cash while placing orders for the 360's. At the time IBM appeared to welcome the leasing firms; their advance orders assured the success of what still was regarded as a chancy venture. Moreover, for once IBM preferred outright purchases to leases since its financial position wasn't as liquid as Watson would have liked. Thus, the leasing firms profited from the 360's—according to some insiders, more even than did IBM.

As for Leasco, it continued to expand, not only by internal growth but through a series of mergers, most of which were leasing firms. Steinberg absorbed Carter Auto Transport & Service, Documentation Inc., Fox Computer, and others like them. In 1968 he astounded Wall Street by successfully acquiring Reliance Insurance, with assets nine times those of Leasco. Hardly stopping to consolidate his holdings, Steinberg set out after Chemical Bank, one of America's most prestigious and powerful institutions, which at the time had more than $8 billion in deposits and one of the directors of which was none other than T. Vincent Learson. Steinberg failed in his bid, but not before becoming headline news in most major cities.

Why had Steinberg gone after Reliance and Chemical Bank? At the time the moves seemed motivated by a desire to obtain control of their assets, which then would be used in more "creative" ways, such as financing computer leases. But there was more to it than that. Having studied IBM's history—and its methods of dealing with challengers—Steinberg was relatively certain that Watson would move to crush the leasing companies and, if not completely successful, at least would cripple them to the point where they no longer were major threats. Leasco then would suffer along with the others. When that happened, he expected to be in a different business or group of businesses. Leasco would provide the vehicle, the means of transporting Steinberg to the heights, and then it no longer would be required. After taking over Reliance, Leasco derived less than 20 percent of its revenues from leases, and had the Chemical Bank take-over worked out, the share would have dropped to below 7 percent. Rather than being a brash upstart, as he often had been portrayed, Steinberg instead was a shrewd young man with ambitions to become part of the establishment. And to a great degree he succeeded. In time most of the other leasing companies would either decline or disappear—when IBM mounted the assault Steinberg had anticipated. By then, however, Leasco had been reborn as the Reliance Group and continued.

That IBM was not to be taken for granted had become a truism within the industry. Whenever there was a dearth of news out of Armonk (that is to say, most of the time) executives at rival companies assumed it meant the troops there were gathering for an assault. "To be a competitor of IBM," said one of them, "is to suffer from a peculiar version of corporate paranoia." Despite setbacks of various kinds in the late 1960's, the company still was considered all-powerful, all-wise, and all but omniscient. When in 1970 it released its first important copying machine, industry analysts reported that although it was faster than some Xerox models, it wasn't unusual in any way and appeared to be overpriced. Yet the stocks of most companies in the industry collapsed; it generally was assumed that IBM soon would take second place in the field and cut into the sales of all companies, Xerox included. The corporate responses were familiar by then. There was much talk of new machines that would make the IBMs appear obsolete, a beefing up of sales forces, higher advertising expenses, and bonuses for salesmen. And lawsuits.

Xerox was quick to join in. The company's lawyers charged IBM with having infringed upon some twenty-two of Xerox's patents. In what had become an almost rote exercise, an IBM spokesman called the action "without foundation" and added that IBM would "defend the suit . . . with all its resources."

Not quite. In this period IBM's considerable legal resources were arrayed against a host of lawyers, including those from the Justice Department's antitrust division. Never before or since had any company been so involved in such a variety of legal actions simultaneously. Around Armonk, jokesters observed that Watson senior had stressed sales, and Tom Watson, technology. The next chairman would have to be lured from the Supreme Court, for the company had entered an age of litigation.

12

A Generation of Litigation

IBM is a multidimensional organism which defies simple analysis. One can consider it a vehicle whereby science is transformed first into technology and then into products, a place where power is created and utilized, a gigantic money machine, or a stage upon which extraordinary individuals play out their roles. It has some of the attributes of a beehive or an anthill, a club or a family. Clearly its social and political aspects are as important as those which are purely economic.

The corporation may also be analyzed as a variant of the nation-state. George Ball and others have observed that in our time the transnationals have taken on some of the trappings of countries, that executives often demonstrate more loyalty to their firms than to their homelands. Certainly the manner by which the computer wars were fought supports such a view.

A Generation of Litigation

The struggles produced heroes, conquerors, turncoats, spies, strategists, tacticians, cabinet officers, and ambassadors—casualties, too, the crippled and those merely bruised. There were surprise attacks and calculated withdrawals to defensive outposts.

There were three important and related differences between political and business conflicts, however. In the first place, no one actually perished during the computer wars; companies and divisions of companies went down the drain, but the individuals involved on the losing sides often reappeared later, to continue the struggle under a different banner and a new army. Except for unusual switches, such as the time when John Burns went to RCA, it was considered altogether proper for the vice-president of one company to accept the presidency of another or for a key individual to go off to start his own corporation. Then, too, the computer wars have never ended. Under the rules of the game as promulgated in the United States participants hoped to win skirmishes and even major battles, but not total victory. To eliminate rivals or even to threaten to do so would involve the third difference between the business and military wars—namely, the presence of government in the arena, in both the form of the antitrust division and the option held by each combatant to use the courts as allies. It was as though, in the midst of a battle, one side or the other were able to call upon a panel of jurors to decide whether or not the opponent was fighting fair. Such an idea is unthinkable in actual warfare today; but it was the norm in the computer wars during the late 1960's and early 1970's, and it continues to the present. At times it appeared the contest might be decided in the courts rather than on the battlefield (for this, read the marketplace).

As has already been shown, the initial barrage in the legal aspect of the computer wars came out of Minnesota, where in early December 1968 Control Data filed a private antitrust action against IBM. It was a two-pronged assault, with the first little more than a diversion and thinly veiled slap at the Justice Department. CDC alleged serious and multiple violations of the

1956 consent decree entered into by the antitrust division of Justice and Tom Watson, implying that Washington had been lax in monitoring the computer industry. On several occasions Norris and other CDC executives had said they would not have gone to court had the government done so. This part of the suit, then, was aimed more at outgoing Attorney General Ramsey Clark than at Tom Watson.

More important, and the heart of the suit, was the allegation that IBM had engaged in no fewer than thirty-four separate practices whereby it sought a monopoly status in the industry (total victory) in order to eliminate or batter into submission all rival firms, while at the same time it discouraged new entities from entering the field. Central to the suit was a contention that IBM had advertised and sold "paper machines and phantom computers" in order to deter customers from ordering the CDC 6600 and other large systems. It had done so by promising "to lease, sell, or make delivery of computers, software or programs . . . not yet in production" and for which "it had no reasonable basis for believing that production or delivery could be accomplished within the time period specified." This, of course, referred to IBM's marketing of the 360/90 family at a time when those machines were still in the planning stages and to the late delivery of models and their early discontinuance.

Additional complaints were made in reference to IBM's massive advertising campaigns, and there were charges that the company encouraged its salesmen to utilize unfair competitive tactics "by imposing unreasonable quotas and severe penalties for the loss of orders, customers, or prospects." Control Data asked for treble damages for injuries, "the exact amount of which remains to be determined," and, more important, "the dissolution . . . or divestiture" of assets by IBM to prevent future abuses.

IBM denied all these charges, and a company spokesman told the press that CDC's allegations would be refuted in a "vigorous and complete" fashion.

Despite their disparate sizes, the contestants appeared

evenly matched in court. Against IBM's in-house law firm and an augmented team from Cravath, Swaine & Moore, CDC deployed a dozen full-time lawyers and 120 paralegal assistants. As for the charges themselves, there was some doubt that they constituted violations of the antitrust laws, even if they could be proved—and that seemed doubtful at the time. It was true, for example, that IBM had accepted orders for the 360/90's prior to their availability, but the company had done so with earlier models, with no protest from CDC or any other computer manufacturer. Deliveries actually were made, and twenty-five of the series had been placed by mid-1966, at which time they were withdrawn from the catalog and production was discontinued. The 90's failed to capture the interest of clients; IBM suffered a loss of close to $110 million on these large machines. Maybe they had been produced to prevent rivals from expanding their markets, but the 90's hardly were "paper machines" or "phantom computers." To this, CDC responded that a firm of IBM's size could afford to take such losses if it thereby defended a client base and inflicted damage upon rivals. Perhaps. But difficult, if not impossible, to demonstrate in court.

The same held true for the matter of unfair sales tactics. It was no secret within the industry that IBM salesmen were strongly urged to expand their placement bases, that they lost points when their machines were replaced by those of competitors. These were aggressive and highly motivated individuals, and many could be ruthless when it came to dealing with rivals. Indeed, it was this very quality that led other firms to seek them out and lure them to their camps. That such people would overpromise and engage in doubtful practices when making their sales pitches might have been expected, but on the other hand, it was against company policy to do so.

All were familiar with the IBM pamphlet *Business Conduct Policies: Responsibilities and Guide*, in which proper conduct in the field was clearly spelled out. In it were discussed two categories of activities which were to be avoided. Not only were IBM salesmen not to engage in overtly illegal practices, but they were warned against going to the edge as well. They were to refrain from doing anything which, though not illegal in itself, "may create a pattern of apparent monopolistic practices. Even though no one will probably start a lawsuit over any one of them, these acts may accumulate into an anti-trust action brought either by the government or by an aggrieved competitor." And this statement was followed by a list of examples of such practices:

A. Unhooking—that is the inducing of a cancellation of a firm competitive order prior to installation.
B. Proposals or mention to a prospect of a commercial product before it has been officially announced when done to thwart a specific competitor.
C. Subtle disparagement of a competitor's products by suggesting for example that his cards may not work so well in our machines.

To underscore this, the *Guide* adds:

Acts in this second category standing alone technically may not be a violation of the anti-trust laws. But when judged by hindsight, a series of several of these acts might be regarded as an indication of an over-all attempt to monopolize and provoke the institution of an action.

Had IBM salesmen engaged in unhooking and related practices in regard to the CDC 6600? Probably some of them had. Was this known in Armonk? It is difficult to imagine top management's failing to know what was happening in the field in regard to so important an issue. Did company folkways and mores encourage such behavior? Decidedly so, but again, other companies in the industry imitated IBM in this regard to the best of their abilities. Finally, was it company policy to engage in such practices? Clearly it was not, but Control Data claimed that practice, not policy, was at issue.

The initial stage of the suit consisted of jockeying for position and fact-finding. Control Data examined 25 to 40 million IBM documents and at a cost of approximately $3 million constructed an index of the more important ones. For its part, IBM pored over 120 million CDC documents, made copies of 6 million of them, and constructed its own index. It also obtained permission to examine specific documents relating to the charges from some 3,400 companies engaged in one way or another with computers, and of course, copies of these documents ran into the millions. A joke made its way around the industry to the effect that the only winner in the case would be Xerox—because of the costs of all those copies.

For a while, as each company made feints at the other, it appeared that some out-of-court settlement was possible. By 1972, however, it was evident that Control Data meant to pursue its suit to the very end, and now IBM mounted its own attack, in the form of two countersuits. Two years earlier CDC had joined with Britain's International Computers Ltd. and France's Compagnie Internationale pour l'Informatique to form the International Data Company, which was to market machines outside the United States. The idea was for CII to produce small to medium-sized computers, ICL to concentrate on larger models, while Control Data contributed its massive systems to the mix. Now, in 1972, IBM charged CDC with participation in an international cartel and restraint of trade via a quasimerger. Furthermore, it claimed misuse of assets by CDC's financial arm, Commercial Credit, a touchy point that had been raised when that large finance company was acquired in 1965.

The second suit, filed three months later, accused Control Data of attempting to monopolize the market for large computer systems. This blast, which was more a harassing tactic than anything else, was thrown out of court on the ground that there simply was no such thing as a large computer industry. And in what might best be described as a countercounterattack, Commercial Credit filed its own antitrust action against IBM, on the ground that as a customer it had been obliged to overpay for that company's equipment.

This kind of parrying continued into late 1972, with each side taking pokes at the other, asking for additional documents, acquiring new platoons of lawyers (IBM had more than 100 of them assigned to the case on a full-time basis), and all the while seeking some kind of behind-the-scene accommodation. Control Data seemed in a strong position by then. IBM was being swamped by litigation and wanted to wrap up the CDC matter in order to devote more attention to the other cases. Norris realized that Watson knew he was determined to pursue the prosecution to its conclusion, and this gave him added incentive to continue. On the other hand, a company with IBM's resources and experience might keep the case in the courts for many years, and there always was a chance that one or more of the countersuits, feeble as they appeared, might strike sparks in one or another courthouse. Trial was set for November of the following year, and as that time approached, both sides intensified their efforts for an out-of-court settlement.

In January 1973 the companies simultaneously announced that an agreement had been reached, one that had little to do with the original charges. CDC had won a victory over IBM, but the latter company was able to make an impressive gain in other areas of its antitrust struggles. For what amounted to its asset value, CDC was to acquire the Service Bureau Corporation, and this, together with its other ventures in the area, made it a leader in the subindustry. This did not mean IBM was taking itself out of the field; for years each division had its own service operations, which competed with Service Bureau. Thus, IBM divested itself of a division it really didn't need, though for a price lower than it was worth. In addition, IBM agreed to pay Control Data $101 million over a period of several years. Most of this money was earmarked to cover expenses relating to the Service Bureau Corporation settlement, but $15 million was specifically to reimburse CDC for part of its legal expenses; thus, IBM tacitly indicated that there was some substance to the original charges. Insofar as costs were concerned, it was estimated at the time that IBM's legal bill was some $60 million and that Control Data came out around $100 million ahead after all payments were made. Norris was pleased, saying: "The decision to file a lawsuit in 1968, although difficult at the time, had proved to be one of the best management decisions in our history." In other words, the courts were a legitimate battle-ground in the computer wars.

As indicated, IBM wasn't too disturbed by this apparent setback, for by then the company was more concerned with the government's antitrust case than with any other litigation. Since the Justice Department's charges ran parallel to several of those set forth by Control Data, it became evident that materials gathered for the earlier case—and never introduced into open court—might be used in the later one. There was that com-puterized documents index, for example; it might prove a pow-erful weapon in the government's hands. With this in mind, the Justice Department asked the court to compel IBM to preserve all materials relating to its case, and an order was sent down to this effect. The government lawyers looked forward to the time they could explore that index, which, according to some rumors, contained sufficient materials to clinch the verdict with no other supporting evidence.

The index might have been the key to the IBM-CDC ac-cord. Under the terms of the settlement Control Data agreed to have it destroyed in the presence of IBM's attorneys. The anti-trust division learned of this after the fact and was irate. Im-mediately the government filed a motion to oblige IBM either to reconstruct the index or to pay $4 million for a new one. The court agreed that the company had violated the order but re-fused to demand restitution. But even had IBM lost this round, all that would have been required was additional work or the expenditure of money, and these were no problem. The effort would have been time-consuming—it could have taken the bet-ter part of three years—in a period when IBM chose to use delaying tactics.

It will be recalled that the Justice Department filed its antitrust brief shortly before the Johnson administration left office. This was not a last-minute decision, however; work on the case had begun in 1965, and in the interim different factions within the department argued back and forth on how best to proceed, on which of IBM's practices should be challenged, and even on whether or not the entire matter should be dropped. Overall, it was charged that IBM had either monopolized or attempted to monopolize the computer industry. Beneath the complex verbiage were four specific allegations.

In the first place, IBM was said to have "impaired" the development of independent service and peripheral companies by maintaining a single price policy for its machines, software, and related materials. Secondly, the company had "used its accumulated software and related support to preclude its competitors from effectively competing for various customer accounts." Next, "by granting exceptional discriminatory allowances in favor of universities and other educational institutions," IBM had influenced these places in their selection of computers. Finally, in an echo of the Control Data charge, the government claimed that IBM had introduced low-profit models knowing that they could not be produced on time and did so to prevent the placement of rival machines.

IBM issued an immediate and categorical denial of each of the charges, conceding only that it indeed "had offices, transacts business and is found within the Southern District of New York" and that the company had been founded in 1911 and had taken its present name thirteen years later. This was reiterated in double-page advertisements placed in most of the nation's leading newspapers. "Has IBM spoiled the computer business for others?" it asked. "Let's look at the record," and this showed that many new firms had entered the field during the past decade and that there were more competitors in 1969 than at any other time in history. This was true not only in the service sector and for peripheral machinery but in the area of mainframes as well. The government's charges were characterized as "unwarranted," and IBM pledged a "forceful defense."

Nonetheless, the Armonk command moved swiftly to strengthen weak points in its armor. In June 1969 IBM "unbundled" its once-unitary package of hardware-software-services-education, establishing separate prices for each component. Simultaneously prices were dropped slightly on hardware, while charges for the other components either remained the same or were boosted. The net result was an increase in prices for those who elected to take the entire bundle, lower charges for users of hardware alone, and benefits for the service companies. Control Data's Norris recognized this immediately. "So far so good," he said. "It's a price increase." So did Walter Bauer, president of Informatics, a California service and programming company. "One of the biggest marketing obstacles is the customer's feeling that computer manufacturers should supply everything from the cradle to the grave," he observed, "and in this business, whatever IBM does has an aura of authenticity. So when IBM says there is such a concept as buying software separately, it makes it acceptable to customers." Yet most of the company's corporate clients continued to want the entire bundle, and some of those who dropped the services to realize economies picked them up again once problems developed. "I'd love to say good morning to IBM systems engineers," admitted Robert Parsons, Jr., of Eastern Air Lines shortly after his company had discontinued the regular service contract; two months later it was restored. Other companies had the same experience. Thus, IBM had it both ways. By its bowing to the government insofar as unbundling was concerned, the company's revenues and profits actually increased.

IBM readily conceded it had given educational discounts and indeed had done so for many years. Early in the computer era the company had provided more than sixty of the first-generation 650's free to colleges and universities offering computer science courses. Later second-generation machines could be obtained for less than half the list price, and there were large discounts for software and special assistance. Other companies did as much, for their own sakes and to help the schools. Many of the more important discoveries in both hardware and techniques came out of the universities, and the companies wanted to tap this source of knowledge and at the same time get to know the important academics in the profession. In addition, it behooved them to have as many programmers, technicians, and researchers in the field with training on their equipment, on the theory that they would demand these machines when in a position to do so. How this constituted a direct violation of the antitrust acts is difficult to say, especially since the practice was industry-wide. Nevertheless, IBM cut back on its educational discounts, to the point where most were lowered to around 10 percent and only a few were above 25 percent. The other companies followed suit. This policy alteration wasn't wholly caused by a desire to respond to the antitrust action, since discounts had been narrowed prior to the announcement. Still, it was difficult to see how any public good was served by these decisions.

There was no obvious, clear-cut method by which IBM could signal its agreement to added competition within the industry. This was a murky area since the company in effect had been asked to prove a negative—to demonstrate that it hadn't behaved in such a way as to discourage potential competitors. Similarly, the government was to have a difficult, if not impossible, task in attempting to substantiate its claim. Later Armonk would note, with sarcasm and obvious glee, that almost a third of the companies the depositions of which had been collected by the antitrust division hadn't been in existence when the original action was filed. Even casual students of the industry recognized that there was a greater proliferation of companies after the introduction of the 360's than at any earlier time.

Finally, there was the matter of phantom computers and paper machines, the most serious of all the allegations, one that went to the heart of the suit, since it dealt with matters of style and tradition as well as with marketing policy. Had Tom Watson and Learson engaged in a knockout strategy similar to that employed by John Patterson and Watson senior a half century earlier? Control Data had claimed this was so, and now the government echoed the charge.

As the case progressed, business publications came to compare it with the famous antitrust action taken by William Howard Taft against the Standard Oil Company of New Jersey. In each case a major corporation was involved, charges of monopoly were presented, and demands made for an industry restructuring in the name of free enterprise. The petroleum company lost its appeal to the Supreme Court in 1911, after

A Generation of Litigation

which it was broken down into several major and a score of minor firms. Now the Justice Department appeared to be asking for what amounted to the same treatment for IBM—at the least, divestitures and at the most, the creation of several firms from the carcass of the giant corporation. Some industry analysts thought that IBM would triumph no matter what was decided. "Instead of facing one IBM, Control Data, UNIVAC, and the others would have to come against four of five of them," thought one such writer. "They hardly could relish such a fate."

As the case dragged on—it still hasn't been settled—comparisons with the Standard Oil case ceased to be made; instead, parallels were drawn with the United Shoe Machinery antitrust action, which was settled by the issuance of a consent decree the very day the Justice Department filed its suit against IBM in 1969—twenty-one years after it had begun. The litigation that had been initiated during the dusk of the Lyndon Johnson presidency continued under the attorneys general of Richard Nixon, Gerald Ford, Jimmy Carter, and Ronald Reagan. *United States* v. *IBM* is now more than halfway toward the record established by Shoe Machinery.

The government case became the centerpiece for the generation of litigation, but the Control Data compromise may have been even more significant for the short run in that it opened the way for other, somewhat similar forays against the Armonk giant. None of these originated from the Seven Dwarfs. Rather, they came from the leasing companies and producers of peripheral equipment. Some were frivolous, but one or two seemed to be based upon realistic complaints. In almost all of them, the complaining parties asked for damages that exceeded their net corporate worths. It soon got to the point where a legal action against IBM caused the price of a company's stock to leap up on Wall Street since it was viewed as being as much of an asset as products and patents.

For example, a month after the filing of the CDC complaint, Data Processing Financial & General weighed in with one of its own. At the time the company's major asset was some $170 million worth of IBM equipment, most of it 360 computers

265

on lease. DPF&G charged IBM with unfair practices insofar as refusing to unbundle software and hardware was concerned, and in addition, it claimed to have been prevented from entering the market for peripheral equipment as a result of unethical tactics. Its complaint asked that IBM be divided into four companies, one each in hardware, software, service, and leasing. How this might be done—and what relations might develop between the four entities—weren't explored. It was no secret that DPF&G was in financial difficulties, however, and that a management shake-up was in the works. Soon thereafter the company announced it no longer could pay for some IBM computers on which it had taken delivery, and then discussions began in earnest between the two sets of attorneys. Originally DPF&G had claimed damages of more than $350 million, and since treble damages were customary in such cases, IBM was being asked to pay more than $1 billion, in addition to being dismantled. As it was, DPF&G agreed to drop its suit in return for a time extension to pay for equipment and an assumption of its legal fees.

Three additional suits entered into in 1969 came to similar conclusions. Two of them, initiated by Applied Data Research and Programmatics, were brushed aside with barely a notice taken of them in Armonk. Then Levin-Townsend filed its brief, which was similar to that presented by DPF&G. In common with the other case, Levin-Townsend soon developed financial troubles, and its president was obliged to resign, after which the matter was quietly dropped.

Greyhound Computer Leasing also mounted a foray against IBM, charging it with having conspired to control the leasing industry and in other ways harass competitors. Greyhound Computer was in better financial shape than Levin-Townsend and DPF&G and, in addition, had the resources of its parent company upon which to draw. This case went before a jury in the summer of 1972 and resulted in a dramatic victory for IBM. Greyhound Computer's presentation was so weak that IBM's attorneys asked for a summary judgment in their favor without even offering a defense. Judge Walter Craig agreed. He found that Greyhound Computer not only had failed to substantiate its claims but had inadvertently demonstrated that IBM was guiltless insofar as violations of the antitrust statutes were concerned. The company's preeminent position in its industry had been obtained "as a result of superior skill, foresight, and industry," said Craig. Its domination resulted from "economic forces over which it had no control." Furthermore, "there is no evidence of an attempt to monopolize." The judge alluded to IBM's market power; but he did not believe it had been misused, and in any case, "size alone does not constitute an offense under the Sherman Act, nor does the mere possession of monopoly power." Greyhound immediately announced it would appeal the verdict, but little more was heard of this litigation.

IBM took a different tack in the Memorex case, which was initiated in 1971. A California concern engaged in the manufacture of magnetic tapes, disk drives, and other components, Memorex had grown rapidly in the 1960's both by providing several of the mainframe companies with its products and by marketing them independently. A number of Memorex systems were designed with the 360's in mind; lower in cost than, and in some ways superior to, the IBM disk drives, they were offered to IBM's customers at attractive rates. The antitrust action was based upon a claim that IBM had used unfair and illegal tactics and practices to prevent such placements. In other ways the charges were similar to those made by previous complainants, and so was the demanded relief—damages and a breakup of the company. This time IBM not only promised a strong defense but issued countercharges of its own, taking the offensive, as it had against Control Data.

Memorex was frightened off. Without the resources to conduct a prolonged case and fearful that its charges wouldn't hold up in court, the company settled for what amounted to a truce. Each side agreed to drop its charges and not to sue the other for at least one year.

Memorex dropped back, hoping to generate sufficient resources for another, more powerful assault. In 1972 the company offered a new disk drive line that was compatible with the lower end of the 360's. Industry magazines agreed the disk drives were technically superior and attractively priced, but Memorex lacked the sales force needed to make sufficient placements. The line eventually was discontinued, at a loss of $40 million. Now Memorex was awash in red ink. The year was up, however, and once again the company looked to the courts for relief from the rigors of the marketplace.

By then IBM was fighting off challenges on a more or less regular basis. It was as though some huge whale were beset by schools of sharks. A group would manage a foray, hoping to rip a chunk of flesh from its flank. Most of the time the whale would content itself with defensive maneuvers, but on occasion it would lash out at an attacker, not only to frighten it away but to warn the others that circled constantly, seeking weak spots in the skin. All would await the first sign of blood, that penetration which would invite a massive charge on the part of every fish in the vicinity.

During the early 1970's it appeared that the antitrust division had the best chance of inflicting such a meaningful wound, one that would show the way to the others. This was a crucial case, and it remained in the preparatory stages for several years. Meanwhile, the peripheral equipment firms made their more or less feeble forays. In addition to those already discussed, there were suits from Advanced Memory Systems and Itel, each a minor entity in the business. These required only supervisory attention from IBM's first line of attorneys and not much more from the reserves. IBM was in the process of developing a version of a farm system for its antitrust team. Lawyers who performed well against one of the leasing companies or producers of peripheral equipment would be marked for advancement to the main arena—the government's case. But even the second team was more than a match for anyone the small companies could locate to prepare and present their cases. It was more than sheer talent, however; IBM simply had a better position than its attackers. Thus, all these cases were settled in ways the company wanted.

The one major exception—and IBM's most surprising and

A Generation of Litigation

unexpected defeat—came in the Telex case. The company was yet another of the many manufacturers of plug-compatible equipment that attempted to produce superior components for the 360's at lower prices. During the 1930's Telex had turned out a line of hearing aids and audiometers, and later the company pioneered in a small way in wire and tape recorders. This experience led Telex into computer memory systems, and during the late 1950's and early 1960's it attempted to sell a family of magnetic tape drives, meeting with indifferent results in a crowded marketplace. After all, Telex was a marginal operation, with erratic leadership and scant financial resources. For a while the company appeared on the verge of dissolution, and in fact, it might have gone out of business had it not been for the advent of the 360's.

Telex was one of the earliest firms to realize there was a market for components that were compatible with the 360 mainframes. Out of its laboratory and factory came a new group of tape and disk drives which, after unbundling, met with a far greater success than management ever believed possible. By the summer of 1969 the firm was able to boast that it had placed 1,000 of the new units, and within the next two years an additional 7,000 were sold or leased. For fiscal 1971 Telex reported revenues of $81 million (of which peripheral equipment accounted for $58 million) and earnings of $5.5 million. By then there were some 100 firms in the subindustry, and Telex had become one of the best-known and fastest-growing of the lot.

It was then that IBM decided to shake up the competition. The name for its semisecret campaign was almost militaristic, the kind that might have emerged from Allied headquarters in Europe at any time from 1942 to 1945. SMASH, as formulated in Armonk, consisted, first of all, of slashes in leasing prices of around 25 percent. This was accompanied by a major sales push and signals that IBM wouldn't renew licensing arrangements then due to expire. S-Day was set for some time in August 1972; but word leaked earlier, and Telex decided to try to prevent the attack.

In January 1972 Telex filed an antitrust suit against IBM,

doing so in Tulsa, a place where companies like IBM often were viewed as part of the eastern enemy camp. The complaints were familiar enough: IBM had monopolized or attempted to monopolize the manufacture, sale, and lease of peripheral equipment through unfair marketing and pricing policies. Telex asked for damages of more than $239 million, which, if trebled as was customary, would come to $717 million. Soon after this the company went to court for a temporary restraining order to prevent SMASH but failed. The IBM campaign started as planned, causing deep distress within the subindustry and the failure of several fairly well-known small firms.

Telex lacked the resources for a concerted effort and decided to campaign "on the cheap." During the discovery phase its case was to be consolidated with that of Control Data, which at the time appeared on the verge of coming to trial. This meant that Telex would be able to refer to the massive and costly brief already prepared by the CDC legal team, including the by then famous index.

In addition, Telex gambled in the way it acquired its own small squad of attorneys. The organizer and leader—and chief strategist—was Floyd Walker, a man who was known for cultivating a hayseed image when he dealt with eastern lawyers before local judges and juries and who had a long string of successes by so doing. Thomas Barr, IBM's lead advocate, was the quintessential easterner and was therefore believed to be at a disadvantage. Walker appeared confident of victory, especially after IBM instituted its SMASH campaign, which to him seemed a clear and unmistakable example of unfair practices. He was willing to accept a small retainer but would receive a large share of the damages should the decision go his way. The actual percentage was unknown, but toward the end of the trial it was rumored to be approximately $60 million.

During late 1972 Walker and his associates polished their arguments, studied the Control Data documents (without paying for the privilege), and monitored the SMASH campaign. By then there was talk of an out-of-court settlement between IBM and CDC, which could mean that Telex would be on its own.

Given all this, Walker decided to move swiftly, and in the following January each side let loose with barrages.

Walker began by filing an amended complaint: Telex now was asking for $416 million in damages, or $1.2 billion on a trebled basis. In order to defend his company against the IBM-CDC settlement, he also asked that the two antitrust cases be separated. Before anything could be done, however, IBM caused the CDC index to be destroyed. Walker issued his complaint before the government organized its own. He demanded the reconstruction of the index, charging that IBM had acted as it had because of a desire to injure his case. The court rejected this argument, noting that by failing to pay any part of the original costs, Telex had signaled a belief that the index was of minor value.

Then Armonk let loose with a barrage of its own. Two countersuits were filed in late January 1973, alleging copyright infringements, violations of patent agreements, and, most important, theft of trade secrets. IBM asked damages in the form of all of Telex's profits from 1970 through 1972 and the issuance of an injunction prohibiting that company from using former IBMers in projects similar to those they had worked on previously. By so charging, IBM opened what might have become a major avenue for future litigation. A victory on this front might deter other firms from raiding laboratories and even sales forces and stem what was becoming a major problem for Armonk. But even should these thrusts fail, Telex would have been placed on the defensive, and that, too, was desirable in the view of IBM's legal brain trust.

For a while almost everything went off according to plan (IBM's, that is). During the pretrial hearing Walker and his colleagues were kept off-balance by switches in policy and surprise motions. But IBM did err in two respects. These tactics irritated several senior judges, who ordered an immediate trial at a time when IBM was switching from one stance to another, and although Barr was able to get the judge he wanted, Sherman Christensen turned out to be the wrong man from Armonk's point of view.

The trial began in April 1973, and all evidence and testimony were completed in less than a month. Christensen then retired to prepare his judgment. For a few months there was little news regarding the case. Within the industry there developed rumors of clandestine meetings between IBM and Telex lawyers who hoped to work out some kind of settlement prior to the decision and of teams of lawyers visiting other peripheral equipment manufacturers, clearly in the hope of obtaining business should Telex win. But such a victory wasn't considered likely. IBM had never lost an important case, the company had some of the nation's top legal talent, and Telex hadn't had access to the valuable CDC index. The betting was that IBM would come through the ordeal without a scar, while Telex might be severely crippled by the countersuits. On Wall Street IBM's stock held firm, while Telex's, already buffeted severely by the SMASH program, declined.

Christensen handed down his verdict on September 14, 1973, and the 222-page document sent tremors through the industry and stunned Armonk. Overall he found both parties guilty as charged. Specifically Christensen said IBM had violated Section 2 of the Clayton Act by attempting to "destroy its plug-compatible-peripheral competition by predatory pricing actions and by market strategy bearing no relationship to technological skill, industry, appropriate foresight, or customer benefit." The IBM marketing strategy, SMASH in particular, was aimed "not at competition in an appropriate competitive sense, but at competitors and their viability as such." That is to say, IBM had set out deliberately to destroy a company that got in its way.

Christensen awarded Telex treble damages of more than $350 million. In the future IBM was to be restrained by a series of alterations in its marketing approach. Further unbundling would be required, and some penalties imposed upon clients desiring to replace IBM equipment with that produced by the peripheral manufacturers would be eliminated. As for Telex, Christensen found merit in the IBM charges and imposed a series of fines that came to slightly less than $22 million; in

A Generation of Litigation

addition, he restrained that company from using IBM patents, manuals, and former employees in certain fashions.

There was no doubt that Telex had won a major victory. The company's common stock immediately rose from around 3 to 8, while IBM common fell by 37 points in the two sessions following the decision. IBM announced that it intended "to appeal the decision," but it soon became evident that a flood of other suits were being filed, almost all of which resembled that of Telex. Lester Kilpatrick of California Computer Products said: "I think almost any company in the computer industry has got to be thinking about bringing suit against IBM, even the big mainframe companies," as CalComp weighed in with a $300 million action. Its time limit on suits having expired, Memorex filed for $3 billion in damages. Marshall Industries asked for $108 million. Itel, which had become a rising force in the industry, joined in soon after. Potter Instruments, all but destroyed by the SMASH program, filed preliminary papers.

The whale had been breached, and the sharks came in for their share of the meat. Most of these suits had at least some merit, but almost all were opportunistic as well, based more upon the Telex decision than any demonstrable violations on the part of IBM. This could be seen in the fact that none of the major companies sought damages; by then most were able to compete on one ground or another and didn't require legal redress. As for companies like CalComp, chairman Kilpatrick was forthcoming in his assessment of his case. The firm's major asset wasn't its patent, product, or anything else that appeared on the balance sheet. Rather, "It's our lawsuit against IBM."

Additional litigation piled up as the Telex case was in the process of being retried. Challenging IBM was a roster of small firms in the peripheral equipment subindustry—DPF, Forro Precision, Symbolic Control, Hudson General, Eaton-Allen, Memory Technology, Saunders Associates—in addition to those previously named. Like Telex and CalComp, these companies were marginal, in most cases weak financially, limited in technology, and thin in management. Some hoped to stave off disaster by coming to a financial settlement; others believed their cases would make them attractive take-over candidates. Their futures, even survivals, rested on success in the courtroom or at the bargaining table, and this in turn depended on the outcome of the Telex case.

In early 1975 a three-judge panel on the Tenth Circuit Court of Appeal reversed the Christensen decision. Finding that the lower court had erred in matters of both fact and law, the court unanimously threw out the quarter of a billion dollars in damages levied against IBM, at the same time ordering Telex to pay IBM $17.5 million in compensation and a punitive award of $1 million.

The news of this reversal caused almost as much commotion within the industry as had the original verdict. IBM couldn't have hoped for a more favorable decision; the company was completely exonerated, and the message could hardly be lost on other litigants. Kilpatrick told a reporter that he was "completely convinced that the appeals court is wrong" and said he would review the decision carefully. "They can't tell me it doesn't hurt," he added. "I've felt the lash." A Saunders Associates attorney thought the reversal would have little impact upon his actions—"Ours is not a Telex-type case. It's much more fundamental"—and he too found it "inconceivable that the circuit court could say there were no predatory acts on IBM's part." Telex vice-president and general counsel J. B. Bailey tried to shrug it off as only a setback along the way, not a major defeat: "It's a shame they made such a mistake. But we won't be gloomy unless the Supreme Court rejects our case. After all, IBM would have appealed it, anyway."

But Telex was in no position to continue. The company simply hadn't the funds to do so or even sufficient capital on hand to pay the damages levied by the appeals court if they were upheld. The contest was strikingly one-sided. IBM could have afforded a payment in excess of $1 billion; Telex had cash items of around $1 million at the time. An out-of-court settlement clearly was necessary. And that October one was announced. Telex would withdraw its petition in return for an arrangement whereby neither party would be required to make payments to the other.

Telex was off the hook. For that matter, so was IBM. Several of the minor cases were dropped immediately, while others would be withdrawn or decided in IBM's favor in the next few years. And all this transpired as the government's case finally came to trial, meaning that most of IBM's augmented legal team could concentrate upon this major assault, which promised to be complex, demanding, and long-lasting.

The government opened its argument before Judge David Edelstein a week after the court of appeals had reversed the Telex decision, so IBM entered the fray in good spirits. But the legal section was troubled by the presence of Edelstein on the bench. An aging jurist known for a generally critical view toward corporate practices, Edelstein had presided over the final hearings which led to the consent decree in 1956 and so was conversant with IBM's history, practices, and approaches. He literally was prepared to devote the remainder of his career to this case.

On January 26, 1981—one day before a retrial in the Greyhound case was to have begun—the two companies announced an out-of-court settlement. Conceding nothing, IBM agreed to pay Greyhound $17.7 million, and in return Greyhound dropped its lawsuit. This concluded the last of the important private antitrust actions, the end of a chapter in the company's history that had lasted more than a dozen years, during which IBM settled or won all of the twenty-four cases brought against it. "From IBM's standpoint, it's one less thorn in their side," said one Wall Street observer. "For IBM, $17.7 million is nothing."

"The deluge of antitrust litigation that hit us in the '70s has been reduced to a trickle," said an IBM report issued a few months prior to the Greyhound settlement. "We have completed six trials, and we have won them all. Ten Federal judges have ruled completely in our favor. It's a relic of the '60s that is now dragging into the '80s—a case that turns on the same issues that we have won time and again." The report went on to quote

Harvard economist Hendrik Houthakker, who initially had supported the government's action but since then had changed his mind. "I have come to the conclusion that there is a lot of competition in the industry," he said. "The industry is not at all like the monopoly depicted by classical economists. IBM is unable to rest on its laurels. It does things all the time to stay ahead of the competition." Of course, Houthakker was referring to technological developments, management techniques, and sales drives, vital ingredients in the computer wars. IBM stayed ahead on the legal front as well. The same sentence would echo through reports, press releases, and related documents: "IBM has denied the charge . . . and is vigorously defending each action."

PART IV

The Way to the Future

13

The Ubiquitous Computer

SCHOLARS DIFFER on the attributes of a mature industry, even when they are in agreement on which ones fall into that category. Certainly canals in the 1850's, railroading at the turn of the century, steel in the 1920's, and automobiles a half century later might be considered mature, even though each was different from the others.

There are several criteria by which young industries may be differentiated from those that are aging, and a dividing line —rough, imprecise, but serviceable—can be established to help determine when the passage from the early stage to the late one begins. Most can be located in such areas as structure, the pace of innovation, and leadership; in addition, there is a qualitative, subjective, and elusive factor which can be discerned in almost all vital, growing industries that is either lacking or found in a faded condition in the others. This is a sense of mystery, freshness, excitement, and originality. When the products or services become familiar, even commonplace, it is a certain sign that the era of youth is passing and that of maturity has begun.

By most ordinary measures, the computer industry was still young in the early 1970's. Scientists who had helped design the initial mainframes were still active, as were several of their products. Relatively few Americans had actually seen computers in operation, and fewer understood the principles upon which they were based. They were still deemed exotic; computerized robots were standard fare in science fiction motion pictures, while in some circles computer engineers and designers were considered on the "forefront of knowledge," sharing the spotlight with atomic scientists and astronauts.

But there were signs of aging in the area of mainframe construction, still dominated by IBM and the Seven Dwarfs. Several early electromechanical computers had been placed in museums, preserved there alongside the horseless carriages, biplanes, and steam locomotives as relics of an earlier era. First-generation machines, which a dozen years earlier had sold for more than $1 million, fetched a few hundred as scrap. No literate American could have been unaware of how computers had altered his life—from processing payrolls, sorting out forms, dispensing checks, and keeping tabs on credit to spewing out data on almost every subject.

Television programs on the computer revolution became a staple on networks, articles about the machines appeared in popular magazines and newspapers, and high school students who a generation earlier might have trained to become typists now took courses in programming. Even then some companies were planning to develop personal computers to market to individuals for use in their homes—placed next to the television set and radio, like them, exotica which had become familiar.

This is not to suggest the computer was about to become commonplace, just another piece of hardware. Rather, some of the mystery was shed as products evolved, new ones appeared, computer language was simplified, and the machines themselves became more accessible.

The pioneering, entrepreneurial spirit remained alive, but to see it in operation, one had to go to the peripheral firms, those turning out components, some of the service companies, and a handful of small units where former IBMers and refugees from the other large firms planned lines of plug-compatible hardware or developed minimachines and giant brains. The major firms continued to innovate; if anything, new product development accelerated in the early 1970's, and for a while proliferation was the rule. But this was done along well-established paths which had been blazed by scientists and managers during the first three generations.

The directions of innovation, paradoxically, were also becoming commonplace, to the point where they almost were predictable. To outsiders it might have appeared that a variety of corporate sclerosis of the imagination had set in. Some who recognized this early attributed it to the letdown after the 360 introduction, an understandable pause after so major an effort. Others took it as another sign of industrial maturity. There never again would be another phenomenon like the 360's, they said, if for no other reason than that of a combination of mature technology and satisfaction with what already existed. It had happened with other products, from light bulbs to jet airliners. After the initial rush of invention and originality, the product line tended to become undifferentiated, the companies started to suffer from signs of gigantism, and a stiff formalism began to envelop the organization.

IBM appreciated the implications of all this, and the company fought the tendency. It long had had a practice of selecting "fellows," whose primary task was the consideration of new ideas. Usually these people asked to work on their own, but they were supposed to discuss the projects with others in the laboratories and offices. Their concepts needn't have been practical or even realistic, but IBM hoped they might serve to stimulate thought throughout parts of the organization, spark imaginative forays elsewhere, and in general keep the company aware of new possibilities in all fields touching upon its business. This kind of approach had obvious limitations. There was no clear method of reviving a mature technology, even had users been willing to revamp their operations to accommodate drastic change—something which clearly wasn't the case. Even IBM balked at suggestions that it reinvent the computer or consider anything that would disturb the 360 client base. That part of the computer revolution at IBM had ended; from the early 1970's onward evolution was the order of the day insofar as mainframes were concerned. The industry had achieved stabilization in this area at least, in large part because of IBM's leadership.

The company provided a clear signal to this effect in late 1970, with the announcement of the 370 series. This was to have been the fourth generation, which would replace the 360's in somewhat the same way the earlier machines had taken over from the 1400's and 7000's. Going over the specifications, a user might easily have discovered that the new computers were more desirable and offered important economies in terms of prices, flexibility, and speed. The price per calculation was cut by as much as 60 percent for some models, and later even deeper slashes were made. While incorporating some of the latest technologies, however, these machines didn't represent a radical break with the past; users of 360's might easily switch to 370's, which took the same software and might even be integrated with the old peripheral equipment. The major change involved the internal storage system, which was much larger and more accessible than that in the 360's. The IBM public relations staff was uncharacteristically modest in its press releases, and Tom Watson spoke of "the new generation" of computers, not "the fourth generation," a term taken up by the business press but soon dropped. For the 370's truly weren't a fourth generation; rather, they were an improvement upon the third, as were rival and imitation machines soon released by other companies. Independent computer engineers, after exploring the new internal storage system, concluded it had been designed more to discourage users from taking memory banks from manufacturers of peripheral equipment than anything else. Technological change hadn't reached a dead end, but clearly the 370's didn't represent a quantum leap in the state of the art.

It soon became evident that no major manufacturer was prepared to stake everything on a truly new generation and that even had this been desired, the technology wouldn't permit it. There wouldn't be a fourth generation in the 1970's, but there would be continual evolution in and additions to existing lines. This, too, was taken as an indication of industrial maturity.

If all this were so, why did IBM insist on providing these machines with a new series number instead of simply adding them to the 360 line? When the question was raised later, company representatives attempted to demonstrate there indeed were significant alterations in designs, but within a few months of their introduction it became clear that pricing and morale had more to do with it than technology and performance. The 370/145, the initial machine in the line, was priced so as to discourage independent leasers from making purchases and then offering the computers to users at attractive rates. IBM lowered its own leasing rates drastically, while it priced the machines in such a way as to remove much of the profit from sales-and-leases. Tom Watson readily conceded his intent. "As long as we operate legally and fairly," he said, "it's not incumbent on us to price our machines to allow the leasing companies to take away our inventory." Watson added that the computers had been announced and then released in such a way as to motivate the sales force. "You have to keep feeding them new things to keep their morale up."

Morale was rather low in the early 1970's. The domestic computer industry was still growing, but the rate had slowed considerably. Some field representatives claimed this was due to an overselling of the 360's in the late 1960's, that in their zeal for placements the leasing companies had "stolen sales" from 1970 and beyond by luring clients into taking more capacity than they really needed. Others observed that the decline was due to the economic recession and that there would be a new boom once conditions improved. Several economists and Wall Street analysts noted that there appeared to be a five-year product cycle in computers and that activity traditionally declined toward the end of the cycle. The 360's had debuted in 1965, so 1970–1971 was destined to be a sluggish period. Such analysts went on to claim that each cycle was more powerful than the one that preceded it, and if tradition held, there would be a rapid improvement by mid-decade. Signs of this were few, however. Rather, the talk within the industry was of how production finally had outpaced placements, another certain indication of industrial maturity.

Forbes put the question bluntly: "Are the days of IBM's great growth behind it?" *Fortune* was more circumspect, but it also voiced doubts about the company's future: "Almost everyone has heard by now that IBM, the great American growth machine, has been sputtering." This might not have been discerned from a casual glance at the firm's consolidated financial statistics, but a detailed examination would have shown that IBM Domestic had peaked in 1968 and remained on a revenue and earnings plateau for the next three years. This stagnation was masked by increased revenues from abroad (by then World Trade was larger than Domestic) and by contributions from interest on the company's cash reserves, which, in the absence of new investment requirements, rose from $933 million in 1969 to $1.5 billion four years later.

Selected Statistics for IBM, 1969–1973

(millions of dollars)

| Year | Gross Revenues | | Net Income |
	Sales	Services, Rentals	
1969	2579	4617	934
1970	2021	5477	1017
1971	2180	6093	1078
1972	2879	6654	1279
1973	3372	7621	1575

Source: IBM 10K, 1973

The Ubiquitous Computer

Wall Street understood this, however, and the malaise was soon reflected in the price of IBM common, which declined sharply in 1970, rallied two years later, only to drift lower once again. IBM remained a glamour stock, but doubts about how long this would continue had appeared. Armonk played all this down and tried to reassure analysts. "Some people would extrapolate a year or two into a trend," said a spokesman in 1972, who thought that "normal" growth would return later in the year, when the full impact of the 370 placements was felt. So it did, but doubts remained.

This apparent loss of vigor was accompanied by a major management change in Armonk which, while carried off smoothly enough, raised new doubts regarding the company's future and was widely interpreted as representing the end of the era of entrepreneurship and the beginning of an age in which professional managers would lead the firm—that unmistakable sign of industrial maturity.

Personality clashes in the upper echelons of large corporations are common; few firms are able to avoid them for more than a year or so. IBM had its share of these, but none was more important than the mutual dislike of Dick Watson and Vin Learson. That the head of World Trade would come into conflict with the chief operating officer of the parent corporation was to have been expected. Their spheres of influence overlapped, and with the growth of World Trade came renewed requests for additional autonomy. But there was more to it than that. During the mid-1960's both men had reason to believe they were in line for the chairmanship when and if Tom Watson stepped down—as he indicated he might upon his sixtieth birthday in 1974. For a while it appeared that Dick had the inside track. World Trade was a thriving organization, he had demonstrated business sophistication, if not the kind of hard-driving enthusiasm that was prized at headquarters, and he was, after all, a Watson.

As for Learson, he was coming to be known as Tom Watson's hatchet man, the kind of person who excelled at cleaning up messes, who had no trouble firing people and shifting them to lesser positions—duties Tom disliked, especially when it came to dealing with individuals taken on by his father. In addition, Learson had created an able staff, which, of course, was dedicated to IBM but, according to rumors, was also personally loyal to him. By recognizing merit and dispensing promotions, he had won the support of several important younger men who were then coming into the inner circles, and he could count on them in any head-on conflict with Dick Watson. This could be seen in Armonk's refusal to permit World Trade a free hand in research and development, the restructuring of the subsidiary, and the diminution of Dick Watson's role within it. Learson's power seemed to grow steadily. Always blunt and forceful, he was the only inside director willing to take on Tom Watson on matters of policy, but he also was astute enough to know when to withdraw. To some it appeared that Tom stood in awe of Learson, viewing him as a force of nature over which he had lost a measure of control.

Dick Watson and Learson each played an important role in the 360 project, which from the first seemed capable of producing IBM's next chief executive officer as well as a new line of hardware. Learson, who was involved from the planning stage, devoted most of his time to the effort, was more conversant than Watson with the problems and personnel involved, and in addition was a far better tactician and more clever infighter. Calculating the risks carefully, he insisted that the third-generation machines be created and produced by both Domestic and World Trade, and so he drew Dick Watson, Gil Jones, and Charles Smith into the planning and execution. The World Trade leaders were flattered and impressed; it appeared that Learson recognized just how important their organization had become. They reasoned that Tom Watson and Learson meant them to have a major role in the project, one that would enhance their positions in Armonk. Learson wasn't dispensing favors or power, however. Rather, he had created conditions whereby credit for success would be his while he shared or even completely avoided blame for setbacks.

Learson's key maneuver came after most of the major decisions on design were in, schedules for production had been agreed upon, and marketing arrangements were in the process of being formulated. Learson and his lieutenants knew the schedule was tight—they had been instrumental in drawing it up. There was little leeway in the manufacturing timetable; any bottleneck or redesign problems could result in months of delay, lost orders, and general embarrassment. Those charged with producing the machines would have to operate under the gun, in an environment in which successes were deemed ordinary and failures rarely forgotten. Furthermore, Learson's estimates of the demand for the new machines proved low. Whether this was done deliberately or was fully appreciated at the time cannot be known. But the scene had been set for Learson's triumph. Should the sales force generate more orders than had been anticipated, credit would be given to those involved in marketing —and additional pressures would be placed upon executives having responsibilities for producing the machines.

The maneuvering for position took place behind closed doors, and those present have never spoken of the way assignments were made. When those doors were opened, however, World Trade—and Dick Watson—came out with important manufacturing tasks, while Learson had major responsibilities in marketing, financing, and placements.

The salesmen had few problems with clients, who literally lined up with their orders. The initial 30's, 40's, 50's, and 65's were placed in 1965, a year when many problems developed in manufacturing, resulting in late deliveries and some cancellations. Schedules had to be redrawn at a time when Learson's star was rising while Dick Watson's was going into eclipse. Later on IBMers would claim that the company truly intended to challenge Control Data in the giant computer field and that the 67's would have done the job had it not been for the inability of manufacturing to do its job well. Thus, indirectly and inferentially, Dick Watson was saddled with some of the blame for the antitrust suit along with everything else.

Dick appreciated what had happened. There seemed little doubt now that Learson was next in line for the succession and that he was being politely shunted aside. Already there were whispers to the effect that the company would benefit if he resigned—Dick was blocking the way upward for the next generation at World Trade—and that his mistakes had to be papered over because he was a Watson. After having spent so many years in his brother's shadow, Dick had taken to brooding, and although he was in control at work, his drinking increased as well.

Meanwhile, Learson's arrogance expanded along with his power. Always abrasive and pugnacious—in Armonk he was known as Attila the Hun—he seemed to dominate the executive suites. Learson's strong competitive drive previously had been seen in the major effort he made to defeat Tom Watson in yachting races; now some of his staff spoke knowingly, if guardedly, about how things would change (for the better in their view) once Watson stepped down. It wasn't simply a matter of personality; Watson and Learson started to clash on major issues of policy, and more often than not, Learson's view prevailed. Watson hoped to come to some kind of settlement with the Justice Department, similar perhaps to that he had worked out in 1956; Learson favored a strong defense, even an attack, without a single concession. The two men had differing views regarding the challenges from leasing companies and manufacturers and marketers of plug-compatible and peripheral equipment. Neither liked losing placements to competitors, but Watson was willing to concede them part of the market in return for industry peace and a series of court settlements. After all, IBM was now in a pioneering stance, exploring new opportunities and developing unique and highly profitable products and services; the company might skim the cream in these areas, leaving a small amount of milk to the others. For his part, Learson instinctively opposed any attempt to draw back from a fight and on occasion appeared eager to destroy any firm so brash as to produce and market machines that competed with those turned out by IBM. The SMASH program was his idea, one that made Watson uncomfortable, although he did not directly oppose it.

The Ubiquitous Computer

What if he had? By the late 1960's there was some question of whether Watson had the troops to head off Learson. This is not to suggest that a coup d'état was in the offing or that the two men were locked in a bitter power struggle; such is not the way at most major corporations, and it certainly would have been out of place at IBM. Rather, Learson was establishing his right to the succession, placing his men in critical areas, winning the confidence of the board, and all the while remaining on reasonably good terms with the chairman. On his part Watson appeared willing to concede powers to Learson so long as he maintained a veto over major decisions and had his way in those areas that interested him the most—namely, new products, ventures, and research.

Some in Armonk suggested that Tom Watson had grown tired of management, that he had slipped somewhat, and that since Learson had a better grasp of current business and immediate prospects, it only made sense for him to assume additional powers. All this may have been so, but Watson might have behaved as he did more because of the calendar than anything else. Learson was ambitious, eager to take full command, but he might be thwarted as a result of a circumstance over which he had no control—namely, that he was one year older than Tom Watson. All the chairman had to do was hold onto his post until he reached the age of sixty and then step down, establishing that as the proper time for retirement. Had he done this—and made it stick—Learson could have been denied the top post. And there is some indication that Tom Watson had this in mind, or at least such was the view commonly held in Armonk in early 1970.

At that time Dick Watson resigned from IBM to take the position of ambassador to France, causing much relief in Armonk and Paris. For the past few years Dick had been something of an embarrassment, more because of his having been ignored and passed over than anything specifically wrong he had done. Like Learson, he had come to the company with a problem he couldn't correct; he was the younger brother, and Tom had been given the command.

Learson had no reason to celebrate, however, for Tom gave no indication of following his brother into some other line of endeavor. Rather, he reiterated his intention to retire in 1974 and implied that with him would go other important executives of his era, Learson in particular. Most of these people accepted this with good grace—they were in that middle period of senior management, too young to retire, too old to be considered for a top post in a rival firm, and in any case all were IBM men and not likely to make the switch. Already Watson had reviewed the coming men in the next generation and appeared to have located there an heir apparent, Frank Cary, who at the time seemed the very model of faceless bureaucrat so often found in the executive suites of major firms in developed industries.

Even meticulous readers of the business press knew little of Frank Cary, who throughout his career had managed to stay out of the spotlight, deferred to his seniors in public, and preferred to perform his tasks with as little publicity as possible. Yet he was well known within the IBM organization and respected by competitors. Former employees who came into contact with Cary during his early years with the company generally characterize him as "a perfect IBM product," meaning he was efficient, ambitious, and willing to make personal sacrifices in order to advance IBM's well-being and his own career (which in his mind often were the same).

After attending UCLA and Stanford, Cary joined IBM in 1948 at the age of twenty-eight and, following the classic path, began as a salesman. Friendly enough but hardly outgoing, he tended to blend in with his background rather than to impress people by force of intellect or imagination. Cary was medium-sized and had a tendency toward pudginess; he had a round face and a receding hairline. Quite a contrast with the matinee idol handsomeness of a Tom Watson and Learson's football captain presence.

But Cary did impress his supervisors with his doggedness and performance, and in the field he demonstrated a talent for organization and administration. So he rose steadily within the organization, to assistant manager, branch manager, and district manager. Then it was on to the presidency of the Service Bureau, that testing place and filter for IBM executives, where he passed muster. In early 1961, with a dozen years at the company behind him, Cary received the call to headquarters; he now became assistant director for the corporate staff, which at the time was involved in planning the 360 campaign. It was the ideal place for an ambitious executive; everyone knew that this would become an incubator for future IBM leaders.

Like most of his generation in this position, Cary became enmeshed in high-level politics, and along with many others, he allied himself with Learson. After proving himself both capable and loyal, Cary was rewarded by being sent back into the field as a vice-president in the Data Processing Division, and from then on his rise was rapid even by IBM standards. Cary became division president in 1964 and general manager of the entire Data Processing Division two years later, and in 1969 he was awarded the penultimate honor of being named to the Management Review Committee, a select body charged with formulating policy and carrying out decisions.

Cary remained close to Learson and generally supported him during debates within the inner circle. He spoke out in favor of the SMASH campaign and early on espoused a hard line insofar as antitrust was concerned. In addition, he was available for special assignments—for a while his rivals called Cary the hatchet man's hatchet man. At the same time he saw the gulf widening between Tom Watson and Learson and sensed that executives too closely aligned with the president might face difficulties later on. Furthermore, although they respected each other's abilities, Learson and Cary were too dissimilar in matters of personality and outside interests ever to become truly close. Increasingly Learson came to rely upon John Opel, who was every bit as ambitious as Cary and whose temperament he found more appealing. Toward the end of the 1960's, then, Cary had put some distance between himself and Learson, though not so much as to alienate his former sponsor.

Tom Watson appreciated what was happening and came to look upon Cary not only as a potential ally but as a possible chief executive officer. Much depended upon what would happen during the next four years, the time Watson believed he had before retirement. He would groom his successor in much the same way he had been brought along. Cary wasn't ready for the top job yet, and perhaps he would never be. Of course, there were other bright middle-aged men Watson could pluck for the post, much to the chagrin of Learson, who by now had no doubts of what was happening.

Everything changed in late 1970, when Watson suffered a heart attack. Although he recovered quickly and soon was back on the job, he clearly could not remain in such a pressure-filled post for much longer, certainly not until 1974. The timetable was scrapped; Watson had to name his successor at a time when no member of the next generation seemed prepared to take over.

Under the circumstances the palm went to Learson, who assumed the chairmanship in the summer of 1971, at which time he was fifty-eight years old. He would command a team of four group executives—Dean McKay, George "Spike" Beitzel, Robert Hubner, and John Opel. Gilbert Jones would remain in charge at World Trade. All but Opel were considered Watson loyalists, and even he, closest of all to Learson, was edging into a more independent stance. As expected, Frank Cary took over as president and chief operating officer, and by then he was pretty much his own man as well as Watson's apparent choice for the succession. Cary was fifty-one years old in 1971 and, if all went as planned, would be fifty-three when he took on the top job, which he might hold until 1980, by which time he would turn sixty. In Watson's view, then, IBM would be taken care of at least insofar as leadership was concerned through the 1970's, and by the close of the decade the company might have been altered so much as to require a fresh set of managers. But that would be Cary's problem, not his.

Meanwhile, Watson would take care of Learson, who even then gave indications he might try to hold on for a few years past his sixtieth birthday. This wouldn't be a major difficulty, however. Watson remained on the board, whose members were loyal to the family, and from there could block any major attempts to go off in new and undesirable directions. In addition, the Armonk staff could be counted on to mark time, knowing that Learson would be gone in fewer than two years and that his successor might change direction once he came aboard. From the first Cary exercised power effectively since both he and the others knew that he soon would take command.

In many ways Learson was at least as well equipped for the top post as any of the three men who preceded him. Few among his contemporaries understood the industry better or had a finer grasp of the marketplace than he. Learson's devotion to IBM was complete and obvious. He was a fierce competitor— William Norris of Control Data, who thoroughly disliked Learson, called him a "primitive" and worse. One company veteran who had known both Watson senior and junior thought Learson would have been more at home with the old man or, better still, with John Patterson, who would have admired his battering-ram approach.

He was, in fact, a throwback to the no-holds-barred era of American business and was out of place in the more polite times of the post-World War II period. Learson simply couldn't accept the idea that other companies should have a significant share of the market or that IBM should concede an inch to anyone, the government included. He was a hard competitor who hated to lose in anything he undertook, who apparently couldn't appreciate the need for tactical withdrawals and concessions. He yearned for complete victories and unconditional surrenders from opponents. "Vin's favorite movie is *Patton*," said one former associate, "and if you knew him, you'd understand why."

Learson wasn't the entrepreneurial type, nor did he fit the textbook definition for professional managers. Rather, he was a shrewd tactician and field commander, an organizer who was able to translate many of Tom Watson's imaginative and daring concepts into actions, often brilliantly. But so far as he was able to demonstrate, he had few new plans of his own, no original vision of where the company should be headed. His tenure as chairman was noted for a recovery from the economic slump and court battles against adversaries, little else. But then, he served for only a year and a half, hardly long enough to make much of an impression upon a firm as large and complex as IBM.

Learson appreciated his situation and stepped down gracefully in early 1973, to be succeeded by Frank Cary. John Opel was named to Cary's old post as president, so inferentially was in line for the succession, which, assuming all went well, would be in 1981. This would provide Cary with sufficient time to make any alterations he felt necessary, while Opel would have ample opportunity to demonstrate both his abilities and his loyalties.

The business publications that had printed major stories about Learson's arrival said relatively little regarding Cary's selection. The reason was obvious: Learson provided good copy, while Cary seemed more like the computers his firm was turning out—coldly efficient but hardly innovative, quirky, or exciting. According to the *Wall Street Journal*, Cary was elevated because he was the "right kind" of leader for that particular season, implying he was there to manage the patrimony, not to alter it significantly.

Was this possible or even conceivable? Perhaps, had Cary chosen to devote most of his attention to the mainframe business, to seek, as Learson had, victories in the field against major competitors such as UNIVAC, Honeywell, Control Data, and NCR, and in the courts against the government. Had he done so, Cary would have signaled that the age of the manager indeed had arrived at IBM and that future gains would come from obtaining a greater share of the mainframe market as well as from the enlargement of volume. There were other areas of opportunity, however, and Cary was well aware of them. The mainframe business may have shown signs of maturity in 1973, but such was not the case with software, storage systems, electronics, and the wide, general area of communications. At headquarters Cary had been considered an able bureaucrat who for all his good qualities was deficient in imagination. Yet he had been elevated by Tom Watson, for whom this trait was a major consideration when it came to leadership. Cary found himself in a position somewhat analogous to Watson's in the late 1940's, when at the latter's urging IBM had turned from tabulators and accounting and calculating machines to computers. Now he would have the opportunity to initiate a move not so much away from computers (which, after all, was still a growth industry) as toward businesses emerging from the technological imperative. This was one of the major management challenges in all American business during the decade, but such were Cary's personality and public image that his way of handling it was all but unrecognized.

Some of the questions regarding the maturity of the mainframe business had been resolved prior to Cary's promotion. As has been alluded to, this segment of the industry underwent a period of overcapacity during the early 1970's, which led to a bitter struggle for placements and, among the Seven Dwarfs more than at IBM, lower profit margins. There had been major shake-outs in other industries under similar circumstances, as weak firms left the field or were absorbed by other, stronger entities. This was deemed the classic indication of maturity. Yet as late as April 1970 it appeared that all the major contenders would survive. All were well funded, each had a defined position and stance, and at stake were matters of prestige and credibility, almost as important as profits.

In early May, however, the industry was swept by rumors regarding shake-ups at several firms and major announcements about to come out of Honeywell. On Wall Street the latter's stock was active, amid talk that the firm was about to cut back drastically on its computer operations or perhaps even to leave the business entirely. Analysts couldn't make up their minds whether the news was bullish or bearish, and while they pondered the matter, some learned that General Electric, too, was considering similar shrinkages for its American operations. Then, on May 20, Honeywell and GE issued a joint announcement to the effect that the former company would acquire most of the computer operations of the latter. It was the largest acquisition in the industry's history, one that made the new

Honeywell Information Systems second to IBM in size, displacing UNIVAC from its traditional runner-up position. Under the terms Honeywell paid $100 million plus 1.5 million shares of its stock for GE's computer operations, meaning that GE had become the major stockholder in Honeywell.

The combination made sense. Over the years Honeywell had developed a superior sales force, which had performed well in match-ups against IBM in the market for medium-sized computers. In contrast, General Electric had one of the spottiest sales organizations in the industry but was as strong as IBM in several key technological areas, and ahead in others; moreover, its quality control was outstanding, whereas Honeywell's was somewhat weak. Honeywell recently had produced the 655, a large machine which, insofar as performance was concerned, was more than a match for the upper end of the 370 line, but few had been placed. Now it was reworked into the Series 6000 and then turned over to the combined sales operation. These machines were very well received, and within two years orders for more than $500 million worth of them had been booked. Quite a number of these came at the expense of IBM, a sore point with Learson. Though hardly anything over which he had control, the success of Honeywell Information Systems took some of the luster from his performance at IBM.

The marriage of Honeywell and GE's computer operation came off smoothly. "It is one of those rare situations where even three years later everybody is happy," said Clarence Spangle, who ran the division for Honeywell. This new entity appeared capable of providing IBM with its strongest competition in the mainframe area since the industry's early days, when UNIVAC led the way. Yet Honeywell was still one of the pack, with no hopes of catching up with the leader.

Nor was it able to claim the runner-up post for long. Burroughs and NCR were undergoing periods of major growth, and another major combination was on the way.

RCA had become the leader in plug compatibles. Its executives boasted that their Spectra machines, patterned after the 360's, offered at least as much performance at a much lower price. "There is a certain disadvantage in looking like a 'me too,' " conceded an RCA executive, "but there are a lot of things working for us." The most important clearly was price. RCA developed the Flexible Accrued Equity Plan, whereby a user might lease a machine under a seventy-two-month plan at rates similar to those offered by IBM but take ownership at the end of the period. During this time RCA guaranteed software compatibility and even offered free service contracts to some who took the plan. "Being easy to switch to makes RCA the only logical alternative to IBM," said the company. "Giving you features IBM doesn't have makes us a better alternative."

Also involved in the contest was the matter of family pride. IBM was a Watson preserve, and in a like fashion, RCA was dominated by the Sarnoffs. Just as Tom junior had succeeded his father, so Robert Sarnoff had taken over from David, and a defeat for "Bobby" would have been galling. Therefore, he plunged ahead, even after it became apparent the company would lose money on placements under the best of circumstances. This is not to suggest that RCA lacked management skills, a strong asset base, good machines, or an aggressive sales force. Rather, in a search for placements and industry status Robert Sarnoff sacrificed profits for volume in the hope that eventually all would turn out to his advantage—and perhaps, too, that he would be looked upon as a worthy successor to his father by matching his successes in radio and television with a triumph in computers.

Just how this was supposed to happen was never made clear, but morale was low at RCA in early 1971, with top executives wondering how much longer such a situation would be allowed to continue. There was talk of a sellout, a merger, and even a palace coup to topple Sarnoff and replace him with a man who would dispose of the computer operations. The Honeywell-GE combination might have been the catalyst for change, but even without it RCA would soon have had to leave the business.

Because customers realized this, too, during the summer of 1971 orders were canceled by executives fearful of being stuck with a machine that lacked a service department. RCA's decline helped the other firms, Honeywell and IBM in particular, and by late summer users were canceling leases on a wholesale basis. Things became so desperate that RCA salesmen were offering two computers for the price of one, and even so, placements dried up.

Unable to bear the pressures placed upon him, Sarnoff announced that RCA would leave the computer business. The company would continue to service its machines and honor all obligations, but nothing more than that would be done.

It was generally believed that RCA had lost more than $250 million on its computer venture, and some estimates ran as high as $450 million. The company still had its computer inventory, production and marketing operations, and a customer base, although at the time the last was eroding rapidly. How much was all this worth—at scrappage prices, that is? "RCA's computer operation has got to be a can of worms," remarked one executive. "I wouldn't touch it if they paid me to take it." But Gerald Probst, head of UNIVAC, had been monitoring RCA for several months and felt otherwise. He wasn't particularly interested in the machines, sales force, and manufacturing facilities; rather, he hoped to negotiate for the customer base. If these clients could be talked into retaining their present machines or replacing them with UNIVACs, that company might once again become the second largest factor in the industry.

Probst approached Sarnoff in late September, and soon teams from both companies met to explore possibilities. Initially RCA insisted upon what amounted to an all-or-nothing arrangement—Sperry Rand would have to purchase plants, inventory, and parts, in addition to assuming responsibility for the entire work force, if it wanted the customer base. Probst rejected this deal out of hand. He was more than willing to hire key scientists, technicians, managers, and salesmen, but he wasn't interested in the factories or assembly-line personnel. Probst was in a strong position, knowing that the longer he held back, the less the property would be worth. But he was also taking a risk since the longer he negotiated, the fewer customers would remain with RCA equipment. He won his gamble; Sarnoff backed down, and Sperry got almost everything it wanted at a surprisingly low price.

The terms were announced on November 19, less than two months after negotiations had begun. In return for $70.5 million down and 15 percent of the revenues derived from existing placements, UNIVAC acquired a customer base of close to 500 companies and government bureaus, along with more than 1,000 computers, the initial cost of which had been more than $900 million. Moving swiftly, UNIVAC executives contacted all these users to assure them of continued service, even better software, and discounts on future machines. Others interviewed RCA personnel, and eventually some 2,500 of them (one-third of the work force) were hired. Probst was delighted with the way things had turned out. Almost all the accounts were retained, and in a swoop UNIVAC had acquired an excellent talent pool. "You could never go out in the open market and get that many people with that type of talent," said a UNIVAC executive. "It's like taking the Eastern Division of the NFL and saying you can take the top ten guys from each team."

UNIVAC had its placements and personnel, at a cost far lower than what Honeywell had paid for General Electric's computer operations or Xerox for Scientific Data. The RCA machines were gradually replaced by UNIVACs, and within a few years most traces of the Sarnoffs' venture into computers had vanished. In the process UNIVAC was invigorated and, as had been the case with the Honeywell acquisition, emerged a much stronger company.

Competition between the old war-horses of the mainframe industry became more polite by mid-decade, and the situation more settled. By then most of the surviving firms appeared secure in their special niches—NCR in banking and retailing, Burroughs in banking, Control Data in major systems, and UNIVAC and Honeywell shadowing IBM, which, of course, was in most areas of data processing. New companies continued to appear—in plug-compatible mainframes, giant and mini-systems, specialized hardware and software, and peripheral equipment. But the industry's old, historic foundation was aging, and looking over the senior executives in mid-decade, one might have been forgiven the conclusion that the era of entrepreneurship had passed and the bureaucrats and managers had taken over. Probst, Spangle, Burroughs's Ray MacDonald, and now Frank Cary seemed of that breed. The only pioneer who remained was Norris of Control Data, and even he was starting to plan for retirement.

In the autumn of 1976, at a data processing seminar, a young technician remarked: "Any idiot can make a computer." Hyperbole, to be sure, but none of those who listened appeared shocked or would disagree. Whatever else computers might do, they were losing the ability to excite the imagination.

14

The Office of the Future

INDUSTRIAL CHANGE often results from a combination of technological innovation and entrepreneurial opportunism. Businessmen seize upon new products and processes to implement decisions made in boardrooms, to tighten a grip on an existing market or open up new markets. The reverse also occurs—the perception of a business need can stir technology and bring forth a wide variety of inventions and related developments. Finally, external forces play important roles, by pressuring both researchers and entrepreneurs into altering their products, developing new ones, and uncovering more appropriate methods of using them.

The process works sluggishly or not at all in truly mature industries. This might be seen by referring to the recent history of the American automobile. The cars produced in 1970 weren't appreciably different technologically from those turned out three decades earlier, and they were sold in pretty much the same ways. There were cosmetic changes and refinements, to be sure, but little else. The technology had hardened, the market for automobiles was well defined, and although several competitors had dropped out, no new ones with fresh ideas in either area had managed to succeed. Technological innovation and marketing development had been profound in the era of Henry Ford and Alfred Sloan; such was not the case under the often faceless managers who succeeded them. Internal stimulation was lacking in the early 1970's, and there was no external one in clear sight. This situation changed with the dramatic increase in the price of gasoline—the external challenge—so that by the end of the decade both technology and structure were undergoing major alterations.

While beneficial in many ways, this quickening of the pace and switches in direction can result in dislocations, pain, and frustration. Gains from new products and services must be balanced by a temporary loss of efficiency elsewhere. Managers and technicians accustomed to a calmer atmosphere must adjust to the new ways, find a haven in the back-line parts of the firm, or be jettisoned. Individuals who yearn for stability and order aren't equipped to provide leadership in a period when imagination is more of an asset than devotion to established norms and when change is the rule. Similarly, bold entrepreneurial types can be destructive when located in industries in which things have settled down—and there were dozens of cases of such people being dismissed from automobile firms in the 1950's and 1960's. Many found positions in the electronics industry and within some of the rapidly growing conglomerates, where their technological and managerial talents were appreciated and might be more usefully employed.

All this had an important bearing upon the situation at IBM and within the computer industry as a whole in 1973, when Frank Cary became chairman. That the essential mainframe business was then more established, accepted, and defined than it had been a decade earlier was fairly evident; as has been indicated, it was in the process of maturation. Except for specialized companies with narrow product lines in ultralarge machines (or boxes, as they were coming to be called) and producers of minicomputers, there would be no new entries into the field. IBM would remain in the lead, while Honeywell, UNIVAC, Burroughs, NCR, and the others scrambled for position behind the Armonk giant. And if the basic machine couldn't be produced by an idiot, at least much of the essential technology held few secrets for educated laymen. As has been noted, advances in mainframe architecture after the introduction of the third-generation machines tended to be evolutionary, based primarily upon the further development of devices and techniques already known toward the end of the 1960's.

To some it seemed the industry had reached a level of stability. Certainly the government's lawyers in the antitrust case believed this was so since they claimed that IBM all but monopolized the computer field and that the company's breakup would restore competition and, so it was assumed, technological growth. Yet even as the case was being prepared, the processes of change were at work, and technological innovation was accelerating rather than slowing. At the same time managers were using computers in different configurations and were quick to appreciate the implications of the developing technologies.

The alterations being made were qualitative as well as quantitative, affecting even the language itself, a certain sign that stagnation had been avoided. This was a familiar process to veterans of the industries. In the 1950's it had been common to speak of the office equipment business. A decade later one heard of the computer industry, and then came data processing, clearly a wider area. "Information" was the key word for the early 1970's—"information processing" implied that more than numbers were being analyzed, and "information systems" indicated that the computer was but one part of a complex of machines. At that time such firms as IBM, Burroughs, and NCR considered themselves manufacturers of computers, which had emerged from the business machines industry of the 1930's and

1940's. Now the cycle was being completed, as each of these firms as well as younger ones rushed to develop what some were calling the office of the future, which incorporated a variety of devices, from computers and copiers to the new word processors (which initially seemed little more than "intelligent typewriters" but clearly were more than that), all of which were linked together in networks by novel communications systems.

At each turn of the wheel IBM had faced new challenges and different sets of competitors. The firm came up against NCR, Burroughs, and Remington Rand in the 1930's and 1940's. UNIVAC was the major challenger in the 1950's, and a decade later there were the likes of General Electric, RCA, Honeywell, and Control Data. By 1970 IBM had to deal with producers of plug-compatible mainframes, manufacturers of peripheral equipment, leasing and service companies, and specialized firms that concentrated on areas it chose to ignore for the time being. The world of the early 1980's was far more complex and even bewildering—amorphous and in a constant state of flux.

Perceptions were shifting rapidly in the late 1970's and early 1980's, so that one could never be quite certain just what elements went into the making of the variegated industry based upon the gathering, processing, and transmission of information. Depending upon how one defined it, IBM appeared either as a giant among pygmies or, in one view, the runner-up to American Telephone & Telegraph. Insofar as computers alone were concerned, IBM had approximately 70 percent of the market. But in the broader area of data processing equipment, it produced some 40 percent of the output. At the turn of the decade IBM trailed Control Data in software and services, followed Digital Equipment, Hewlett-Packard, and Data General in minicomputers, and was far behind Wang Laboratories in word processing. Datapoint showed the way in distributed data processing, AT&T led in communications networks, while Apple, Commodore, and Tandy were far ahead in microcomputers. There even was a threat from Exxon; the world's largest corporation became involved in information systems, in what for it was a small way, but clearly an indication of what might be expected in the future. And behind them all, on the periphery of the industry according to most definitions but already in it according to other, broader ones, were such technologically proficient firms as Texas Instruments, Intel, and Motorola, leading manufacturers of what had become the central element in all this—the integrated circuit.

Integrated circuitry was not a new idea or product in the late 1960's. Millions of the chips had been used in the third-generation machines, and they clearly would be employed on computers to be manufactured in the future. As has been discussed, the initial idea behind these circuits was to place several electronic components on a single surface, in this way saving space and money and enabling the operations to be conducted more rapidly than was possible with transistors. The first of the chips, assembled in part by hand at Texas Instruments and Fairchild Camera, were relatively limited, large, expensive, and subject to failures. In 1963, a year during which some 300 million transistors and diodes were turned out at an average cost of slightly more than $1 each, Fairchild and TI produced less than 500,000 integrated circuits, almost all of which cost more than $25 apiece. The price declined rapidly as technology advanced, new companies entered the field, and economies of scale came into force. Just as transistors had replaced vacuum tubes, so the chips took over from transistors. In 1967, for the first time, total production of transistors and diodes declined; that year almost 69 million chips were produced at an average price of $3.32.

By then industry insiders had come to appreciate the potential of integrated circuits. If enough components in the proper configuration could be crammed onto a silicon chip, the unit might perform some of the functions of a computer—it would be, in the lexicon of the industry, a processor. All that would be required would be an input mechanism, a display, and a memory to provide a user with what already was being called a computer on a chip. This concept was being discussed at several companies, IBM included, toward the end of the 1960's, and work was progressing on increasingly more complex chips. Out of this came the technology of large-scale integration

(LSI) of circuitry, which became one of the most exciting areas in computer research. Within a decade researchers had placed the equivalent of 100,000 transistors on a chip, and the unit had more power than the 7070's, which a generation earlier filled an entire room. Moreover, scientists already had begun work on very large-scale integration (VLSI) and talked confidently of creating units at least twice as powerful as the largest 370, at a cost of a few hundred dollars, which would be capable of being carried in the user's vest pocket. They implied that these micro-processors would not only replace all existing hardware and thus revolutionize the industry but also provide anyone who needed such a service with a convenient, easy-to-program device with a self-contained power source, at so low a price as to make it all but disposable.

The general public had its first encounter with micro-processors in the early 1970's, when they appeared in the form of pocket calculators and digital wristwatches. The early ones were little more than simple adding machines and time displays, purchased more out of curiosity than need. By mid-decade, however, it was possible to obtain what amounted to a pocket computer, complete with memory banks, readouts, and scores of programs. Hewlett-Packard and Texas Instruments led the way, with several Japanese firms close behind. In 1981 one could purchase a hand-held computer based upon LSI with the capability of the early ENIACs for less than $200. The memory systems of such devices were relatively small, however, and software remained limited. Given the rapid pace of technological advances, however, these problems seemed capable of being overcome within a relatively short period.

By the early 1980's, too, the initial digital watches had given way to complex, preprogrammed devices more akin to computers with a time readout than the simple analogue, spring-driven models of the 1960's. These watches were programmed to change days, months, and years automatically, and some came equipped with calculators as well. As is the case with the hand-held computers, these are based upon LSI technology, a key element in the emerging microelectronics industry, which in 1979 accounted for sales of more than $11 billion and was expanding at an annual rate of around 20 percent. Microprocessors, its major subindustry, led the way in growth, with production doubling every eighteen months.

Texas Instruments had started out as a supplier of seismic services and then entered and assumed leadership of the transistor industry; at one time IBM was its major customer. The next step, to integrated circuits, was easily made. Then, in the 1970's, TI turned to the production and marketing of instruments under its own name, while it continued to supply components to others. By the early 1980's it was ready for the next step: entrance into the computer market. Along with several other former components manufacturers, such as Intel and National Semiconductor, it was prepared to go into the field against IBM itself, and in fact, National was already there, selling and leasing plug-compatible machines based upon its components but manufactured by others. Thus, one of the next challenges to IBM would come from the broad area of microelectronics, which today holds greater promise for growth than even information processing.

Toward the end of the 1970's microelectronics was employed in the design and production of games, such as basketball, football, or baseball. The "player" would match himself against a preprogrammed computer, which in some models could be set at the required degree of difficulty. Computerized chess games followed, along with a wide variety of offerings under the general heading of amusements. Although they had no direct bearing upon the information processing industry, such toys prepared the general public for what came to be known as the home or personal computer.

In 1974 a small New Mexico-based electronics firm, Micro-Instrumentation Telemetry Systems, produced the first of its Altair 8800 microcomputers, designed to sell for $400. More for the hobbyist than the general public and lacking software, the Altair clearly had limited appeal, and MITS couldn't afford an advertising campaign. Yet 1,500 of them were sold within a year, encouraging others to enter the field. The most important of these was Radio Shack, the largest American retail electronics firm, which catered to hobbyists and did a sizable business with the general public. Radio Shack offered its microcomputer in 1977, at a time when demand for the systems was expanding faster than supply. The following year it accounted for half of the 200,000 machines sold nationally, and it was evident that a new subindustry had emerged.

The transition from electronic games to home computers wasn't difficult to assay. More troublesome was the matter of exploring the uses for such machines. Clearly one might play games on them, and the memory systems could store recipes, telephone numbers, tax records, and the like. In time software was developed to offer language instruction and even to create a home security system. Had this been all, however, the appeal of such computers would have been extremely limited, and the market soon saturated.

Radio Shack and the many other companies in the field appreciated the problem and developed not only software for home or personal uses but programs that might appeal to professionals and small businessmen. Given the proper instruction, these microcomputers might handle accounts receivable and payable, maintain inventories, keep records of correspondence, and provide financial information for tax purposes. But even with all this, the personal computers had clear limitations and remained halfway between business tool and toy.

This changed toward the end of the 1970's, when it became possible to link a personal computer with a central data base by means of a modem (modulation/demodulation device) which enabled it to communicate over telephone lines or other means of transmission. Thus, the inexpensive home machine could be connected—for a fee—to some of the most sophisticated and advanced programs available.

The development of microcomputers that could be utilized as terminals that had access to huge storage facilities was soon recognized as one of the most important developments in the industry, the central one in helping transform information processing into information communications and one which will have profound implications for every major firm in the field.

As with all such subindustries, there was much experimentation and innovation in the early years of microcomputers. Entry into the field was relatively easy, but the mortality rate for fledgling companies was high, both typical of periods of industrial youth and great growth. Relatively minor miscalculations in design, production, marketing, or pricing could mean bankruptcy for an undercapitalized firm. Price cutting was the rule; the computer which sold for $8,000 might be discounted to $4,000 within a year and be considered obsolete six months later.

By 1979, however, the subindustry was taking shape, and several strong leaders had emerged. Tandy, the parent company for Radio Shack, reported microcomputer revenues of $150 million, twice that of Apple Computer, the runner-up. Such was the nature of the industry that within two years Apple—the fastest-growing firm in the business—was running neck and neck with Radio Shack, and it appeared it would soon take the leadership position. Then came Commodore International, BASF, and Verbatim, each with a special niche, but none close to the two leaders in revenues or placements.

All these firms had learned important lessons. Good distribution was required, for example, and customers insisted upon standard typewriter keyboards and a complete array of software. Also, the market for microcomputers was different from that for minis in that it was broader and shallower. For example, sales increased substantially in December 1978, 1979, and 1980, indicating that parents were purchasing them as Christmas presents for their children, and as prices came down, the numbers of hobbyists increased. Thus, simplicity in programming was vital.

Within the industry it generally was conceded that Apple had the most advanced equipment, while Commodore's was rugged and dependable. As for Radio Shack, its position was earned through services, in much the same way IBM had come to dominate computers in the 1950's and 1960's. By 1981 the company had some 7,000 shops and more than 50 specialized computer centers. Potential buyers—people who knew little about the machines and their capabilities—understood they could receive guidance and assistance at the many retail outlets, and by then Radio Shack had a good reputation for servicing its products. For all its assets Apple couldn't match Radio Shack in this regard; the company had to rely on its superior technologies and trouble-free hardware and, in addition, had to create an extensive service network. As for Commodore, in spite of its having developed machines specially suited for schools, it had a poor reputation for service. More even than was the case with business computers, microcomputer owners demanded a strong backup from the manufacturer, which in this case meant highly visible retail stores.

The lesson wasn't lost on other companies considering selling or leasing information processing machines to the general public, and among these were the giants of the industry, most of which had no direct experience in the area and little to guide them. Still, in 1979 Xerox took the plunge, announcing its intention to open service centers, some of which would be in shopping malls, where potential buyers might see the machines in operation, learn of their attributes, and even place orders. Xerox salesmen who previously had made the rounds of offices now had to learn to sell machines for home use—as though they were sewing machines and dishwashers.

Texas Instruments was next to enter the retailing effort, making the move shortly after marketing its initial consumer products. Then Digital Equipment, with one of the weaker sales forces in the industry and a reputation for concentrating on sophisticated users, made a turnabout and announced it, too, was preparing to serve the amateur market. Other important minicomputer manufacturers followed suit. Clearly they believed that personal computers would prove a large market and that with the proper orientation, tens of thousands of Americans would not only purchase them but become continuing customers for software and services. A strong indication of this came when Sears, Roebuck said it would offer computers through catalogs, with models to be displayed and demonstrated in selected stores as well.

By 1981 almost all the old-line mainframe companies either had announced intentions of entering the field or were in the process of drawing up plans for such ventures. With the exception of Sperry, none had much experience in the area, and that company's had been limited to typewriters and office supplies. Now, along with the others, Sperry drew up sketches of "computer stores" and spoke with advertising agencies about the best methods of luring potential customers inside.

IBM followed suit. The organization that had instructed the others in marketing skills announced it, too, would take the plunge and for the first time create stores geared to serve the general public. This move provided the concept with legitimacy and appeared to be an important shift in Armonk's thinking. Not even during the 1950's and 1960's, when its electric typewriters had achieved important penetration in the nonbusiness sector, had IBM attempted to create a consumer marketing branch, but now the firm appeared about to do so for computers. Furthermore, within the industry the announcement was taken as a sign that IBM was preparing to enter the microcomputer market.

This wasn't the case. Rather, as had become traditional with the company, IBM left the pioneering to others and would jump in with a significant effort to grab a large share of the business only after their concept proved both valid and profitable. To be sure, the initial shops represented a beachhead, but they didn't signal a major push into the lowest and most competitive segment of the computer business. IBM would display, demonstrate, and sell or lease minicomputers from these facilities, but the machines and their software were geared toward the needs of small businessmen and professionals, not the hobbyists and games players who constituted a large part of Radio Shack's sales or the high schools which purchased thousands of Commodore and Apple machines. Armonk still wasn't concerned with this part of the industry.

From the start several IBM executives had been intrigued

by one aspect of microcomputers—namely, their ability to be linked by means of modems to data banks. In this way the processor could be transformed into a terminal, which could have access to powerful memory systems or could even exchange information with other computers in various parts of the world. This wasn't a new idea, and in fact, according to one industry estimate, in 1970 there already were 100,000 terminals attached to IBM machines alone. All the major firms were experimenting along these lines. What the development of the microcomputer market had done was to indicate that potential purchasers of access to software were greater in number than had been imagined.

Although IBM wasn't particularly interested in microcomputers, it was vitally concerned with new uses for its products, especially the medium-sized and large computers which were the heart of its operations. The 360 program had been predicated upon the belief that these machines might be sold or leased to individual businesses or government agencies; IBM had little interest in terminal systems or time-sharing in the mid-1960's.

By 1970, however, as the rest of the industry started to move into this emerging area, IBM started to take notice. Cary was one of the first to appreciate the potential of what already was known as distributed data processing, and he worked hard to win Learson over to his view. "The market will move toward remote computing," he predicted in a 1971 memo to the chairman, "and noncentral processing unit equipment will be a continually increasing portion of the business." With Learson's grudging approval, Cary went ahead with the AQUARIUS (A Query and Retrieval Interactive Utility System), a prototype operation that linked computers and terminals and was supposed to pave the way for IBM's commercial ventures into distributed data processing.

There was a basic flaw in the AQUARIUS concept and execution, however, which wasn't evident at the time but became glaringly so later on, as IBM failed to make the kind of inroads into the field it had expected. It seemed that

The Office of the Future

AQUARIUS and other ventures that flowed out of it were based upon a technology that was becoming outmoded and that in any case was inappropriate for such systems.

In order to understand this, one must first appreciate the fact that in the late 1960's and early 1970's Armonk was still basking in the afterglow of the 360 revolution, Learson's greatest triumph and the campaign and gamble upon which his reputation rested. The 360's had changed the company's orientation in ways that often had been painful. Many top executives had won their battle stars during the third generation's struggles, and they had strong emotional ties to the 360's and 370's.

The Data Processing Division, IBM's heart, from which Cary emerged, was a complex and varied operation. Within it scores of scientists and technicians were working on a wide variety of original concepts. But the main drive there was to find additional uses for technologies and devices developed and perfected in the mid-1960's. Meanwhile, other major firms, with less of this kind of emotional baggage, were making fresh studies of the minicomputer market and were attempting to adjust to the coming evolution from data processing to information systems. Newer firms with young entrepreneurs, with no representation in the third generation but a clear interest in distributed data processing, were grabbing large segments of that market. Such people could be found at Data Processing, but not in positions of major authority; these were held by 360 veterans.

These individuals were responsible for IBM's initial foray into minicomputers. In 1969 the company organized the General Systems Division, to be based in Atlanta. Out of it came the System/3, which incorporated a good deal of the 360 design and concepts. This was a small but powerful machine, one that appealed to programmers trained on the 360's. As such it required professional handling and was almost impossible for neophytes to use. Thus, it was rejected by some IBM customers who wanted small machines to use in remote offices and by a good many businessmen who hoped their initial computer could be operated by retrained bookkeeping personnel. The System/3 was, in reality, a scaled-down version of the 360 and as such might have appealed to those who found the bigger machines too powerful for their needs. Armonk understood this and, to prevent "downgrading," constructed the System/3 in such a way as to make it incompatible with the 360's and 370's. Thus, the machine was too complex and big for the minicomputer market and wasn't appropriate for many users of larger machines. IBM was able to carve a place for the System/3 as a result of an intense sales effort and price cuts, but it never threatened its Digital Equipment counterparts as was the original intention.

This was the situation Cary inherited. Data Processing was dominated by the 360 establishment, and the System/3 was something of an embarrassment. AQUARIUS was workable, but based upon the wrong kind of technology and concept. Cary had been one of the major movers during the 360 campaign but earlier than most had come to realize that its technology was limited. More than most IBM veterans he was interested in distributed data processing and was willing to mount a major campaign in this direction. It would be going too far to suggest that in this respect Cary bore a relationship to Learson similar to the one Watson junior had with his father in the early 1950's. For one thing, the decision to enter the computer market was far bolder than Cary's plan to stress distributed data processing, and for another, IBM was a much larger and more complex company in the early 1970's than it had been two decades earlier. In addition, Cary had other ideas for the firm, some of which were at least as important as a move into DDP. Still, his assumption of the chairmanship did signal the beginning of a change in this area.

Cary understood that initially at least little could be done with the old Data Processing establishment. But he knew that within the group were scientists and marketing personnel interested in new approaches to distributed data processing and convinced IBM had to mount a major effort in minicomputers. So in 1974 Cary restructured that part of the corporation, in effect unraveling the operation Watson and Learson had put together for the 360 campaign and returning to the old days, when both General Products and Data Systems produced computers and products tended to overlap.

Data Processing would continue to work on such centralized systems as the 360's, 370's, and successor machines and, in addition, take on assignments in DDP based upon such hardware. An upgraded General Systems would assume responsibilities for System/3, create new small computers, and attempt different approaches to distributed data processing. Into General Systems Cary placed most of the dissidents, along with several brilliant mavericks who were having a difficult time with Armonk. In order to place distance between the two divisions, General Systems was to remain headquartered in Atlanta, while the major research centers were in San Jose, California, and Boulder, Colorado. Within a few months General Systems had the nickname of IBM/West, and the San Jose installation became one of the most unorthodox elements within the corporation, known for its air of informality, internal squabbles, colorful characters, and novel approaches to problems. Old-timers visiting San Jose were surprised by what they encountered, and some remarked that such antics wouldn't have been tolerated in the Watson era. This wasn't so. From his perch on the board, Tom Watson gave his approval. Both he and Cary felt the firm needed a shaking up, and General Systems provided some of the stirring.

The following year General Systems was made part of a new major division, the General Business Group, with a mandate to undertake a wide variety of projects. Structurally it was the equal of Data Processing. Each was headed by a senior vice-president—the veteran Spike Beitzel was at General Business, and Paul Rizzo, one of the most prominent executives in IBM's next generation, commanded Data Processing. That their areas of responsibility overlapped was evident and not accidental. For the first time in its history IBM encouraged divisional rivalries —what was known as the General Motors pattern. The lower end of the Data Processing line would come head-on against not only Burroughs, Digital Equipment, and the others but also the upper end of General Business's machines and services. Salesmen for each division would compete against those from the other. This was yet another method Cary employed to stimulate innovation and keep the company alive to new opportunities.

Meanwhile, work on distributed data processing continued, and out of the AQUARIUS project came the Systems Network Architecture (SNA), immediately hailed as IBM's entry into this rapidly growing segment of the market. Based upon the 360's and 370's, it hardly was unique and didn't represent an advance in the state of the art. SNA was erected from the top down—that is to say, it was centered upon the host computer, to which was added peripheral equipment of various kinds. This proved an effective selling point. The system was offered to data processing managers who were accustomed to the 360's and tended to look upon SNA as a logical outgrowth of previous designs with which they were familiar. Since these were the people who made purchase or lease decisions, SNA did quite well.

General Systems took another approach. Initially it revamped the System/3, while it worked on new models geared more to users of minicomputers than anyone else. Out of this came System/34 and System/38 and the Series/1 line. In 1978 it announced the 5110, which sold for less than a third of the price of the System/3's, and was more powerful and flexible. Furthermore, these new machines might easily be linked together to form a distributed data processing system—one that was constructed from the bottom up. Just as Data Processing offered its SNA complexes to data processing managers, so General Systems geared its placement efforts at department managers eager to have their own information system and use it to draw upon materials available throughout and even outside the organization.

As expected, the intracompany rivalry shook up things at Data Processing. Rizzo turned out the 303X line, machines that were a direct outgrowth of the 370's, but, in addition, prodded his researchers into new efforts in distributed data processing. In the autumn of 1978, while General Systems was taking orders for its System/38's and 5110's, he announced the availability of the 8100, a machine that might be used in the conventional fashion but was specially designed to function as part of a network. In writing of the 8100's, computer expert Larry Woods said that they were some of the most important machines in the industry's history, that their introduction may mark "a turning point in the general direction of worldwide computer development. With the 8100 announcement, IBM legitimized the concept of DDP, and gave notice to the rest of the minicomputer industry that it is serious about entering this marketplace."

Some of this was hyperbole. Distributed data processing was well entrenched both as an idea and in practice and didn't require legitimization by IBM or any other firm. Thus, the 8100's may have changed the direction of IBM, but hardly of the industry. Also, there never was any doubt about Cary's seriousness in matters that required so great an investment and diversion of resources. Many other companies had a head start and had established solid positions within the subindustry. The major question in 1978 was could IBM catch up with the leaders.

The market for distributed data processing was small in 1978—some $1.6 billion worth of hardware and software was sold that year. But it was growing rapidly, with most experts agreeing that expansion would be at the rate of 35 percent annually. Among the leaders were such fairly young companies as Datapoint, Four-Phase, and Wang, while minicomputer companies such as Digital Equipment and Data General also had entries. Some of the older firms were in the business, too, with complex systems in advance of anything IBM possessed that year. Burroughs, which had undergone a renaissance in the 1970's and now was the second largest firm in data processing, was about to unveil SWIFT. Created for the Society for Worldwide Interbank Financial Telecommunications, this system would link computers in some 700 of the world's largest banks. UNIVAC was in the process of establishing DCA, which stood for Distributed Communications Architecture. A consortium comprised of Xerox, Digital Equipment, and Intel had plans for local networks. Tymshare, a small firm in the service area, developed TYMNET, which, in addition to processing information, had the capability of sending and receiving electronic mail. General Telephone & Electronics was perfecting a similar system, called GTE Telenet. The most important of them all would come out of American Telephone & Telegraph. Known as Advanced Communications System (ACS), when completed it would have the capability of placing data banks in all parts of the world at the disposal of users of its terminals.

Cary understood all this but appeared confident his new entries would capture a large share of the market. He had good reasons for optimism. In the first place, IBM's reputation was such as to give it an edge over competitors. Then, too, placement of terminals required a large and experienced sales force, and IBM retained its advantage in this area. Finally, he had created a structure to direct the company's efforts in DDP, and judged by the steady stream of new products coming out of Data Processing and General Systems, it appeared to be working well. It still wasn't clear whether the major thrust would come from Armonk or Atlanta, and Cary made certain no favoritism was shown in the contest. Whenever he praised the products of one division, he took care to say something positive about those of the other. He called System/38 "one of the best products we've ever had because it is so easy for the customer to use." On the other hand, he said that "the 8100 is our *networking* product."

Industry analysts speculated on the meaning of this and other Cary moves. Had he set up and maintained the two divisions to stimulate competition, was this a prelude to a corporate split-up in advance of a decision in the antitrust case, or might it be a way of responding to the government's charges? Would General Business become the dominant division within IBM, and if so, did this imply that in the future the corporation would downplay hardware in favor of greater stress upon software and DDP? Cary obviously considered DDP an initial step toward the creation of some kind of global telecommunications network and believed IBM would have to enter this new competition.

"It's not a question of whether we're going to do it," he said, "but a question of when and how."

If this were the case, what kind of company would he have to create to bestow upon his successor in 1981? At a computer seminar held in the summer of 1980 one seer suggested that within a decade mainframes would become a relatively small part of IBM's total business and that by 1990 most of the firm's operations would revolve around services, software, and communications. By then, he went on to say, many of today's companies would have been merged out of existence, and those that remained would have become specialists in one or more sub-industries. At the apex of a new information processing and dissemination industry would be two firms, IBM and AT&T, each having invaded successfully the domain of the other.

All this is conjecture, of course, but the idea isn't as far-fetched as it might have appeared when Cary took office. During the 1970's the industry was transformed into something different from what it had been in the third generation. If Cary lacked the charisma and flash of the Watsons, he at least had the imagination and drive to restructure IBM in such a way as to enable it to take the lead in whatever paths technology would guide it. Given the nature of the challenges he had to face, it well might be argued that his accomplishments were on the same level as theirs.

15

Microworld · Macrosystems

IN 1980 IBM reported gross revenues of more than $24 billion, twice what they had been six years earlier. By most yardsticks this might have been considered an impressive showing—but not by those usually employed in the data processing industry. Not only was IBM's growth rate far lower than those of the small new companies in distributed data processing, word processing, and microcomputers—Datapoint, Wang, Apple, and Tandy among others—but it was below each of its older rivals in mainframes—Burroughs, NCR, Control Data, Sperry, and Honeywell.

There were other signs of trouble. In 1979, for the first time in a generation, net earnings had declined from the previous year's mark. IBM had blundered in the pricing of new products, had committed costly, if not crippling, financial errors, and had angered and wounded institutional and private bond buyers. The company's stock was in trouble, too, ending the decade pretty much where it had been at the beginning; Wall Street's once-premier growth and glamour issue was badly tarnished. Moreover, IBM seemed to have failed in putting down upstart companies in America, and there were rumblings from overseas, Japan in particular, which indicated that a new invasion of the American market was about to commence. Meanwhile, the Justice Department's antitrust case continued, sapping corporate energies and taking time from other business in Armonk.

Selected Statistics for IBM, 1975–1979

(millions of dollars)

| Year | Gross Revenues | | Earnings |
	Sales	Services, Rentals	
1975	4549	9891	1990
1976	5959	10345	2398
1977	7090	11043	2719
1978	8755	12321	3111
1979	9473	13390	3011

Source: *IBM Annual Report*, 1979

From all this one might have been justified in concluding that IBM was faltering. In mid-1979, when several brokerages were removing the stock from their recommended lists, *Business Week* wondered whether IBM was "about to become just another stodgy mature company." Other publications, however, presented a different view. *Datamation*, the respected industry organ, ran an article by Gideon Gartner purporting to show that the firm would double in size by 1983. Both cases might be found in financial, business, and technological publications, and those who read all of them might have become more confused than informed. How was it possible for so many industry insiders to draw such disparate conclusions from the same mass of evidence?

There was a clear pattern in the analyses, however. Most Wall Street advisories tended toward the pessimistic, while industry insiders usually highlighted positive elements in the corporate picture. By 1981, as IBM emerged from what some considered its worst period of sluggishness and others called one of consolidation and regrouping, the reasons for this dichotomy had become clear. The company had suffered through a temporary slowdown, which discouraged the investment community, but its new products and ongoing research thoroughly impressed professionals in the field. Moreover, some of them had come to realize that during the Cary regime IBM had reshaped itself to a greater extent than at any time since the early 1950's.

Obviously any firm the size of IBM is bound to be complex and contain contradictory elements; this was to be expected in a company with more than 340,000 employees and 33 vice-presidents of various descriptions. Yet 80 percent or so of the business was in the single area of information processing and communications, and much of the rest was related to it, so that IBM was far more homogeneous than the many multi-industry firms that had developed during the post-World War II period. In attempting to understand the company, analysts dissected it in several ways, each to illustrate a particular point of view. One might study Domestic and World Trade separately and divide World Trade further into Americas/Far East and Europe/Middle East/Africa. Or each division could be analyzed as a discrete unit. According to one's point of view, IBM might be seen as a services company that sold supporting hardware or as a hardware manufacturer that offered software to obtain placements. At one time in the late 1970's, when IBM had cash items of several billion dollars, it was fashionable to interpret the firm as a bank that made its profits through sales and leases of products that happened to be computers.

Each of these approaches is valid in its own limited way, but none offers a rounded picture of IBM. A handful of those in power in 1980 could appreciate it in all its complexities, and of these, only Cary and Opel could do so from the pinnacle. Tom Watson, who left the board the previous year to accept the ambassadorship to the USSR, might have accomplished this from yet another vantage point. At the close of the Watson era he might have reflected upon the differences between the company he had helped create and that which was emerging as Cary prepared to step down in favor of John Opel.

IBM wasn't comprised of a handful of separate and distinct firms, to be sure, and the distinctions could be made for almost every other company in the industry. Still, it is a useful way to understand where IBM is in the early 1980's and where it is headed. Parts of each division were involved with products and problems inherited from the Watson, Learson, and Cary regimes, while others were busily pushing ahead into several new areas, which to a degree were conceptually divorced from much of what had gone before.

The centerpiece in that legacy is mainframes. Not even the most sanguine minicomputer manufacturer seriously doubted that the medium-sized and big machines would continue to occupy the central position in information processing. Readout equipment, word processors, and terminals doubtless would show more rapid growth, but all of them plus other peripheral equipment were dependent upon the central processing units and their memory banks. Moreover, while distributed data processing was one of the more rapidly growing segments of the industry, freestanding machines still accounted for the larger share of sales and leases. Thus, mainframes weren't yet the "cash cows" some ardent advocates of DDP made them out to be—to be used to provide revenues to fund other, more promising segments of the business—but rather were the heart of the operation, one that IBM had to defend against rivals.

A 1978 industry survey indicated that IBM had 65.2 percent of the worldwide market for large-scale general-purpose mainframes. Among them Honeywell, Burroughs, UNIVAC, NCR, and Control Data accounted for 32 percent of placements, while other manufacturers of non-IBM compatible machines took another 2.5 percent. That year firms in the business of turning out and marketing IBM plug-compatible mainframes had a minuscule 2.3 percent of the market.

Two years later they had slightly more than 4 percent of

placements. Industry observer Sanford Garrett predicted their share would double by 1983, when IBM's market slice would come to 60 percent.

This didn't mean that IBM would sell and lease fewer machines, but rather that its portion of the rapidly growing market would shrink somewhat, while several small firms would experience exponential growth. In 1978 the problems posed by the plug-compatible-machine manufacturers were minor, but the implications were profound and called for a serious, concerted response.

Plug compatibility wasn't a novel concept. As has been seen, Honeywell and RCA had turned out machines during the 1960's that could utilize IBM software. Control Data and several younger firms had had complete lines of peripheral equipment designed with the 360's and 370's in mind. For the most part these companies had advertised their products as less expensive replacements for existing IBM counterparts, and in the wake of IBM's unbundling operation they did a brisk business. However, none dared challenge IBM insofar as the 360 mainframes were concerned. Within the industry it was generally understood that Armonk would use all its formidable resources to turn back such a blatant attack. Everyone recalled that RCA had resorted to such an approach—and soon after had been obliged to leave the industry.

Gene Amdahl, who had been the major designer for the 360 series, was prepared to assume such risks. After completing work on that assignment, he moved up quickly within the organization, with much of his work revolving around new ideas for large machines. Then Amdahl became an IBM fellow, which meant he was freed from all direct responsibilities and encouraged to investigate any ideas that interested him. Out of this came a proposal to produce an advanced large-scale computer, one that would utilize LSI technology and might become the basis for a fourth generation. This was in 1970. Sales and leases of 360's were going well, and top management saw no reason to take a step which surely would result in declining popularity for this line. Amdahl was made to understand there was no chance of his machine going into production, and the laboratory he had established for his researches was closed down. Fast to anger and in any case eager to put all such controls behind him, he resigned and set about obtaining funds for his own company.

Amdahl received backing from the Heizer Corporation, a Chicago-based venture capital firm, from Nixdorf, a German manufacturer of small computers, and from the large Japanese conglomerate Fujitsu. The understanding was that Amdahl would establish a plant in California from which he would produce large and medium-sized machines, all to be advanced technologically but compatible with specific IBM hardware. Furthermore, some of the components would be manufactured in Japan, and Fujitsu would have a say in international placements. There was some evidence that the Japanese firm hoped to obtain ideas and patents from Amdahl and eventually use them to make a foray of its own into the American market.

Amdahl's strategy was simple and straightforward. One of the major design flaws in the 360's had been their use of hybrid integrated circuits, and in other ways the line was based upon technologies which by the early 1970's were outmoded. By utilizing current LSI capabilities and other ideas he had been working on, Amdahl would design and then produce computers that were smaller, simpler, faster, and more powerful than their 360 and 370 counterparts. Moreover, they would be offered at far lower prices than the IBM machines, mainly to customers who felt they didn't require extensive services. Amdahl was prepared to repair his own machines but wouldn't develop software—all his computers would operate on IBM programs.

Some users feared that Amdahl might be forced to bow once Armonk launched its counterattack and that they would be stuck with hardware that couldn't be serviced. Amdahl resolved this by entering into an arrangement whereby in such an eventuality Fujitsu would assume all such contracts, acting for Amdahl as UNIVAC had for RCA. Some industry observers took this to mean that the company eventually would become a front for the Japanese company, the initial spearhead in what would be a major invasion of the American market. This Japanese connection became well known and generally worked in IBM's favor. When, in 1980, a proposed merger between Amdahl and Storage Technology was called off as a result of objections from Fujitsu, talk of Japanese arrogance flared. Amdahl spokesmen brushed this aside, and in fact, few technology transfers actually occurred. In any case, thought one executive, dislike of Armonk more than balanced fears of the Japanese. "The animosity toward IBM is broad, deep, and worldwide."

All such issues would have been moot were it not for the fact that Amdahl more than delivered on his pledges. Not only were his machines superior in performance and lower in price than their IBM counterparts, but they had far better service records. This was due in part to the ways Amdahl utilized LSI technology and also to the fact that his computers didn't run as hot as the 360's. The IBMs were kept cool by use of expensive plumbing; the Amdahls featured air cooling, thus saving users additional funds.

Amdahl's most important early machine, the 470 V/6, was introduced in mid-decade, to compete with the 360/168. Placements weren't as difficult as might have been expected; from the first AT&T proved a willing customer, and others followed. A *Fortune* survey taken in 1977 indicated satisfaction on the part of users. "Our V/6 is unbelievably reliable," said a Hughes Aircraft data processing manager. "I've been in this racket for twenty years, and it's the most incredible engineering feat I've ever seen." Others felt the same way. The 470 V/6's were taken by General Motors, NASA, and similar blue-chip clients. By the spring of 1977 Amdahl had installed some fifty units and had cut deeply into IBM's position in large-scale computer placements.

Of the older, established firms only Control Data attempted to follow Amdahl's lead, and even then it limited its plug-compatible foray to the lower end of the computer spectrum. The reasons were obvious. Business was excellent and prospects in other areas were alluring during the second half of the 1970's. Burroughs and NCR had large order backlogs from customers in banking and insurance and were fighting off strong challenges in retailing. UNIVAC had won significant contracts from airline firms and was mounting a major push in this market. These companies and others were exploring the potential of distributed data processing and specialized machines. None felt any need to mount a direct challenge to IBM in this field, especially when they considered their lack of success in previous head-on confrontations.

The more important firms in this new phase of plug compatibility were new to the experience. Itel, which for a while grew even more rapidly than Amdahl, had begun as a leasing company; now it marketed a line of machines designed and produced by National Semiconductor. Later such small, virtually unknown firms as Two Pi, Cambridge Memories, Kardios, Citel, Magnuson, and Nanodata prepared to challenge specific IBM hardware with their own versions. For the most part these companies were headed by young technicians—Gene Amdahl's son was a Magnuson executive—who had little or no marketing experience and in any case never had undergone the frightening experience of an IBM assault.

That such small firms could and did survive in the late 1970's indicates that IBM's response might have been inadequate or botched or that contrary to the Justice Department's contention, the company wasn't able to exercise the traditional control of a monopolizer. Or it might have been that Armonk had decided upon a limited counterattack, one that would ward off Amdahl but not destroy the company. By early 1977 Amdahl was boasting that his firm had close to a quarter of the market for machines in their categories, and Wall Street took note that his profit margin was half again as large as IBM's. Amdahl counted upon a continuance of this to fund his research, development, and expansion programs. Any diminution of the margin would oblige his company to cut back drastically. It was a soft spot that Cary meant to probe.

The campaign began in a conventional fashion. IBM

salesmen and executives visited clients who were thought to be considering plug-compatible machines, to warn them of problems that might arise should Amdahl or National Semiconductor leave the business. There was talk of reduced maintenance on IBM peripheral equipment hooked onto other mainframes, of software changes to eliminate or reduce compatibility, and of alterations in hardware that could make the Amdahls less compatible than advertised. None of this was very effective and was more in the nature of a skirmish than anything else. What IBM learned from this was that the customers found the Amdahls appealing, and most would not be swayed by words alone.

The important push came in March 1977, when IBM introduced a new machine, the 3033, which was almost twice as powerful as the 360/168. By itself this was no surprise. The computer was evolutionary, insofar as design was concerned, and in no way would make obsolete either the 360/158 or the 370/168, key elements in IBM's hardware array. What shocked the industry was the matter of prices: The 3033 sold or leased for two-thirds the posted figures for the 360/168. Never before had IBM or any other firm slashed so deeply the costs of computations per second. There was more to come. In the same announcement IBM said there would be a 30 percent across-the-board cut in the prices of 370/158's and 370/168's.

Traditionally IBM had maintained a "price umbrella" for the industry, setting charges high enough to enable its competitors to remain in the field. This enabled IBM to show a large return on operations, and by allowing others a share of the market, it reduced charges of monopoly. To some, the new pricing structure appeared to be a declaration that IBM had decided to set off an industry shakedown. All the other old mainframe firms would have to follow its lead, and they did. Each of these had become quite diversified, however, and a majority of their models weren't affected by the price changes. Their profits might decline somewhat, but hardly enough to cause distress. As far as IBM itself was concerned, margins actually rose, as did net income.

From the first it was obvious the action had been aimed squarely at the leasing companies and Amdahl, almost all the products of which were affected. Within a year several major leasers were in trouble and soon after would leave the business. But Amdahl's response was prompt, direct, and even a trifle cocky. Three days after the IBM announcement Gene Amdahl told customers of two new machines. The 470 V/5, plug-compatible with IBM's 370/168, would be lower in price. More important, the 470 V/7, plug-compatible with the 3033, would be close to half again as fast as the IBM model, but cost only 3 percent more. Finally, there would be a 25 percent price reduction on the workhorse 470 V/6s. Then Amdahl turned around and negotiated a 20 percent price reduction on components purchased from Fujitsu. Technological improvements led to further economies. In the end, margins held up, and as a result of lower prices, sales and leases expanded. Revenues went from $93 million in 1976 to $189 million the following year and to $321 million in 1978. In this same span net income rose from $29 million to $110 million. Clearly Amdahl was in the race to stay.

IBM conceded nothing to its adversary. The initial price reduction apparently had little impact, so Cary opened a sustained campaign meant to wear down but not destroy Amdahl and the other plug-compatible manufacturers. He had vastly greater resources than his competitors and knew that IBM was bound to win any contest of this nature. In the end Cary had what amounted to a victory—Itel came close to bankruptcy, and Amdahl's growth ground to a halt. But IBM paid a price for this in the form of what amounted to a series of self-inflicted wounds.

Armonk announced the 303X line in 1977. Evolutionary in design but lower in cost and higher in performance than the 370's, it was priced in such a way as to invite a response from Amdahl. That company accepted the challenge, matching IBM price cut for price cut. Orders poured into both companies, and the following year Cary announced that the computing power of all 303X's for which placements were being arranged came to four times the total for all computers IBM had installed in its history.

There were problems, however, which were either ignored or unappreciated. First of all, industry insiders knew that IBM was preparing two additional series, the 4300's and the large H computers, and given the experience of the past two years, their prices could be expected to be lower than those for the 303Xs. Thus, more clients than usual leased rather than purchased. This would assure the company a steady revenue flow for a number of years, and eventually the line proved quite profitable. But initially the cash drain was severe.

Armonk hadn't anticipated this shift, but even so, the company might have come through it all unscathed had it not been for a series of financial moves begun in 1977. In part because of the price war that year, IBM's common stock had fallen sharply, to the point where management considered it greatly undervalued. At the time the company had cash items and equivalents of close to $6 billion, more than any other firm in the nation. Cary earmarked more than $1 billion of this cache for a repurchase campaign. Thus, at a time when Armonk should have been gathering its substantial financial resources to pay for what most people within the company understood would be a costly expansion of facilities and personnel, IBM was spending money to reduce its equity base. Not since 1963, when Williams had accelerated the repayment of the Prudential Insurance $160 million loan, had IBM committed such a financial mistake.

As noted IBM's earnings declined in 1979, in part as a result of the switch from sales to leasing. Income and reserves weren't sufficient to finance expansion, so, as indicated earlier, the company went to Wall Street to float a $1 billion debt issue. This was a few weeks prior to Federal Reserve Board Chairman Paul Volcker's announcement that monetary policy would be tightened. Interest rates rose, and the quotations for the two new IBM issues plummeted, leaving sour tastes in the mouths of investors and underwriters. That year, too, IBM split its com-

Microworld · Macrosystems

mon shares on a four-for-one basis. Presumably this was done to make the shares more accessible to small investors, and the shareholder population did expand somewhat. But for the first time in the memory of most Wall Streeters, the stock sold for below 100. During most of the last half century IBM had been the first or second highest-priced issue listed on the New York Stock Exchange, and this provided it with a form of status. Now it was just another stock, selling in the same price range as other aging blue chips like AT&T, Exxon, and General Motors. This was more symbolic than real, perhaps, but the 1979 split also helped diminish the IBM image on Wall Street.

The year's biggest blunder, however, was the way the 4300's were priced. As heralded, these new machines were far more powerful than the middle segment of the 360, 370, and 303X lines, which they were to replace or augment. More important, however, was the fact that the line was priced to offer close to eight times as much capacity for the same dollar as did some of the older models. IBM had thought the market could absorb 20,000 of the 4300's. Within three weeks of their introduction in January the company had orders for 42,000 of them, with some deliveries scheduled for as late as 1983. Would-be buyers and leasers were selected by lot, and this resulted in a fiasco. Some firms placed multiple orders to have a number of places on the line, in this way bettering their chances for an early delivery. They did this knowing that the other orders would be canceled. Thus, IBM couldn't be sure how many of the orders constituted true placements. Some of the firms which drew low numbers were able to sell their places for as much as $20,000 to others who needed the machines as soon as possible. Within a few weeks IBM was obliged to close the order books and tried to make sense of the situation.

By then, as the dust cleared somewhat, questions arose whether the 4300's could prove profitable at these prices. One analyst called the campaign "a poorly thought-out strategy that made investors ask for the first time whether IBM's planning is on target," while another called the price and lease schedule "the worst mistake in the company's history." Moreover, despite

331

Cary's attempt to reverse the trend that began with the 1977 price cuts, the lease-to-sales ratio increased. The huge order backlog meant that production facilities had to be expanded at a more rapid pace than previously had been planned, and this indicated that additional borrowing would be required; the large number of leases indicated that insufficient funds would be generated from this source for the first few years.

IBM was in the unusual position of being strapped for cash. In addition to the bond sales, the company borrowed $300 million from the Saudi Arabian Monetary Agency, placed its paper in several European financial capitals, and enlarged its lines of credit at American banks. Then, to shore up its position in the market, the company raised its prices on the 4300's to a point where some semblance of order was restored.

Conditions had calmed down somewhat by 1981, at least to the point where Armonk could assess the situation more realistically than had been possible two years earlier. On the positive side, it appeared the 4300 series would prove a financial success. The outlook was bright for the Series H machines as well as for other new products IBM was bringing to the market. The company's cash-flow squeeze had eased, and industry sources were predicting that IBM would have large reserves by mid-decade, more than enough to fund new programs in other areas. But Armonk had given the appearance of being an awkward giant, and this remained. On the eve of his retirement Cary might boast that he had beaten off challenges in mainframes and from the leasing companies while he had pioneered in new areas, but the company had paid a large price for what still seemed an uncertain victory. Profit margins had been slashed, earnings were lower than they might have been, the company had incurred a large debt, and with all this Amdahl was still there, not merely intact but growing rapidly once again. Insofar as mainframes were concerned, IBM no longer appeared invincible.

Could it have been that Amdahl—which in 1979 was only the thirteenth largest factor in data processing—had succeeded where such well-funded giants as RCA and General Electric failed? Perhaps, but this was more a result of the times and the ways technology and the markets had developed as anything else. RCA and GE had mounted their challenges when mainframes were central to the data processing business and when technology was more revolutionary than it would become, and the industry itself far narrower. They had been obliged to make enormous investments in their hopes of gaining the number two position in data processing. Gene Amdahl's ambitions were more limited. There were few secrets in the industry by the mid-1970's, no startlingly new technologies on the horizon. Amdahl couldn't know precisely what IBM was planning to produce in the way of mainframes, but he had a pretty good idea. Thus, he was able to track the company and produce what many users obviously considered a superior version of the standard model and to offer it at lower costs. For the time being at least, he wouldn't pioneer. This proved to be a recipe for success. By using it, Amdahl was able to win a place in data processing denied companies with larger asset bases and greater reputations.

As noted, the business of mainframes was declining in growth in the late 1970's, while it had been expanding rapidly when the earlier challenges had been mounted. According to *Datamation*, revenues from the sales and leases of data processing equipment rose from $31.1 billion in 1977 to $45.7 billion in 1979, for an advance of 47 percent. In this same period mainframe revenues fell from $7.4 billion to $7.2 billion, from 24 percent of the total market to 16 percent. From 1977 to 1979 minicomputer sales advanced by 74 percent, and those for peripherals and terminals, 49 percent. Service and software revenues went from $5.7 billion to $11.8 billion, more than doubling. The fastest-growing firms in the data processing industry were Apple, Commodore, Tandy, and Tandem, not Amdahl.

The press and even most of the general business magazines had become accustomed to considering the mainframe computer industry, and so they focused on Amdahl and the plug-compatible business during the late 1970's. In a like fashion, they looked overseas, drawing from the experiences of other industries—automobiles, television, calculators—and predicting foreign invasions of the American market. In 1969, for example, *Forbes* ran a story entitled: "Japan's Computer Industry—Wait until 1980," implying that by then that country, and perhaps others, would be formidable competitors for IBM and the rest. This ignored the special nature of the computer business, the large technological lead enjoyed by the Americans, their superior sales and service forces, and related factors. Still, by 1981 Fujitsu had drawn even with IBM Japan in terms of placements in that country, and there were rumors (later denied) that IBM would market a small Matsushita computer under its own logo in the United States. What did happen was an agreement between IBM and Minolta under which the Japanese copier would be sold here under the IBM trademark.

Notwithstanding this, the foreign computer manufacturers remain small compared with their American counterparts. In 1978, for example, Hitachi, then the largest of the group, showed revenues of $1.8 billion from this segment of its business, or less than Burroughs, NCR, or Control Data. France's Cii-Bull, and Great Britain's ICL, each had barely more than $1 billion in revenues. Siemens, the leading German firm, reported data processing revenues of $703 million. None of these was an important factor in the American market, nor did any seem capable of making a serious bid there in the early 1980's. In fact, IBM remained the leading force in the industry in every country in which it functioned with the exceptions of Great Britain and Japan. Even then, IBM Japan had revenues of more than $1.5 billion in 1979, had a third of that country's mainframe placements, was its eleventh largest firm, and accounted for almost all its computer exports.

Not only was IBM dominant in the national and international markets, but it also plunged ahead strongly in the newer areas to be found in information processing and communications, which were constantly expanding to incorporate other technologies and concepts. Further, it was the only firm that came close to blanketing the field. IBM didn't produce microcomputers and several other hardware products and continued to lag behind Digital Equipment in minicomputers and Xerox in copiers, but it might be found leading in most other technologies, especially those relating to the now-familiar office of the future. Here, too, the old pattern was followed: Others would do the pioneering, after which IBM would come in and take over.

For example, in 1978 the Qyx division of Exxon Enterprises had most of the market for electronic typewriters, while IBM hadn't a model in the field. Two years later the IBM electronics had more than 70 percent of that category's placements, while Qyx held onto 17 percent and was losing both personnel and money. Initially it seemed Exxon had the power to take the lead in selected segments of the office equipment industry; today this is recognized as a chimera. Nor was Armonk content to let it go at that. By 1981 the company was close to perfecting a typewriter capable of transcribing human speech and already had a model that could isolate spelling errors.

Expansion continued at an accelerating pace, in both scope and depth. Research and development expenditures for 1979 came to $1.4 billion, three times that of a decade earlier and more than the rest of the industry combined. Capital expenditures, affected by tool-ups for the 4300 and H programs, were $6 billion, half again that for the previous year—and almost as much as worldwide revenues had been in 1968. Some critics argued that IBM was overbuilding, but others, who approved of this heavy investment in plants, laboratories, and personnel, considered this a prudent policy, in view of IBM's growth and the inflationary atmosphere of the times. By 1981 Gideon Gartner's thought that IBM might double in revenues every five years or so no longer seemed as reckless as it had been two years earlier. In fact, some within the industry thought the pace might quicken somewhat if one or more of the newer ventures caught fire.

Some of these were minor by IBM standards. Cary purchased several small firms in the scientific instrumentation field and out of them fashioned a new entity, IBM Instruments, which by 1980 was introducing new products of its own. A modest operation which accounts for less than one-tenth of 1 percent of the corporation's revenues, it nonetheless is growing rapidly and shows signs of breaking out into new areas, some on its own, others in conjunction with other IBM divisions.

More important for the immediate future was a foray into data storage undertaken in conjunction with MCA Inc., the entertainment conglomerate. In the late 1970's MCA's affiliate, DiscoVision Associates, was developing on its own and in conjunction with others a new system whereby motion pictures and other shows might be placed on discs resembling phonograph records to be played on augmented television sets. This was a highly competitive field, one with great promise. According to some industry estimates, revenues for players and discs could come to $20 billion by 1990. Cary purchased a half interest in DiscoVision, with both companies announcing there would be a melding of IBM technology and MCA entertainment expertise—the former company would stress hardware; the latter, software. But there was more to it than that. In addition to containing movies and "video magazines," the discs might store information, for both businesses and governments, in a far more efficient manner than anything currently available. "Optical discs will impact everything from word processors to large-scale computers," said Michael Ettenberg, who headed the RCA projects in this new area. Control Data, Honeywell, and Exxon were also involved in disc research, while Xerox, in conjunction with a French electronics company, announced it would have an office disc recorder ready for placements by 1982. Xerox is aiming at the computer peripheral market, and disc systems also could become the hearts of distributed data processing networks.

As before in other areas, IBM initially is one of the pack. But if the pattern holds, sometime in the mid or late 1980's, after Xerox and others open the market, it will step in to take a majority of the business.

IBM's key future project, the one which has attracted the most attention and which offers the greatest promise, is in the telecommunications area. In 1973 the company purchased a majority interest in the CML Satellite Corporation, the initials of which derive from the fact that it was organized by Comsat General, MCI Communications, and Lockheed. CML had ambitions of establishing a worldwide telecommunications network based upon satellite systems, one that clearly would rival the American Telephone & Telegraph operations and run parallel to work being conducted by that firm. MCI, which was challenging AT&T in long-distance operations, was a small company, while Lockheed was in financial and operational disarray. Thus, they were willing to sell out to IBM for $2.5 million each. In this way, IBM not only for the first time entered a field regulated by the government but also came into a head-to-head confrontation with AT&T.

Out of this came a new entity, Satellite Business Systems, and another partner, Aetna Life & Casualty, whose interest in the firm was basically financial. In plans submitted to the Federal Communications Commission SBS indicated that its system will consist of satellites circling the earth filled with the necessary electronic gear and that in a decade or so it would be possible for virtually any computer to transmit data to any other on the globe. As for AT&T, it is in the process of dividing itself into two entities, one to oversee traditional telephone operations, the other—"Baby Bell"—to engage in data transmission and, according to an October 1980 Federal Communications Commission decision, to produce computers. In effect, each giant is invading the territory of the other and, in so doing, heeding the technological imperative. As management theorist Peter Drucker put it, "IBM clearly is at a point where its product is becoming the 'wrong' product. Even the American Telephone Company, despite the intelligent management of its monopoly position, is now at the point where its product is becoming the 'wrong' product." In 1981 each company was beginning to enter what Drucker clearly considers the "right" area, setting the stage for one of history's greatest business confrontations.

16

Transition and Beyond

ACCORDING TO the carefully worked-out plan, Frank Cary relinquished his post as chief executive officer and turned over leadership of the corporation to John Opel on January 1, 1981. He would continue as chairman, but Cary stepped down from the powerful Management Review Committee. Then he set off for an extended vacation, the first in several years, as if to provide another clear signal that he no longer was in command.

The transition was smooth, as might have been expected given the nature of the corporation and the personalities of the two men involved. All that was required was some shuffling of papers, changes in letterheads, movements from office to office, and the like. As one industry observer suggested, it was as if a section of a large computer system had been replaced by another, almost identical one. Such is the way power is transferred at IBM today.

Transition and Beyond

This isn't to suggest that Opel in any way is a carbon copy of Frank Cary or that he has patterned himself deliberately upon his predecessor. Rather, each man is a product of the system; they fitted the profile the corporation required when each entered the sales trainee program, Cary in 1948 and Opel the following year. Neither man had any significant business experience outside IBM, both had earned M.B.A. degrees, and each demonstrated the kinds of talents which the IBM imperative insisted upon and which earned them steady promotions. They shared many experiences; both were veterans of the 360 campaign, in which they earned battle stars and achieved recognition. Cary and Opel worked well together, with the chairman making certain that Opel was involved directly in every major decision the corporation made in the 1970's. Given IBM's penchant for secrecy, there is no way of knowing whether or not he differed with Cary on any significant policy or program, but Opel is generally considered the more imaginative of the two and less rigid in his approaches, while Cary is famous for his bluntness, an attribute that might have been honed while working under Vincent Learson. Opel appears an easygoing individual, who doesn't flare up at what may have been an unintentional slight, as Cary is known to have done on occasion. But neither man suffers fools gladly. When working together, they function harmoniously, and they clearly have come out of the same mold. Opel wouldn't have risen to the presidency or lasted as long as he did as heir apparent were this not so.

More than any of his predecessors as chief executive officer —more even than Tom Watson—Opel came to command after an intensive apprenticeship, and his experiences within .the corporation were diverse. At various times he served in marketing, finance, and manufacturing, and for a while in the early 1960's he even did time in public relations, something very difficult to imagine with either Learson or Cary.

No one expects dramatic changes at IBM for the first two or three years of the Opel regime. In part this is because, as indicated, he generally agrees with, and had a part in shaping, the present courses of action, but also because research and development already has placed on stream the products and services IBM will introduce during the first half of the 1980's. Then, too, there are forces over which IBM has relatively little control, such as government interventions both in the United States and in other parts of the world. Justice Department claims notwithstanding, IBM faces keen competition in most of the areas in which it operates and will have to make responses in the area of prices and products. The technological imperative must be dealt with; IBM will have to absorb new discoveries and incorporate them into its machines and services. Finally, there is the matter of size and complexity. Altering the direction of a supercorporation has been compared with shifting the course of an ocean liner. Both tend to move sluggishly, as orders are implemented down the line and the machinery moves into the new path. Rapid shifts are possible at such firms as Tandem, Apple, and Prime, but not at IBM. These smaller firms are headed by entrepreneurs—innovators who can stimulate others by setting examples and who rule their firms with a strong hand. Opel faces a different situation at IBM, a widely dispersed entity beyond the day-to-day administration of any single individual. Nor can he lead the way in technological innovation; even had he the talents and knowledge, Opel would lack the time. Rather, he will have to be a manager, hoping to direct departmental entrepreneurs engaged in projects down the line. There seems no reason to believe he will falter in the task. The mechanism to accomplish it is in place and functioning well, provided by Watson, Learson, and especially Cary.

IBM's major business in this period will be the familiar one of producing, selling, and leasing computers and related equipment as well as software. By early 1981 it was clear that the new big and medium-sized machines would be major successes and that profits from them would flow to the bottom line late that year and accelerate in 1982 and 1983. One major problem in this area will be to turn them out more rapidly and provide financing for customers. Because of this, IBM is engaged in one of the greatest construction and expansion programs in corporate history, one far larger in magnitude and scope than the one attending the creation and introduction of the 360 series. During the past three years manufacturing plant and laboratory space have expanded by more than a quarter. During 1980 alone, more than 4 million square feet were completed, and an additional 8 million square feet of plant and laboratory space were under construction in eight countries. At the end of 1978 IBM reported a net investment in plant, rental machines, and other property of $4.3 billion; two years later the figure was $15 billion. Only a small portion of this effort could be financed by cash flow, so IBM had to go to the money markets more often and for larger bites than ever before. The corporation's long-term debt rose from $285 million at the end of 1978 to $1.6 billion a year later, and by early 1981 it stood at $2.1 billion, with the company about to borrow an additional $200 million in Europe to finance plant expansion in Latin America and Asia.

Most of the money will be used to erect and expand facilities and finance equipment leases. Research and development programs account for much of the remainder, and from this area will emerge products and services that will characterize the middle and late years of the Opel regime.

As always, Armonk is tight-lipped about its specific programs; little of the details are known at this time. But a giant entity can no more keep its research and programs secret than an elephant can hide in the bush. Moreover, IBM's present commitments must be continued in such a way as to militate against any sharp changes in direction. It would appear, then, that Opel's options are restricted. For the most part he will likely hew to the Cary line, while he awaits new developments from the laboratories and the universities.

IBM's leaders have been most comfortable when concentrating upon innovations in pricing, distribution, and services rather than in high technology, even though its research and development expenditures are greater than the combined total of all its major competitors. This, too, will likely continue under Opel. The corporation has a clear idea of what it can do best, and it possesses no major subsidiary from which a different thrust might be expected. It also has a well-known self-imposed mandate, to which it has hewed throughout the computer age. The basic statement has been altered in minor ways over the years, but the message has always been the same: "IBM's operations, with very minor exceptions, are in the field of information-handling systems, equipment and services to solve the increasingly complex problems of business, government, science, space exploration, defense, education, medicine, and many other areas of human activity."

One can assume the corporation will continue as the undisputed leader in these fields. IBM equipment helped direct every one of the space shots, including the Explorer series. Its machines are in use in hospitals, oil and natural gas fields, schools, banks, libraries, retail establishments, government agencies, and, in fact, every enterprise in which quantification is possible and information can be processed. A 1979 Department of Commerce report indicated that growth in these established and well-defined areas should be in the 25 to 30 percent range throughout the 1980's, and historically such projections have been on the low side.

Certainly the cost of such services will continue to decline. It is well known that some of today's hand-held machines, available for around $100 and for which interesting software exists, possess the data processing powers of the giant electromechanical marvels of three decades ago. Several industry figures have observed that had the automobile makers duplicated their feats, we would have Cadillacs costing $50 or so, capable of cruising at 700 miles per hour, sipping gasoline at the rate of one gallon per 1,000 miles.

There might be discerned in the early 1980's the coming together of three related forces: lower computation costs, simpler and more flexible software, and an enlarged public not only aware of information processing but capable of utilizing at least some parts of it. That the office of the future will be highly automated, more complex, and based upon information-processing systems is now fairly obvious, as is the fact that IBM will be the dominant force in this evolving field. What is not yet clear is how the technological imperative will affect the home. Computers and related equipment certainly can monitor and control home energy utilization, store information regarding household management, and provide family members with information regarding taxes, expenditures, travel, and dozens of other areas. Moreover, there is emerging a new relationship between office and home, as much the result of sociological change as technological development. Computer-oriented workers are applying knowledge learned in offices to solve problems at home, while homemakers are reaching out to the new technology to facilitate their work. Clearly a generation of children reared on electronic, programmable toys will be psychologically ready to carry this development forward.

As has been indicated, Apple Computer probably will be one of the leading forces in this expanding field. Its machines are easy to understand and low in price, and the software is flexible and available. Even the name is right: NCR, Burroughs, and UNIVAC smack of the office and factory, while Apple is familiar and even "friendly."

Along with others in the personal-computer business, Apple awaited a move from Armonk, but none came, not even the usual rumors. All involved understood this meant little. IBM never telegraphed its punches. In this promising field, in many others, the corporation sponsored research, constructed prototypes, and monitored the market. Then, when the time appeared appropriate, IBM would move in.

As it happened, the announcement regarding the IBM personal computer was made in early August 1981. While no one in the industry was really surprised, at least insofar as the hardware was concerned, the corporation's approach was somewhat different this time and indicated a previously unappreciated flexibility at IBM headquarters and in the field.

IBM announced that its new small machine would be sold, not only at company outlets, but at Sears Roebuck and computer stores throughout the nation, providing IBM with a retail network larger even than those of Apple and Radio Shack. Moreover, IBM would encourage independents to create software programs for the machines and submit them to Armonk. If accepted, they would be "published," and "authors" would receive royalties for their work. In this way, IBM planned to draw upon a large army of freelance operators and reward them for their product. Apple had done as much in its early days and now IBM was imitating the subindustry's leader and in the process signaling an intention of beating it at its own game.

IBM's dramatic move into the consumer market signaled a sea change in the company's image and attitudes, and industry experts concluded that IBM had decided to concentrate on selling the machines to small businessmen, farmers and farm combines, stores, scientific organizations, and large offices where individual desk-top computers might prove useful. Taken together, these leading business and organizational markets accounted for some $900 million worth of machines in 1980, and some predicted they would grow, with IBM's entry, to $5 billion by 1985. The home and school markets, however—where Apple, Radio Shack, and Commodore were well entrenched—took $155 million worth of machines in 1980, and was expected, with IBM, to "only quadruple" by 1985.

While students and hobbyists may or may not prefer their friendly Apples, data managers and businessmen will probably feel more comfortable with the familiar and tested IBM logo. Warren Winger, chairman of Compushops, a chain of stores in Texas and Illinois, told a *New York Times* reporter that IBM strategy was geared to achieve dominance in the more promising business and scientific fields which hadn't been sufficiently exploited by the smaller companies. "It appears that IBM has a better understanding of why the Apple II was successful than had Apple" was his verdict.

The decision to enter the personal-computer market was made by Cary, even though the announcement was released during the Opel regime. And, clearly, the personal computer will be one of IBM's major efforts in the 1980's. But it is well to remember IBM's size. So large is IBM that no single new product can achieve a dominant role. Even if the company posts annual sales of $2 billion worth of personal computers by 1985—a distinct possibility—this would come to less than 5 percent of total IBM revenue. The small machines may bring IBM into previously untapped markets, but they won't alter the corporation's direction or orientation, established by Cary in the 1970's and carried on by Opel in the early 1980's. It is part of a harmonious whole which outsiders can comprehend only in retrospect. This, too, is part of the IBM mystique.

In 1980 Opel told IBM's stockholders that the company faced two sets of problems and challenges in the years ahead. The first was inflation, and to meet it, the corporation was instituting economies in many areas. Then, with a steady glance in the direction of the Justice Department, he spoke of the challenges of increased competition:

> In addition to the many veteran companies in our industry, we see new and growing competitors all around the world, especially the Japanese. They come to the market alone, and they come with American and European partners.
>
> Then we see the PCMs—the plug compatible manufacturers. They are proliferating. They are the kind of companies that offer equipment in substitution for IBM products interconnected in IBM systems.
>
> AT&T and other telephone companies, both here and abroad, are expanding horizontally into our business.
>
> The semiconductor manufacturers are integrating vertically into our business.
>
> Even an oil company, Exxon, is diversifying into information processing.
>
> A great number of well-managed business enterprises in the United States, as well as around the world, often supported by their governments, continue to enter our industry.

Thus was presented the very picture of a citadel under assault, of a colossus in a chronic state of siege. Those who understand the industry best, however, know that IBM is not seriously threatened by other domestic data processing firms, that the Japanese computer challenge—trumpeted for more than a decade—has yet to materialize on the world scene in any serious fashion, and that Armonk always has proved more than capable of turning back those who tried to poach on its preserve. Within a year Texas Instruments, consciously modeled after IBM insofar as management and style were concerned, stumbled badly in its attempt to enter the data processing industry. And Exxon, after a promising start in office automation, had to cut back as a result of management defections and production and distribution bottlenecks.

Top executives and technicians at IBM seem to thrive in such an atmosphere. The firm often greets new challenges in the computer wars as though its industry position were in peril, but thus far along this has never been so. Perhaps it is because the company's actual adversaries are so limited in power and resources that Armonk may feel it necessary to inflate awesome ghosts and images out of wraiths and then behave as if each illusion had size and substance.

If IBM is involved in what often seems like the business equivalent of warfare, it is against foes that often are imaginary, with exaggerated strengths, which in press releases and speeches are made to appear formidable. In fact, there is no such competitive colossus. The enemy is a mirror image of IBM itself. And there is only one IBM.

Acknowledgments

IN THE COURSE of conducting research for this volume, I interviewed some fifty former and present IBM managers, salesmen, and scientists and twice as many individuals connected in some way with other firms in the information processing industry. In addition, there were conversations with journalists and academics with interests in the field. All were told that the present book was to be a history of data processing centered on IBM, but not a study of the corporation itself.

The reason for this approach will be clear to all who know or have worked within the corporation. More perhaps than any other major American business enterprise, IBM enforces a code of secrecy regarding its operations. Dozens of researchers have approached Armonk asking for permission to explore archives and to conduct interviews. To the best of my knowledge few interviews have ever been granted, and then only under strict understandings and limits of the kind that no scholar willingly accepts.

What is puzzling about all this is that IBM probably has less to hide or fear from articles or books than almost any other major American corporation. There are no significant scandals in its past, no inept or corrupt leaders, not even a major blunder which could embarrass someone past or present in the corporation. One might criticize IBM for its aggressive marketing practices, scour the antitrust docket for tales of unfair competition, and speak with leaders of rival firms to gather tales of how the behemoth blind-sided them. In fact, some of this has been done. But from every quarter there emerges a consistent picture of an organization efficient despite its giant size, one that has managed to retain the respect, if not always the admiration, of most who have left it, and a succession of IBM leaders all of whom have been judged competent and even outstanding when compared with their counterparts elsewhere.

Those who know or who have had dealings with IBM are aware of the corporation's intense dislike of publicity. Its leaders are far from willing to cooperate with journalists and others in the preparation of articles on its activities, a phenomenon which has been noted and commented upon in various parts of this work. All the research for this book, then, has been gathered from the outside, and from some of those within the corporation who were willing to contribute informally to what they believed would be an accurate and impartial history of the data processing industry and its lead company, IBM. At their request these individuals have not been named. But many will, I think, recognize their contributions on one or more of these pages. Finally, in no way has IBM seen, had access to, supported or subsidized any part of this book.

A work dealing with a corporation like IBM necessarily must come to terms with scientific, technological, legal, and even accounting matters, but the focus here has been upon leadership and its implementation, the ways entrepreneurs and managers deal with rivals, and the processes by which techno-

Acknowledgments

logical discoveries are transformed into products and services which are marketed to customers.

Students of management will recognize the influence here of two scholars, Peter F. Drucker and Alfred Chandler. Along with Drucker I am interested in the ways modern corporations justify their existences and practices, provide rationales for those who work within them, set their objectives, and exercise power. Just as Chandler is concerned with the means by which large business enterprises define their strategies and structures, so have I attempted to perform this task for IBM when dealing with the rationales and practices of the Watsons, Vincent Learson, Frank Cary, and John Opel, as well as dozens of other businessmen who worked with them or competed against IBM in the marketplace.

Two practitioners have read the entire manuscript and in the process have provided me with what amounted to a much-needed short course in data and information processing. My thanks to Alice and Edmund Berridge for their invaluable assistance.

Selected Bibliography

Books

Allyn, Stanley. *My Half Century with NCR*. New York: McGraw-Hill, 1967.

Alterman, Hyman. *Counting People: The Census in History*. New York: Harcourt Brace & World, 1969.

Bain, Joe. *Barriers to New Competition*. Cambridge: Harvard University Press, 1970.

Belden, Thomas, and Marva Belden. *The Lengthening Shadow*. Boston: Little, Brown, 1962.

Bell, William. *A Management Guide to Electronic Computers*. New York: McGraw-Hill, 1957.

Berkeley, E. C. *Giant Brains or Machines That Think*. New York: John Wiley, 1949.

Bernstein, Jeremy. *The Analytical Engine*. New York: Random House, 1963.

Bliven, Bruce, Jr. *The Wonderful Writing Machine*. New York: Random House, 1954.

Booth, Andrew, and Kathleen Booth. *Automatic Digital Calculators*. London: Butterworth's Scientific Publications, 1956.

Bowden, B. V., ed. *Faster Than Thought: A Symposium on Digital Computing Machines*. London: Pitman, 1953.

Bridge, James, ed. *The Trust: Its Book*. New York: Arno, 1973 ed.

Brock, Gerald. *The U.S. Computer Industry: A Study of Market Power*. Philadelphia: Ballinger, 1975.

Selected Bibliography

Byrn, Edward. *The Progress of Invention in the Nineteenth Century*. New York: Munn, 1900.

Crowther, J. G. *Discoveries and Inventions of the Twentieth Century*. New York: Dutton, 1966.

Crowther, Samuel. *John H. Patterson: Pioneer in Industrial Welfare*. New York: Doubleday Page, 1923.

Diebold, John, ed. *The World of the Computer*. New York: Random House, 1973.

Eckler, A. Ross. *The Bureau of the Census*. New York: Praeger, 1972.

Edward, Perry, and Bruce Broadwell. *Data Processing*. Belmont, Calif.: Wadsworth, 1979.

Engelbourg, Saul. *International Business Machines: A Business History*. New York: Arno, 1976.

Fields, Craig. *About Computers*. Cambridge, Mass.: Winthrop, 1973.

Flint, Charles. *Memories of an Active Life*. New York: Putnam, 1923.

Foy, Nancy. *The Sun Never Sets on IBM*. New York: Morrow, 1975.

Giedion, Siegfried. *Mechanism Takes Command*. New York: Oxford University Press, 1948.

Gilchrist, Bruce, and Milton Wessel. *Government Regulation of the Computer Industry*. Washington: AFIPS, 1972.

Gilfallan, S. C. *The Sociology of Invention*. Cambridge: MIT Press, 1935.

Goldstine, Herman. *The Computer from Pascal to Von Neumann*. Princeton: Princeton University Press, 1972.

Greenberger, Martin, ed. *Computers and the World of the Future*. Cambridge: MIT Press, 1966 ed.

Greenwood, Ernest. *Aladdin U.S.A.* New York: Harper, 1928.

Gropelli, Angelico. "The Growth Process in the Computer Industry." Ph.D. dissertation. New York University, 1970.

Gupton, James, Jr. *Getting Down to Business with Your Microcomputer*. Northridge, Calif.: Sourcebooks, 1979.

Halacy, D. S., Jr. *Computers—The Machines We Think with*. New York: Harper, 1969.

Hall, Courtney. *History of American Industrial Science*. New York: Library Publishers, 1954.

Harmon, Alvin. *The International Computer Industry*. Cambridge: Harvard University Press, 1970.

Kaempffert, Waldemar, ed. *A Popular History of American Inventions*. New York: Burt, 1924.

Malik, Rex. *And Tomorrow . . . the World?* London: Millington, 1975.

Marcosson, Isaac. *Wherever Men Trade*. New York: Dodd, Mead, 1948.

National Industrial Conference Board. *Mergers in Industry*. New York: National Industrial Conference Board, 1929.

Phister, Montgomery, Jr. *Data Processing Technology and Economics*. Santa Monica, Calif.: Santa Monica Publishing, 1976.

Popkin, Gary, and Arthur Pike. *Introduction to Data Processing*. Boston: Houghton Mifflin, 1977.

Pyke, Magnus. *The Science Century*. New York: Walker, 1967.

Pylyshyn, Zenon, ed. *Perspectives on the Computer Revolution*. Englewood Cliffs, N.J.: Prentice-Hall, 1970.

Ridgeway, George. *Merchants of Peace*. New York: Columbia University Press, 1938.

Riley, Robert. "A Case Study of a Differentiated Monopoly: The Computer Time-Sharing Industry." Ph.D. dissertation. University of Cincinnati, 1970.

Rodgers, William. *Think: A Biography of the Watsons and I.B.M.* New York: Stein & Day, 1969.

Rosenberg, Jerry. *The Computer Prophets*. New York: Collier-Macmillan, 1969.

Sackman, Harold. *Computers, System Science, and Evolving Society*. New York: Wiley, 1967.

Selected Bibliography

Scherer, F. M. *Industrial Market Structure and Economic Performance.* Chicago: Rand McNally, 1970.

Sharp, William. *The Economics of Computers.* New York: Columbia University Press, 1969.

Soma, John. *The Computer Industry.* Lexington, Mass.: Lexington Books, 1976.

Stevens, William, ed. *Industrial Combinations and Trusts.* New York: Macmillan, 1914.

Turck, J. A. V. *Origin of Modern Calculating Machines.* Chicago: Western Society of Engineers, 1921.

Usher, Abbott. *A History of Mechanical Inventions.* Cambridge: Harvard University Press, 1962.

Van Tassel, Dennie. *The Compleat Computer.* Chicago: Science Research Associates, 1976.

Voth, Ben. *A Piece of the Computer Pie.* Houston: Gulf, 1974.

Wilkins, Mira. *The Emergence of Multinational Enterprise.* Cambridge, Mass.: Harvard University Press, 1970.

————. *The Maturing of Multinational Enterprise.* Cambridge, Mass.: Harvard University Press, 1974.

Wooldridge, Susan, and Keith London. *The Computer Survival Handbook.* Boston: Gambit, 1973.

Wright, Carroll. *The History and Growth of the United States Census.* Washington, D.C.: Government Printing Office, 1900.

Wu, Margaret. *Introduction to Computer Data Processing.* New York: Harcourt Brace Jovanovich, 1975.

Magazines and Journals

Barrons
Business Automation
Business Week
Byte
Computer Decisions
Computer Design
Computers and Automation
Computers and People
Computerworld
Data Communications
Datamation
Duns Review
Forbes
Fortune
Harvard Business Review
Infosystems
IBM Data Processor
IBM Systems Journal
Mini-Micro Systems
Think

Index

Index

Index

Index

Index

IBM 360 and, 223–24, 256, 257, 267, 268, 269
lawyers in, 224, 257, 259, 268, 270–71, 275
leases vs. sales in, 144
of leasing companies, 265–66
of Memorex, 267, 273
of 1930s, 90–92
of 1950s, 142–47
1956 consent decree in, 143–44, 145, 146, 176, 275
paper computers and, 212, 213–14, 228–29, 230, 256, 264
patent licensing and, 145–46
of peripherals manufacturers, 267–75
salesmen's practices and, 256, 257–58
Service Bureau Corporation and, 144–45, 260
settlements of, 259, 260, 265, 266, 270, 274, 275, 288
SMASH campaign and, 269–70, 272, 273, 288
software/hardware packages and, 225, 226
of Telex, 269–75
unbundling and, 262–63, 266, 272
IBM AQUARIUS, 312–13, 314, 317
IBM Data Processing Division, 313, 314–16, 318
IBM Deutschland, 197–98, 200–1, 203, 206, 214
IBM Electric Accounting Machines Division, 125, 130
IBM Electronic Data Machine Division, 125, 128–29, 130
IBM Federal Systems Division, 161
IBM Field Engineering Division, 161
IBM France, 197–98, 199, 201, 203, 214
IBM General Business Group, 315–16, 318
IBM General Systems Division, 313–14, 315, 318
IBM Instruments, 335–36
IBM Japan, 195, 334
IBM leases, 76–77
  depreciation methods in, 235, 251
  finance charges in, 77
  income of, 77, 81, 83, 128, 221
  price structures of, 125–26, 128, 156, 157, 283, 328, 331–32
  sales vs., 144, 332
  of tabulating machines, 80–81
IBM Research Division, 162–63, 335
IBM salesmen, 76, 154, 160–61, 162,

163, 183–84, 243–44, 315–16
  ethical guidelines of, 257–58
IBM Series H, 330, 332, 335
IBM Service Bureau Corporation (SBC), 144–45, 162, 237, 260, 291
  revenues and profits of, 145
IBM STRETCH, 156–57, 161, 213, 217
IBM Systems Network Architecture (SNA), 316
IBM System/3, 245, 313–14, 315, 316
IBM System/38, 316, 318
IBM tabulating machines, 80–81
  accounting machines of, 80–81, 83
  keypunchers of, 80–81, 83
  sorters of, 80, 83
  verifiers of, 80
IBM Tape Processing Machine (TPM), 123, 124
IBM Time Recording Division, 78, 162
IBM United Kingdom, Ltd., 136–37
IBM World Trade Corporation, 131–32, 134, 137, 162, 184, 196–207, 285
  American/European domination of, 202
  Americanization of, 204–5
  British market of, 135–36, 195, 196
  financing of, 199
  French market of, 190, 191
  headquarters of, 197
  IBM 360 and, 214, 219, 230, 286, 287
  Italian market of, 192
  Japanese market of, 193, 194
  national differences in, 202–3
  predecessors of, 134–37
  research and production of, 201, 205, 207, 286
  revenues and profits of, 134, 197, 199, 204
  structure of, 197–99, 200–1, 203–4, 322
  in undeveloped countries, 201, 202
  U.S. market and, 206
  West German market of, 193
  See also specific national companies
Integrated circuits, 211–12, 227, 305–6
  LSI, 305–6

Index

Index

Index